GREAT BOOK OF
Woodworking Tips

GREAT BOOK OF
Woodworking Tips

OVER 650 INGENIOUS WORKSHOP TIPS, TECHNIQUES, AND SECRETS

from the experts at American Woodworker

Introduction by Randy Johnson
Editor, *American Woodworker* Magazine

FOX CHAPEL
PUBLISHING

Published by Fox Chapel Publishing Company, Inc., 903 Square Street, Mount Joy, PA 17552, 717-560-4703, www.FoxChapelPublishing.com.

American Woodworker, ISSN 1074-9152, USPS 738-710, is published bimonthly by Woodworking Media, LLC, 90 Sherman St., Cambridge, MA 02140, www.AmericanWoodworker.com.

ISBN: 978-1-56523-596-0

Publisher's Cataloging-in-Publication Data

Great book of woodworking tips : over 650 ingenious workshop tips,

techniques, and secrets from the experts at American Woodworker /

introductions by Randy Johnson, editor, American Woodworker. --

East Petersburg, PA : Fox Chapel Publishing, c2012.

p. ; cm.

ISBN: 978-1-56523-596-0 ; 1-53523-596-7

1. Woodwork--Handbooks, manuals, etc. 2. Woodwork--

Amateurs' manuals. 3.Woodwork--Technique. 4. Woodwork--

Equipment and supplies. I. Johnson, Randy. II. American

woodworker.

TT185 .G74 2012

684/.08--dc23 1204

To learn more about the other great books from Fox Chapel Publishing, or to find a retailer near you, call toll-free 800-457-9112 or visit us at *www.FoxChapelPublishing.com.*

We are always looking for talented authors. To submit an idea, please send a brief inquiry to acquisitions@foxchapelpublishing.com.

Printed in Singapore
Fifth printing

Contents

Introduction

It's about the aha!

Everyone loves a clever workshop tip. An ingenious solution to a vexing problem brings an aha! to the lips, and with it the resolve to try the trick for oneself, or perhaps to go one better by creating an improvement. Or, if the shop tip is obvious, we salute with a slap to the forehead, wondering why we couldn't have thought of that for ourselves. But we didn't, and that's one reason why woodworkers treasure collections such as this book.

The other reason, of course, is wrapped up in today's workshop reality. It's not like it was in Grandpa's day, when skills and workshop practices were passed from master to apprentice and father to son. This is the era of the amateur craftsman, mostly self-taught, working alone in his or her home workshop, and most likely without much contact with other woodworkers. In lieu of Grandpa, we rely on woodworking magazines to provide this all-important sharing of information and shine a light on the conundrums that dog the path to prowess. Every magazine and journal in the field boasts a tips column, largely driven by the readers themselves and their urge to share hard-earned knowledge. Along with shop tips, readers frequently ask good questions, giving the editors the additional challenge and opportunity of finding and presenting equally good answers.

It's often said that skill has two components: know-what, plus know-how. You have to know what to do, as well as how to do it. It's not always easy to glean both components from the printed page, but a sharp photograph certainly does help. Photography is where this collection of workshop tips really shines. Since 1999, editors at *American Woodworker* magazine have invested heavily in creating clear photo illustrations for reader-submitted tips and questions. When it's only a drawing, you're never quite sure about the underlying reality. But the photo removes that uncertainty, making the answer clear on the page.

We've emphasized photo illustrations in this huge collection of workshop wisdom. I'm personally grateful to my predecessors and colleagues for their determination to grace each chunk of solid advice with photographic clarity. Our team certainly has enjoyed gathering, illustrating and organizing this priceless information. We hope you enjoy the succession of aha! moments that you're sure to receive as you turn these pages.

—Randy Johnson, editor-in-chief,
American Woodworker magazine

Bandsaw

New Bandsaw Tires

My bandsaw has developed tracking problems to the point that the blade won't stay on the wheel. I checked everything and can't seem to clear up the problem. What's going on here?

Because these problems developed over time, I suggest you check your tires. The tires on your bandsaw provide traction for the blade and, like the tires on your car, they wear out and the rubber degrades with time. A new set of tires will likely put your saw back on track.

"Obvious signs of worn tires are cracks and tears," explains Peter Perez, president of Carter Products Inc., a bandsaw accessory manufacturer. "A good wear test is to sink a fingernail into the tire. A good tire will rebound with no visible mark on it. If your fingernail leaves an impression, it's time to replace the tire."

It's easier to replace the tires with the wheel removed from the saw. Taper the end of a dowel, clamp it in a vise, and set the wheel on it. We recommend replacing both rubber tires with urethane tires. Urethane offers two big advantages: It lasts longer and it doesn't require adhesive to install. Clamp the new tire on the wheel and stretch the tire over the rim. Urethane tires can be made more flexible by soaking them in hot water before you put them on the wheels.

Tapered Dowel End

New Urethane Tire

Spring Clamp Blade Storage

I like to keep my bandsaw blades on the wall next to my saw. To save space, I fold them into coils. The trouble comes when I hang the coiled blade on a peg or nail. I've had the blades suddenly come uncoiled and spring off the wall! That's unpleasant and potentially dangerous. I tried using twist ties, but they wore out quickly and it was a pain having to tie up and untie the blade every time I used it.

I came up with this handy hanger made with a 2x4 and some very small spring clamps. I notched the edge of the 2x4 with a dado blade and screwed a spring clamp into each notch. Now when I go to change blades, all I have to do is squeeze the spring clamp to release the blade.

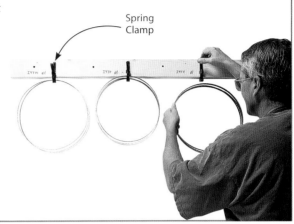

Spring Clamp

Can a 2x4 Dull a Blade?

After resawing some pine 2x4s, my bandsaw blade smoked and seemed mighty dull. How can that be?

Chances are your blade wasn't dull at all. It's teeth were probably coated with pine pitch, which you should remove with blade cleaner. Other woods, such as cherry, also deposit pitch on bandsaw blades.

Like any sawblade, a bandsaw blade's teeth won't cut properly if they're caked with pitch. Pitch fills in the clearances necessary for the blade to cut with a minimum of friction. This makes the blade run hotter, which creates even more buildup. Blade cleaner removes all traces of pitch, making your blade feel much sharper. You should remove the blade for cleaning to avoid potentially damaging your wheel's tires.

Tooth with pitch buildup

Tooth after cleaning

Clean Bandsaw Tires

My bandsaw tires have a buildup of pitch and sawdust that seems to be embedded right into the rubber. What's the best way to clean my tires?

An excessive buildup of sawdust and pitch on your tires can lead to tracking problems, so it's a good idea to clean them periodically.

Start by unplugging your machine. Then remove the blade and tilt the table out of the way. You'll find the buildup to be much worse on your lower tire where sawdust tends to get trapped under the blade as it travels around the wheel. Use some 120-grit sandpaper or synthetic steel wool and a light touch to clean the wheel as you turn it by hand.

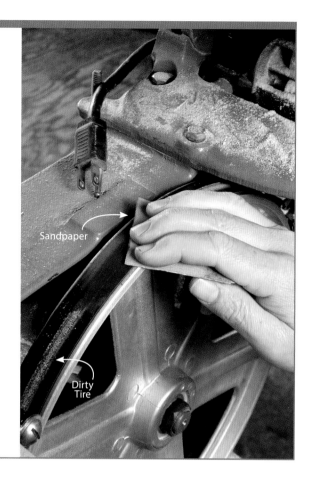

Sandpaper

Dirty Tire

Disposable Guide Blocks

I've bandsawed hundreds of puzzle pieces using very small blades. I gave up on the steel guide blocks that came with my saw because when those little blades came in contact with the blocks, they'd dull right away. And, when I wanted to back out of a cut, the blade would pop out of the blocks.

Now I make my own guide blocks from scraps of hardwood. My blades last longer and don't pop out or wander because they're trapped between the wooden blocks. The blocks wear, but it's so easy to just re-cut their ends or make new ones altogether.

With the bandsaw unplugged, I install the new blocks by pushing them toward the blade until they're lightly touching it. Then I lock the blocks in place and spin the upper blade wheel to make sure they don't drag on the blade.

Captured Blade

Wood Guide Blocks

Align Bandsaw Wheels

I've tried everything to get good resaw results on my bandsaw, but the blade still wanders. What gives?

If you use a sharp blade designed for resawing, compensate for drift angle, and set the proper tension and still get bad results resawing, there's only one other possibility: Your wheels need alignment. Pop the hood (well, the wheel covers) on your saw and put a straightedge across the rim of both wheels (Photo 1). If there's a gap, your wheels are not operating in the same plane.

Misaligned wheels are a problem for bandsaws with crowned wheels. If your saw is 16 in. or smaller, chances are it has crowned wheels. A crowned wheel has a slight hump where the blade rides. The crown is designed to force the blade toward the center of the wheel and aid in tracking the blade. If the two crowned surfaces are not in the same plane, they pull against each other, robbing the saw of power and accuracy.

Fortunately, the problem is easy to fix on most saws. First, measure the misalignment (Photo 2). Next, remove the blade and the wheel and apply the appropriate shim(s) (Photo 3). Most saws have thin washers behind each wheel. You may find removing the stock washer and replacing it with a thicker one is just the ticket.

Reattach the wheel and give your saw a spin.

Note: Some saws have an adjustable bottom wheel. Just loosen the setscrew and slide the bottom wheel in or out the appropriate amount.

Check the wheel alignment with your resaw blade mounted and tensioned. It may be necessary to adjust the tracking of the upper wheel to make the faces of both rims parallel.

Measure the gap with a ruler calibrated to at least 1/32 in. or with a dial caliper.

Add or replace washers behind the wheel to achieve alignment. For small adjustments, use metal shim stock or metal dado blade shims behind the washer.

Hassle-Free Blade Mounting

I don't know how many times I've struggled to put on a bandsaw blade. When I get it placed on one wheel, it just pops off the other. My solution? I temporarily hold the blade on the top wheel with spring clamps. Then I thread the blade through the guides and onto the bottom wheel. I crank the tension lever, remove the clamps and, sure as Bob's your uncle, I'm ready to go.

Bandsaw Table Lock

Before I installed this device, I couldn't lock my bandsaw's table securely enough for resawing. If I banged a heavy board on the outboard side, the table would always tip out of adjustment. Now the table stays fixed at 90 degrees.

After removing the table, I drilled and tapped two ¼-in. holes and bolted on a 3-in. length of angle iron with a slot cut in the long leg. After reinstalling the table and locking it perpendicular to the blade, I used this slot to locate and drill another ¼-in. hole in the saw casting. I tapped this hole and installed a length of threaded rod, which I locked into place by tightening a nut against the frame. To lock the top at 90 degrees, I installed two additional nuts and a washer underneath the angle. When I want to tilt the table, I just remove the knob and its washer.

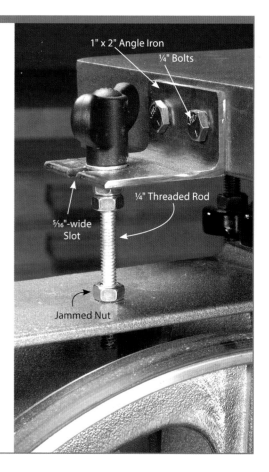

1" x 2" Angle Iron

¼" Bolts

¼" Threaded Rod

⁵⁄₁₆"-wide Slot

Jammed Nut

Folding Bandsaw Blades

I once saw someone fold a bandsaw blade for easier storage— how was that done?

Folding a bandsaw blade can be a bit intimidating when you first attempt it. Armed with sharp teeth and a spring-like tension, the blade deserves respect. At the same time it's an easy trick for entertaining your non-woodworking friends!

Be sure to wear leather gloves and eye-protection. Stand behind the open blade with the teeth pointing away from you. With one foot, gently step on the blade just enough to keep it secure to the floor (if your floor is cement, use a piece of plywood to protect the blade). With the palms of your hands facing away from you, grasp the back of the blade at two and ten o'clock. Your thumbs should be pointed away from you (Photo 1). With a firm hold on the blade, roll your wrists inward so your thumbs end up pointing toward each other

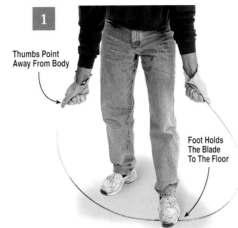

Thumbs Point Away From Body

Foot Holds The Blade To The Floor

Turn Thumbs In Toward Each Other

(Photo 2). At this point you will feel the resistance in the blade give way. Gently push the folding blade toward the floor as you lift your foot off the blade (Photo 3).

It may feel awkward at first but after a few tries you'll be folding blades with the best of them.

Speedy Blade Tensioning

Changing bandsaw blades used to be a pain, because my bandsaw doesn't have a quick-release blade-tensioning mechanism. I finally got tired of hand-cranking, so I replaced the tensioning rod with a ⅜-in. threaded rod. I locked two nuts against each other on top of the rod, making sure their faces lined up. Now a ⁹⁄₁₆-in. socket operates the tensioning system and only my trigger finger gets tired.

⁹⁄₁₆" Socket

Threaded Rod

Friction-Free Resaw Fence

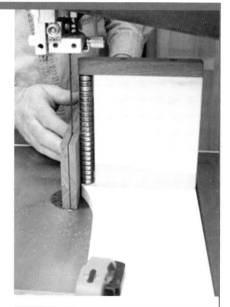

Resawing a board is tricky. Most blades drift, so that you must angle the board to get a straight cut. Standard bandsaw fences can't be angled to compensate for drift, so many folks use a single-point fence instead, like this one. The point on my fence is a tall stack of machine bearings, which gives me effortless, resistance-free cutting.

To build the fence, you'll need a ⁵⁄₁₆" steel rod, ⁵⁄₁₆" i.d. bearings, ⁵⁄₁₆" i.d. washers, a base 6" to 8" wide and as long as the depth of your saw's table, an upright (its height depends on your saw's capacity), and a hardwood cap to house the steel rod and hold the bearings in place. The steel rod and washers are available at any hardware store for a few bucks or try an auto parts or surplus store; the exact i.d. and o.d. of the bearings aren't particularly important.

Drill a ⁵⁄₁₆" hole at the base's point to house the steel rod's bottom end. Position the hole to allow the bearings to overhang the point by ⅛". Glue and screw the upright to the base, ⅛" behind the bearings.

Insert the rod in the base's hole and stack the bearings with a washer between each one. Insert the top end of the rod in the cap's hole, and then screw the cap to the upright, making sure it's positioned so the bearing stack is square to the saw's table.

Bandsawing Inside Curves

This is a useful trick when bandsawing inside curves. It requires no marking and no special jig. First I cut a shallow slot in a piece of scrap and attach it to the bandsaw fence, as shown. The radius of the cut, "R," is the same as the distance between the fence and the blade. The notch acts as a pivot point as the workpiece is rotated around the cut.

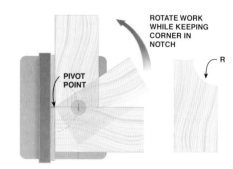

1/8" PIVOT NOTCH

R

PIVOT POINT

ROTATE WORK WHILE KEEPING CORNER IN NOTCH

R

Pattern-Cut Finials

The traditional way to make a square finial on a bandsaw is to mark and cut the pattern on one side of the blank, then tape the offcut back on to the blank in order to guide the cuts on the adjacent side. This is difficult to do with an intricate pattern because it's hard to keep the offcut in one piece.

I use a sled with a handle for steering it. First, I screw the finial blank to the sled (Photo 1). Next, I screw a pattern to the top edge of the sled and follow the pattern to cut the first side of the finial (Photo 2). Then I unscrew the finial, rotate it 90°, screw it back on the sled, and cut the next side (Photo 3). The sled's side supports are an important safety feature—they keep the finial from being pulled down by the saw's blade during the second cut.

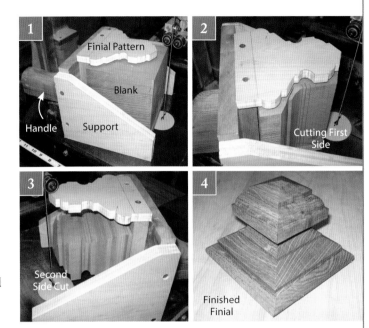

1 — Finial Pattern · Blank · Handle · Support

2 — Cutting First Side

3 — Second Side Cut

4 — Finished Finial

Blade Pop-out

When cutting a shallow angle, my bandsaw blade won't follow the line. When I approach the end of the line at the edge of the board, the blade pops out of the cut. What am I doing wrong?

A fresh, sharp blade shouldn't have this problem, but even a moderate amount of use can dull a blade sufficiently to cause it to pop out. The best solution is to make a habit of beginning the cut at the shallow angle, as shown at left, rather than exiting from it. If your cut has a shallow angle at both ends, start from one end, stop halfway, back out slowly, and start again at the other end.

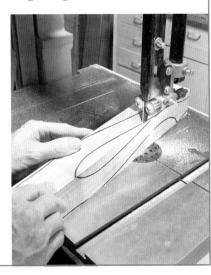

Zero-Clearance Bandsaw Table

I like to cut tenons with my bandsaw, but the little cutoffs tend to fall down in the space by the blade and get in the way or bind the blade. I found a slick fix. Tape a piece of thin cardboard (from something like a manila folder or old cereal box) to the table. The trimmings stay on top of the table and are easily pushed out of the way.

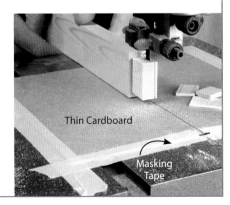

Thin Cardboard

Masking Tape

Bandsaw Offcut Tray

While sweeping up offcuts from around my bandsaw, I realized two things: First, I hate sweeping. Second, a dustpan-shaped tray attached to the bandsaw would catch most of the offcuts I was sweeping.

I made my tray from scraps of ½-in. plywood and ¼-in. hardboard. I fastened two pieces of ⅛-in. x 1-in. steel to the tray and bolted it to my saw through the rip fence mounting holes. In addition to catching offcuts, this tray also offers convenient storage when I'm cutting numerous small pieces.

Mounting
Hole

Resaw Without Warp

I've had a few bad experiences with wood warping after I resaw. Is there any way to tell whether a board is a good candidate for resawing?

The warp you refer to is case-hardening. A case-hardened board looks like any other board but has internal stresses caused by improper drying techniques. These stresses lay hidden until resawing releases them causing the board to warp.

Unfortunately, there's no way to visually tell if a board is case-hardened or not, but there is a simple test. Go in about 6-in. from the end of the board and cut a ¾-in.-thick section. Go to the bandsaw and cut out about one half of the width from the middle. If case-hardening is not present, the fork will remain stable. If there are internal stresses present, they will manifest themselves in forks that either pinch together (case-hardened) or bow outward (reverse case-hardened).

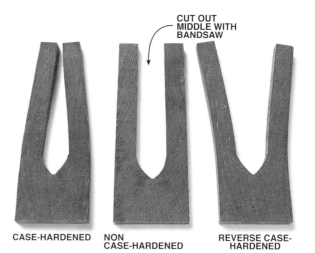

CUT OUT
MIDDLE WITH
BANDSAW

CASE-HARDENED   NON
                 CASE-HARDENED   REVERSE CASE-
                                   HARDENED

Slice Steel on Your Bandsaw

I've heard of a technique called friction-cutting that allows you to cut steel on a woodworking bandsaw. What is friction-cutting and does it really work?

Friction-cutting is used in industry for cutting iron-base metals, also called ferrous metals, such as steel. You can adopt the technology to your woodworking bandsaw to do limited cutting of ferrous metals in your home shop. Here's how it works: Mount a metal-cutting blade in your bandsaw. The woodcutting bandsaw's high speed—3,000 feet per minute (fpm)—will cause the blade to dull quickly when cutting steel (see photos, below). However, the friction generated by the dull teeth will heat the metal to molten red, allowing the blade to slice through the steel. It's amazing when you first try it. You'll feel some resistance before the metal reaches the molten stage, but once it does, you can cut ⅛-in.-thick steel as though it were 1-in.-thick oak. I tried this in my own shop and had great results in steel ⅛ in. or thinner. Thicker metal diffuses too much heat so the metal doesn't become hot enough to melt.

Friction-cutting on a woodworking bandsaw requires a few precautionary measures. Sparks fly using this method, so be sure to vacuum up all the saw dust in and around your saw beforehand. Also, the blade can be quite hot after continuous cutting, so keep your saw running but give the blade a break from cutting from time to time to let it cool. Otherwise the rubber tire on the wheel could melt. We recommend using ceramic blocks or the stock metal-guide blocks that came with the saw.

CAUTION Be sure to vacuum the dust from your machine before trying this procedure and disconnect dust-collection hoses from the saw.

New Metal-Cutting Blade

Cutting steel at high woodcutting speeds turns a new metal-cutting blade into a dull but effective friction-cutting blade that can cut up to ⅛-in.-thick steel.

Blade After Cutting Steel

Cabinet Making

Better Drawer Sides

I like using ½-in. birch plywood for drawer sides because it's so inexpensive, but when I rout dovetails sometimes it chips out like crazy. For a cleaner cut, should I be using solid wood instead?

No, you can stick with plywood, but switch to a different type, such as Baltic birch or AplePly. Technique may not be the problem; it could be the material.

Most standard birch plywood has very thin face veneers glued to three thicker layers of softwood or utility hardwood veneers. These inner layers could contain rough areas, knots, voids and splits. When you hit those areas with a router, the result is chip-out.

Baltic birch and ApplePly are made from many more layers of thinner veneers. The inner veneers of both of these high-density plywoods are very smooth, and the greater number of thin inner plies makes chip-out much less likely.

The top edges of your drawers will look better, too, because there are fewer and smaller voids in high-density plywood. You won't have nearly as many unsightly holes to fill.

Baltic birch is a generic term for imported plywood with birch faces and birch-core veneers. ApplePly is a trade name for one domestic manufacturer's plywood with maple faces and birch- or alder-core veneers.

Baltic birch is available at many lumber dealers in various thicknesses, but it only comes in 5-ft. by 5-ft. pieces (about $25 for one sheet of ½ in.). One annoying problem: a whole sheet may not fit into the back of your truck or van without cutting first. ApplePly also comes in a variety of thicknesses and is made in standard 4x8 sheets (about $60 for one sheet of ½ in.).

A Bead in any Board

I wanted an antique beadboard look for my cabinet doors, but stock beadboard didn't work out with my door size. Here's what I came up with: I glued up a solid door and cut ³⁄₁₆-in. x ³⁄₁₆-in. dadoes at each glue joint. Then I chamfered the edges with a sanding block (or you could use a plane). Finally, I ran a thin bead of glue in the bottom of the dadoes and laid in ³⁄₁₆-in. dowels. Could it be any simpler? Now I can have any width beadboard I need and I'm not limited to the wood species available at the lumberyard. I have a few more ideas to try, like using rope instead of dowels.

³⁄₁₆" Dowel

³⁄₁₆" x ³⁄₁₆" Dado

Chamfer Edges

Good-Looking Panels

Nothing makes a cabinet look worse than door panels with unattractive grain that runs at weird angles. It pays to be picky about grain direction, even if it means wasting some plywood.

After assembling your door frames without glue, slide them around on the sheet of plywood until they frame attractive panels. Look for symmetrical grain patterns that you can center. Avoid patterns that run off one side.

I try to find grain that resembles mountains or cathedral arches. These A-shaped patterns make doors and cabinets appear taller and more graceful. Tight grain patterns, where the early and late growth is closely spaced, usually look better than patterns with wide grain.

Mark your good-looking panels by tracing around the inside of the door frames. Cut out the traced panels at least ½ in. larger on all four sides. Then trim them to fit the frames. Use the ugly plywood that's left over for jigs or in other places where appearance doesn't matter.

Door Frame

Beautiful Button Knobs

As a kid, I used to play with my grandmother's button box every time we visited. I loved all those bright, shiny colors! Now that I've inherited her treasure hoard, I found a way to display these beautiful antiques on a sewing cabinet I made for my wife.
Old buttons make fascinating knobs.
I turn or buy a set of wooden knobs and then drill out the centers of the knobs with a Forstner bit. I finish the knob and epoxy the button into the recess. Of course, new buttons work fine, too, and are easier to buy in a complete set.

Jazzed-Up Drawer Fronts

When I told my wife I was going to build her new kitchen cabinets she was delighted. I really surprised her when I dressed up the drawers with a little carving. It wasn't that hard either and I only used one carving tool; a V-gouge. It sure jazzes up the kitchen!

Secure Knobs

I'll never forget the time I tried to yank open a stuck drawer on my homemade dresser and ended up holding only the knob! I'd pulled the knob right off the screw. Determined to solve this problem, I went to my lathe and designed a knob that'll never come off. As a bonus for the extra work, my two-part knob combines the ease of turning an end-grain knob and the beautifully grained top of a face-grain knob.

I removed the spurs from a standard T-nut with a pair of pliers and epoxied it into the base of the knob. I made a face-grain cap for the knob with a plug cutter installed in my drill press, epoxied it into a recess above the T-nut, and turned it smooth. When the cap is made from a highly figured contrasting wood, you've got a beautiful knob that'll always remain firmly attached to your drawer.

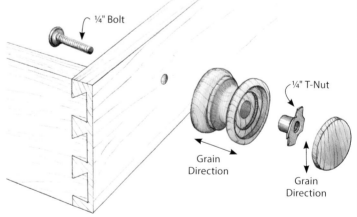

¼" Bolt

¼" T-Nut

Grain Direction

Grain Direction

Easy Drawer Dividers

Help! The junk drawer in our kitchen is out of control! I have trouble finding anything in there. Is there a simple way to add dividers to my kitchen drawers without taking them apart?

You bet! Here's a way to control the clutter in less time than it takes to find the potato peeler.

To make the brackets that hold the dividers in place, groove the edge of a ¾-in.-thick board on your router table and round over the outside edges. Then rip the grooved edge off the board and crosscut to length. I like to attach the brackets with double-faced tape or a little hot-melt glue. That way you can reposition them to suit your ever-changing collection of kitchen junk.

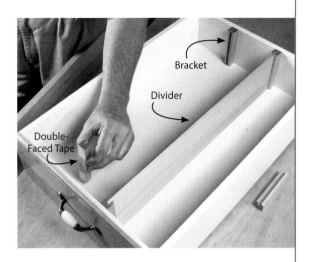

Worn Drawers

I've noticed in some antique chests of drawers that the pine drawer sides are really worn. I want to build a chest of drawers meant for daily use but don't want the drawers to wear away before my grandchildren get to use it. Is there a way to build better, long-lasting drawers?

Yes, there is. Furniture makers often used wood that was fairly soft for drawer sides because it was easy to work with. These sides wore away because the pine couldn't handle the repeated rubbing of soft wood on soft wood. (As a cure, some Shaker cabinetmakers even tried tapering the drawer sides to make a wider bearing surface, as shown above.) Sides made from a soft wood are still a good idea, but for the longest-lasting drawers, add a strip of wear-resistant wood only where needed: on the bottom of the drawer side.

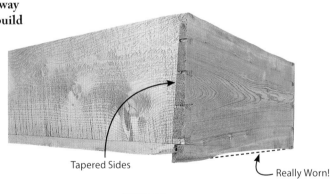

Tapered Sides

Really Worn!

Wear-Resistant Strip

Before building the drawer sides, glue a ¼-in. strip of a hard wood to the bottom of the drawer side blanks. Build the runners from the same wood.

Why not make the sides entirely from a hard wood? Here are three good reasons:
- Softer woods are less expensive.
- It's much easier to cut dovetails in a soft wood.
- Soft woods usually weigh less, causing less wear.

Cabinet Jacks

I usually work alone, but when I install upper cabinets, I always enlist the help of two shop-made cabinet jacks. They're steadier than an extra pair of hands. The jacks stand on the lower cabinets. To position and level the upper cabinets, I just turn two bolts in each jack.

The jacks are 15" tall and 12" deep. Make them from 2x4s, with 2x6 bases. In the jack's top members, pound two ½" x 2" coupler nuts into tight-fitting holes. Thread a ½" x 6" full-thread hex-head bolt through each coupler nut and cap it with a rubber chair-leg tip.

Chair Leg Tip

Coupler Nut

Full-Thread Hex Bolt

Comfortable Dovetails

Like the majority of workbenches, mine is fine for planing but too low for cutting dovetails without prolonged stooping. My answer is to clamp a heavy backing board, as shown in the sketch, and clamp the workpiece to it. I usually tilt the work so half the dovetail-cutting lines are vertical and then, after sawing, tilt it the other way for the second set. A refinement is to draw layout lines on the backing board for reference.

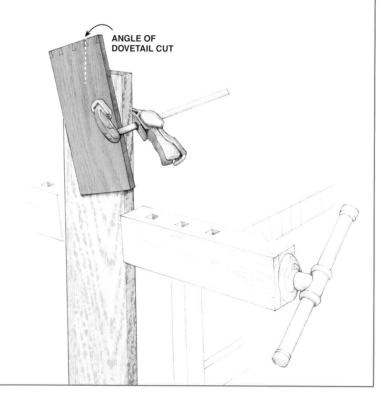

ANGLE OF DOVETAIL CUT

Pin Board Marking Jig

My task: 28 kitchen drawers of different sizes, all with hand-cut dovetails. The thought of laying these out was overwhelming, so I designed a jig to simplify the process. To make the jig, carefully lay out and cut a piece of ¼" hardboard as if it were the pin board for the tallest drawer. Glue and nail the hardboard to a ¾" plywood backer. Fasten a stop on each side.

Place an actual pin board into the jig with the outside face against the backer board and one side against either stop. Clamp the whole thing into a vise and use a chisel to mark the end grain, defining the pins. Scribe a depth line, and use a square to mark saw lines and cut the dovetails as usual. Since my drawer heights and my dovetail spacing were in ½" increments, the jig worked for all the drawers.

Stop

Backer Board

Drawer Stop Screws

Making an inset drawer line up flush with the face of a cabinet can be fussy work. To make it easy, I just install two screws on the back of the drawer and turn them until the drawer's front is perfectly aligned.

Screw

Tight Knobs

Drawer knobs that work loose and spin around drive me crazy. So instead of drilling a hole through the drawer front and screwing the knobs on from the back, I fasten them to a post that's securely anchored in the drawer front. I drill a pilot hole two-thirds of the way through the drawer front and thread in a pan head sheet metal screw (these screws have sharp threads that really grip). I cut off the screw's head and file the rough edges. Then I thread on the knob.

Chop Saw

Adjustable Chop Saw Stop

This handy stop grips tightly and is easy to adjust, so you can lock in crosscuts. A spacer the same thickness as the saw's auxiliary fence is the key. Sandwiched between the two clamp faces, this spacer makes the stop fit the fence perfectly. Sandpaper affixed to the stop's front face provides a secure grip.

Glue the spacer and front clamp face together, making sure their edges are flush. Then glue on the plywood top. Align the back clamp face flush with the glued-up front assembly and drill a ¼-in. hole through all three pieces. Glue sandpaper to the front clamp face. Install the carriage bolt, set it with a hammer and attach the knob. I mounted the knob on the back face so it would be out of the way. The top's overhang keeps the back face from spinning as you tighten the knob.

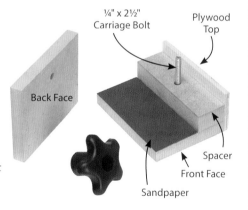

Back Face

¼" x 2½" Carriage Bolt

Plywood Top

Spacer

Front Face

Sandpaper

Double-Duty Edge Guide

Instead of measuring for my circular saw's offset each time I need to make a cut, I use a modified edge guide. I screwed two ¾" x ¾" x 12" hardwood blocks to the front and back clamp bars of the guide and clamped the guide to a board.

Next, I placed the saw's base against the edge guide and made a cut through the blocks and the board. The end of each block now indicates exactly where the saw will cut. I just line up the end of one block with a pencil mark on the panel, clamp the guide, and turn on the saw.

I also routed a dado in the other end of the hardwood blocks, using the same method. Again, instead of measuring my router's offset, I just position the dadoes in the blocks next to a pencil mark on the panel, and rout away.

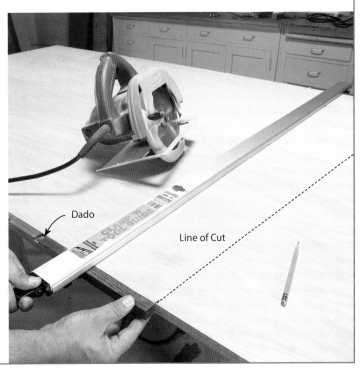

Dado

Line of Cut

Quick-Action Miter Saw Stop

I got tired of clamping a block to my miter saw fence every time I wanted to make a stop cut, so I made this adjustable quick-action stop. Unlike a spring clamp, once this baby's clamped to the saw fence, it stays put!

My stop is based on a locking welding clamp I found at the hardware store for about $24; imported knock-offs cost a lot less. This weird-looking clamp has adjustable jaws and locks just like vise-grip pliers do.

First, I cut the front tongs from the clamp's upper jaws. They're hardened steel, so I used an angle grinder equipped with a cutting wheel. After cutting, I ground the surfaces flat. Then, using my drill press, I drilled holes for the screws.

For the clamp to work, the stop board must be ⅜ in. taller than the fence, because the clamp's lower jaws have an offset "sweet spot." Before mounting the clamp, I notched the stop board's bottom corners to prevent sawdust buildup.

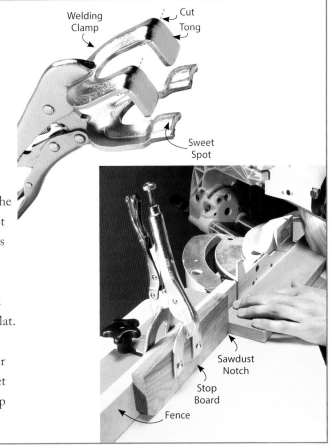

Welding Clamp

Cut Tong

Sweet Spot

Sawdust Notch

Stop Board

Fence

Doweling Jig Saw Stop

My doweling jig ended up in the junk drawer after I bought my biscuit joiner. I brought it out of retirement though, when I set up my chop saw bench. That old doweling jig has become a very useful saw stop. I simply clamp it to my 2x2 fence. I added a tape measure to the top of my fence, which makes setting the stop quick and accurate. It's simple to remove the jig if I need to use it for doweling.

Stick-On Tape Measure
Doweling Jig
2x2 Fence

Sawing Aluminum

Can I cut aluminum with my chop saw?

Yes. Most carbide blades work fine for occasionally cutting aluminum, but we recommend using a special, non-ferrous metal-cutting blade (about $70) if you cut a lot of aluminum or brass. It's safer to use than a standard blade because the geometry of the teeth makes it less likely to kick back when cutting a soft metal. And it will last longer than a standard blade because the teeth are made of a softer carbide.

No matter which blade you use, feed the saw about one-third slower than you do when cutting wood. Coating the blade with a regular dose of WD-40 (when the saw's not running) prevents the gullets from clogging.

Flip-Up Miter-Saw Fence

I was so excited when I bought my sliding miter saw, until I realized how much bench space it took up. My Bosch needs a bench at least 38-in. deep. I also wanted an extension fence on both sides, but this made my benchtop almost unusable for other work. I fixed my problem by hinging the fences to the walls. Now when I want to use the benchtop for something else, I just flip up the fence. I hold it to the wall with a simple wooden turnbuckle.

Turnbuckle

Hinge

Stop Block That Stays Put

When making repetitive cuts, I found that my stop block would shift. With a hardwood cutoff, a leftover piece of T-track, a ¼–20 hex head bolt and a jig knob, I constructed a stop block that doesn't move and is super easy to adjust.

First, drill a hole in the saw's fence, then groove the block for the T-track. Slide the head of the bolt into the T-track and insert the threaded end through the hole. Tighten the jig knob on the back of the fence, and the stop block doesn't move!

One-Switch Chop Saw Station

I decked out my chop saw station with a shop vacuum for dust collection and a shop light so I can see where I'm cutting. It worked great except for one thing: I had to flip two switches just to make one cut. The solution was simple. I bought a power strip, with keyholes for mounting, for about $6 at the hardware store and plugged everything into that. Now when I want to make a cut, I flip a single switch on the power strip and my chop saw station springs to life. No more fumbling around.

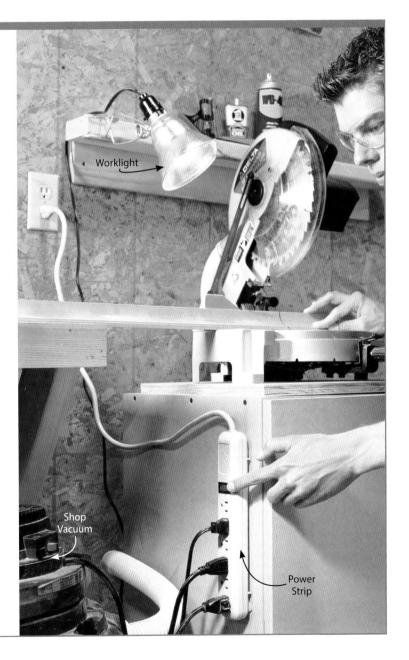

Worklight

Shop Vacuum

Power Strip

Super Chop Saw Stop

This stop slides along a rail that's screwed to the top of my chop saw fence, and I can lock it in any position. The hinged block is locked in the down position with a trunk latch. When not needed, the stop can be flipped up out of the way or removed altogether. The miter attachment is quickly installed with a single bolt and two wooden locking pins keep it from swiveling.

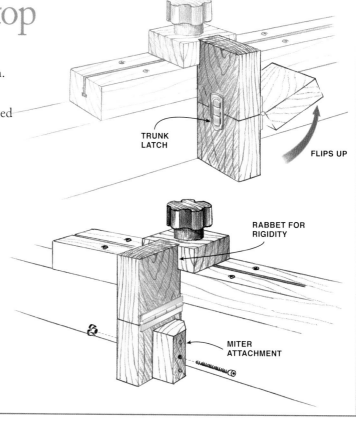

TRUNK LATCH

FLIPS UP

RABBET FOR RIGIDITY

MITER ATTACHMENT

Zero-Clearance Miter Table

Here's a dirt-simple but effective accessory for your miter saw. It eliminates tear-out, allows you to make precision cuts by aligning a pencil mark with the kerf, and provides room to screw or clamp a stop block anywhere along the fence.

Originally, I built this table for extra support when cutting long pieces. But it's such a great addition that now I leave it on my saw all the time.

You could use ¾" stock, but I made my table from ½" plywood to minimize the decrease in my saw's crosscut capacity. It can be any length you want. For stability, make the bed about 3" wider than the maximum length of the saw's kerf.

Glue and screw the fence to the plywood bed at 90°. Screw the table's fence to the saw's fence, and you're set.

Portable Miter Saw Station

I just don't have room in my crowded shop for a permanent miter saw setup. Consequently, I designed this miter saw station to easily knock down when I'm not using it.

I started with an 8-ft. 2x12 that was flat and straight. (A couple of pieces of ¾-in.-thick plywood glued together would also work.) I routed a groove down the middle of the 2x12 for the metal T-track. Then I screwed my miter saw to a plywood carriage board, which I fastened to the T-track with T-bolts and knobs. This allows me to slide my saw to either end when cutting long boards. I added two sliding support brackets which are also attached with T-bolts and knobs. The brackets support the ends of my boards when I'm sawing. I added a flip-up stop to each bracket so I can make multiple parts of the same length. When I'm not using my miter saw station, I simply remove the saw and stand the 2x12 on end, secured against a wall. The whole setup cost me about $50.

Adjustable Saw
Carriage Board

Flip-Up Stop

Sliding
Support
Bracket

Wingnuts

T-Knob on
T-Bolt

T-Track

Clamps & Clamping

Mobile Clamp Carousel

I've got a pile of K-body clamps that I use all the time. This clamp carousel guarantees they're always close at hand. It stores 18 clamps in a 2-sq.-ft. space, and I can roll them right to the job.

My carousel consists of two ¾-in. plywood discs securely fastened to a center post by glue, screws and braces. The top disc has a 1½-in. square cutout in the center so it will slip over the post. Both discs are divided into 18 segments, each spanning 20 degrees. I cut notches for the clamp beams in the top disc and glued wedge-shaped spacers on the bottom disc to corral the clamp heads. The carousel rolls on five 3-in. swivel casters. To hold the clamps in place, I screwed a strip of plastic cut from a food-storage container around the edge of the top disc and cut a slit at each notch.

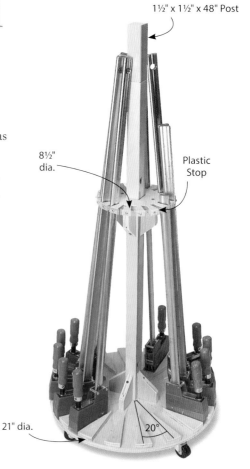

1½" x 1½" x 48" Post

8½"
dia.

Plastic
Stop

21" dia.

20°

Cut Notches

Without notches on a mobile cart, one bump can send your clamps flying. The boards that you notch should be wide enough to fully support the clamps' heads. The trick is to make the notches deep enough for a clamp's head and wide enough so the clamp's bar is easy to insert and remove.

To make half-round notches for pipe clamps, drill holes down the middle of a wide board. Rip through the center of the holes to make two support boards, each with half-round holes.

Make Big Brackets

These sturdy 12-in. x 16-in. brackets are great for storing lots of long, heavy clamps in a narrow space. The 2x4 brackets are wide enough for pipe and bar clamps. Use 2x6s to store K-body-style and deep-throated adjustable clamps.

Dado a 45-degree support board into each bracket. Screw the brackets to the cleats from the back, leaving 2-in. spaces between for the clamps' bars. Then fasten the brackets to the wall.

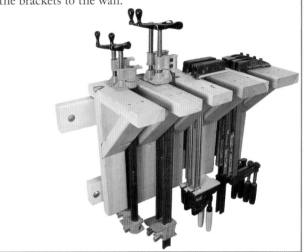

Conduit Fits All the Shorties

If you have room for only one rack for your short clamps, build this one. It accommodates a wide variety of shapes—almost anything that has jaws. The rack even holds C-clamps and quick-release clamps, which usually have to be tightened to stay on a board for storage. Simply hook them over the metal conduit. Conduit is superior to using a wooden dowel rod because it is stiffer and more durable.

For most clamps, position the conduit 2 in. from the wall. Strategically locate a second length of conduit to support the bars of long clamps.

Metal Brackets Serve Double Duty

Got long clamps you want to keep handy? Use heavy-duty 12-in. shelf brackets. (They're great for lumber, too.) This rack works well for long, heavy clamps because it stores them horizontally, making it easy to remove, use and return them. When you need one, simply pick it up and lay it down on your project. You won't have to twirl or hoist them the way you would if you stored long clamps in a vertical rack.

Heavy-duty shelf brackets are available at home centers; the slotted standards come in short lengths for a dedicated clamp rack.

Double Duty Clamp Rack

One sure thing about clamps is that they're never close enough when you need them. That's why I devised this rolling rack. Its 4-in. locking swivel casters easily plow through sawdust and over cracks and power cords. To make this rack doubly useful, I designed it to work as an outfeed support for my tablesaw. Its 2x6 top inclines at a 5-degree angle so its top edge matches my tablesaw's height.

I made the rack from 2x4s, a 2x6 and ⅝-in. electrical conduit. Drill ¹¹⁄₁₆-in. holes for the conduit in the doubled-up 2x4 rails, spaced to suit your clamp lengths. Then cut the conduit in 18-in. to 24-in. lengths as needed and install them. To keep the clamps from sliding off, cap the conduit support arms with rubber chair leg caps from the hardware store.

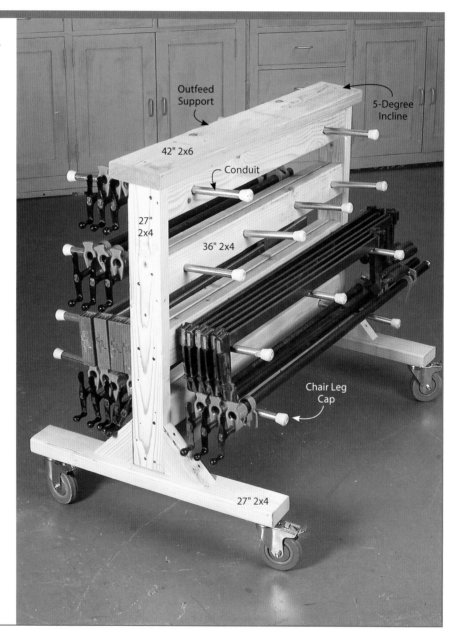

Outfeed Support

5-Degree Incline

42" 2x6

Conduit

27" 2x4

36" 2x4

Chair Leg Cap

27" 2x4

Mobile Clamp Rack

Tired of dragging clamps around my shop, I built this rack that brings them right to the job. It takes up only 21 x 32 in. of real estate and can handle 36 adjustable clamps and 12 4-ft. pipe clamps.

I assembled the side frames separately before screwing them together with gussets at the top and a plywood shelf at the bottom. I tapered the ends of the 1x4s at the top to fit. Before installing the 3-in. swivel casters, I glued on plywood pads to reinforce the corner joints.

Each frame consists of 2x4 and 2x6 rails screwed to 1x4 ends. I ripped the 2x6s in half to make the clamp rails. I staggered the top rails so the pipe clamp rail sits higher.

To make the half-round cutouts that hold the pipe clamps, I drilled centered holes in the 2x6 before I ripped it in half.

On the other frame, I cut slots in the rails for adjustable clamps. I cut the slots on my tablesaw, using my dado set and the miter gauge.

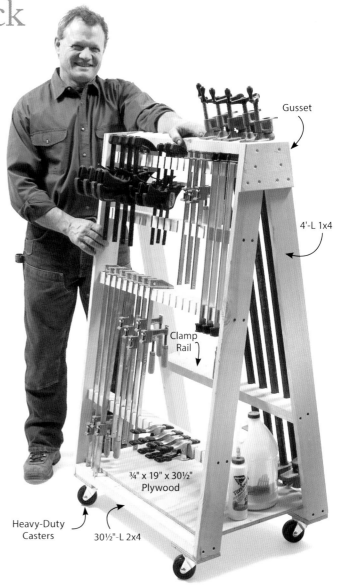

Gusset

4'-L 1x4

Clamp Rail

¾" x 19" x 30½" Plywood

Heavy-Duty Casters

30½"-L 2x4

Throw 'Em in a Tub

Oddball clamps won't become lost if you keep them together in a utility tub, which costs about $3 at a discount store. Tubs are a great way to store and transport spring clamps, C-clamps and small hand screws. Lidded tubs can even be stacked.

Clamp Blocks Plus

Bessey K-Blocks are great for holding K-clamps in position for glue-ups, but they're also quite handy for other things. I milled hardwood strips the same dimensions as my K-clamps and use them to raise work pieces for stacked glue-ups. I also use the blocks and strips for pocket-hole assembly, so I don't have to hang a joint over the edge of my workbench to clamp it. Shop-made blocks like these, made in maple, would work just as well.

Cauls Distribute Pressure

It's not easy to get enough squeeze in the middle of a big box to force home dado or biscuit joints. Big cauls are the answer.

A caul is simply a thick, straight board. I make my cauls from stiff wood, such as hard maple, but any wood will do. The wider and thicker the caul, the less it flexes and the better it delivers pressure far from the clamps. I made a set of eight, each measuring 1¾ x 3 x 24 in., to have around the shop whenever I need them.

Stout cauls like these should provide plenty of pressure, but you can get extra pressure in the middle by inserting one or more shims (I use playing cards). You can also round or taper one of the caul's edges from the middle to each end to create a crown. I do a dry run with cauls top and bottom, without shims, and place a straightedge on the cabinet to see whether the sides are flat. If one side bulges and needs more pressure in the center, I loosen the clamps, insert shims and retighten.

Caul

Another Angle on Flat Glue-ups

To keep panels from bowing under clamp pressure while gluing, I install lengths of angle aluminum on each end. I clamp the angle pieces just firmly enough to hold things in place. Then I tighten the pipe clamps. Unlike iron or steel, aluminum won't leave black marks where it contacts squeezed-out glue. Unlike a wooden cleat, it won't become glued to the panel.

Aluminum Angle

Blocks Center Clamping Pressure

Uneven clamping pressure can easily draw offset joints, such as the one shown here, out of square. A block aligned with the joint properly directs the clamp's pressure.

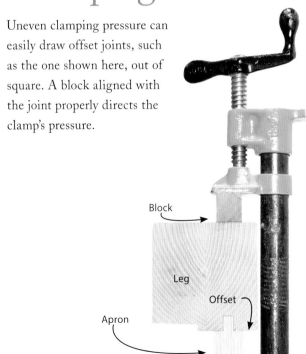

Block

Leg

Offset

Apron

90-Degree Brackets Simplify Complex Clamping Jobs

Clamping together a cabinet with numerous shelves and rails can be a real pain. Shop-made 90-degree brackets allow assembling the cabinet one joint at a time and keep the joints square while you clamp the cabinet together.

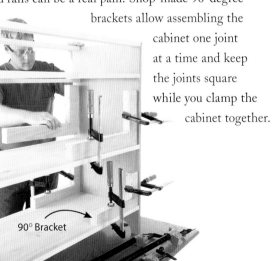

90° Bracket

Clamp Table

Cradle

Screen
Hinge

Spreader

I don't have room in my garage shop for a permanent clamp table, so I made this folding version from a leftover 2-ft.-wide sheet of ¾-in.-thick plywood. Folded, it's less than 2 in. thick, so it stores neatly in a narrow space.

First, I crosscut the sheet to 60 in. in length. Then I made a rip cut to create the 16-in.-wide base.

Next, I drilled 1⅛-in.-dia. holes at 4-in. intervals down the middle of the remaining 8-in.-wide piece. Ripping this piece down the middle created two racks with half-round cradles for pipe clamps. I attached these racks to the base with screen hinges, which are flat on the outside, so they can be surface-mounted (I bought four 3-in. screen hinges for less than $4 at my local home center). I mounted the hinges on the inside of the racks, so the racks sit on the base when they're open.

Friction-fit spreaders lock the racks in position during use. I made the spreaders 3 in. wide so they sit below the half–round clamp cradles. When the table folds for storage, wing nuts hold the spreaders on the base.

Box Beams Guarantee Flat Glue Ups

Made by gluing rails of equal width between two faces, box beams work like thick cauls to evenly distribute clamp pressure. They're great for gluing veneered panels or torsion boxes.

Face
Rail
Box Beam

Support Unwieldy Clamps

Without help, it's tough to hold a long, heavy pipe clamp level while you draw it tight. By supporting one end, a spring clamp eliminates the need for help from extra hands.

Check Edge Joints With One Centered Clamp

Like dry-fitting a joint before you glue, this technique highlights imperfectly jointed boards that may otherwise be hard to see. Here, one slightly crowned edge causes a noticeable gap. Even if no gaps appear, test all the joints by lifting one board while lowering the other. If the boards move without resistance, the joint is too loose. Re-joint one or both boards and try again.

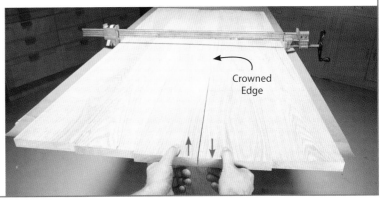

Crowned Edge

Clamp Jaw Binder

When I loosened my adjustable clamps to make minor adjustments, they frequently slipped all the way open. Sometimes my hand got whacked, sometimes the clamp fell and sometimes entire clamped-up assemblies crashed to the floor. Limiting the lower jaw's travel with a rubber band solved the problem. Now I can easily adjust my clamps using one hand.

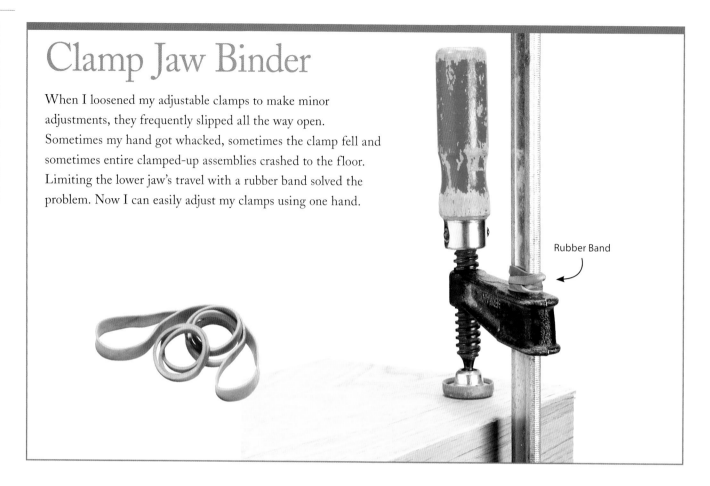

Rubber Band

Clamp Traction Pads

My spring clamps wouldn't work on an acute-angle joint I needed to clamp. Even though their jaws had swiveling pads, the clamps just slipped off.

Nothing worked to hold the clamps in place until I made my own traction pads by gluing strips of coarse abrasive together back to back. When the glue was dry, I cut the strips into squares and stuck them between the clamp pads and the wood.

Traction Pad

Corner Clamp for Thick Stock

Thick stock is no problem with this quick clamping setup. Cut the notches so they line up with the center of the miter. This helps the joint come together evenly and reduces joint slippage when the handscrew clamp is tightened. A piece of folded sandpaper (180 or 220 grit) placed between the clamping boards and workpieces also helps.

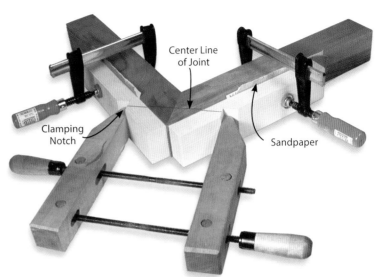

Center Line of Joint

Clamping Notch

Sandpaper

Clamps by the Roll

Tape works wonders when it comes to clamping together small projects like jewelry boxes. Regular clamps can be cumbersome and simply too big and heavy. By contrast, masking tape, is easy to use. When you stretch the tape a little it exerts sufficient pressure for small projects. As always, make sure your project is square before setting it aside to dry.

Create Parallel Clamping Shoulders For Curved Shapes

Make custom clamping blocks by tracing and cutting the curved profiles. Then mark and cut clamping shoulders parallel to the joints. Be proactive: Self-hanging clamp blocks free both hands for clamping. trimmings stay on top of the table and are easily pushed out of the way.

Home-Made Deep Reach Clamps

Like most woodworkers, I never have enough clamps. Adding to a clamp collection is expensive, so when I needed some deep reach clamps, I made these auxiliary hardwood jaws. You can make them whatever size you like. The jaws are mortised to slide on the clamp's bar. A stiff wood that resists splitting, like maple, is ideal.

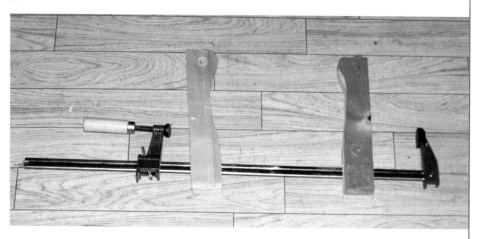

Masking Tape Clamps Edgebanding

Thin stock doesn't require lots of clamping pressure. Simply draw the tape across the edgeband and firmly down both sides of the panel guide, simply saw off the end. As long as your blade is set at 90 degrees to the table, you should get near-perfect results.

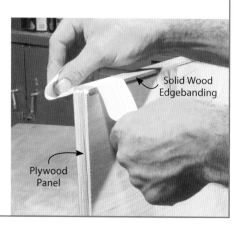

Solid Wood Edgebanding

Plywood Panel

Make Short Clamps Go Long

You don't need super-long clamps to clamp super-long glue-ups. Just gang your regular clamps together.

Knock-Off Blocks for Long Miters

Long miters are a nightmare to clamp, but adding temporary triangular blocks makes it a snap. The key is to use paper from a grocery bag. Dab some wood glue on both sides of the paper, stick the blocks wherever you need them and let the glue set overnight. When you're done clamping, remove each block with a hammer blow. The paper creates a weak spot in the glue bond, so the blocks break away without damage to the wood. Use hot water to soften any paper or glue left on the wood, then scrape it away and sand as usual.

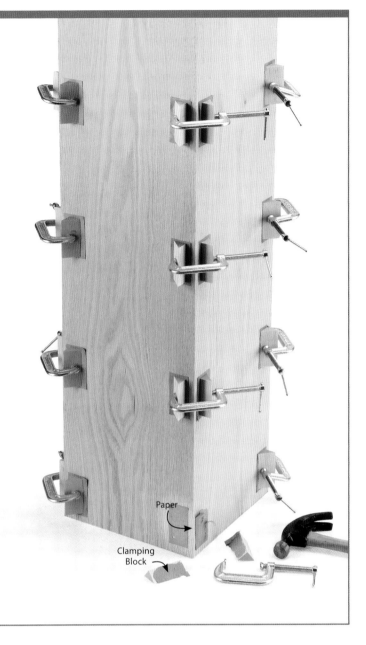

Paper

Clamping Block

Paper Towel Pads Keep Corner Joints Clean

Here's a trick for managing glue squeeze-out when you clamp dovetails or box joints: Face your clamp pads with paper towels. They absorb glue so it doesn't soak deeply into the wood. After the glue has dried, the papered blocks knock off easily. Dampen any paper that remains on the joint. After about a minute it'll scrub right off.

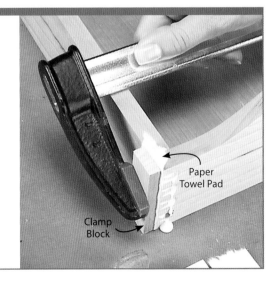

Paper Towel Pad

Clamp Block

Masking Tape Miter Clamping

This is the simplest way to glue and clamp a long miter. Lay the parts mitered-side down on a flat surface. Now use masking tape as both a hinge and a clamp. Apply a couple of strips of masking tape to pull the parts close together. Add a long strip of tape for the hinge. Carefully turn the assembly over and spread some glue on the miters. Fold up one half and add some more masking tape to hold all the parts together.

Step 1

Step 2

Notched Blocks for No-Rush Glue-Up

Getting all four corners of a box or frame aligned and clamped before the glue sets can be a frantic rush. Four notched blocks lower the frustration level by letting you tackle glue-up in manageable steps. Start by joining two corners to form the two halves of the box or frame. Allow those first two glue joints to cure for 30 minutes or so. Then rotate the notched blocks and complete the assembly by gluing the two halves together.

No-Slip Taper Clamps

Every woodworker eventually comes across an angled or tapered clamping task. Wedge-shaped clamping blocks place the clamps at a right angle to the joint, which is what you want. But the wedged parts are still likely to slip and slide when pressure is applied. The real secret to keeping things from moving around is to add a stop cleat to each clamping block. Now the parts will stay put.

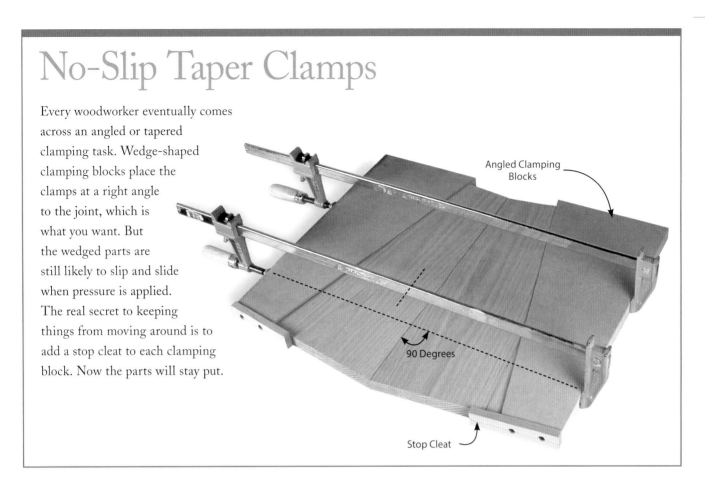

Angled Clamping Blocks

90 Degrees

Stop Cleat

Perfect Frames Every Time

If you make a lot of small picture frames, here's an excellent shop-made clamp. Make the corner blocks from 2-in. x 2-in. x 1½-in.-thick stock. Drill holes for the threaded rod and a 10mm hole for the cross dowel. The four corner blocks all have the same shape and drilling pattern. The threaded rod is held on one end by the cross dowel and by a wing nut on the other. The wing nut is used to tighten the clamp and can be adjusted to pull the frame perfectly square.

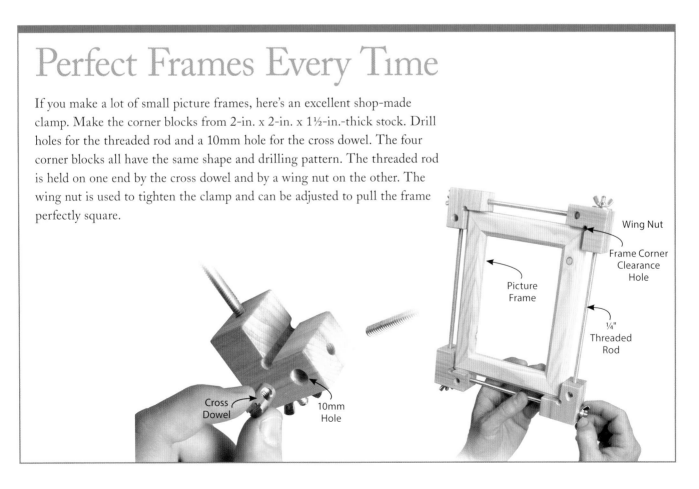

Cross Dowel

10mm Hole

Wing Nut

Frame Corner Clearance Hole

Picture Frame

¼" Threaded Rod

Plastic Laminate Clamps

When shimmed under cauls clamped on wide cabinet sides, plastic laminate pieces act as deep-reach clamps, providing pressure in the middle of the joint.

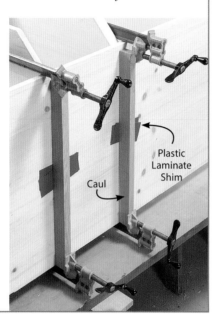

Plastic Laminate Shim

Caul

Refrigerator Magnets Make Instant Clamp Pads

They're readily available, a snap to install and they effectively insulate clamp pressure!

Permanent Clamp Pads

I lost the rubber pads that came with my clamps. I liked the way the pads protected the wood, so I decided to make my own. After a couple dips in liquid plastic ($9 at a hardware store), my clamps have cushy pads that don't slip off. They work great!

Power-Grip Clamp Handle

I love adjustable clamps, but I used to have trouble gripping and tightening the handles, especially at the end of a long day. Glued-on pieces of drawer liner ($5 per roll at most home centers) make them much easier to use. Two or three wraps make a comfortable grip that you can really put the squeeze on.

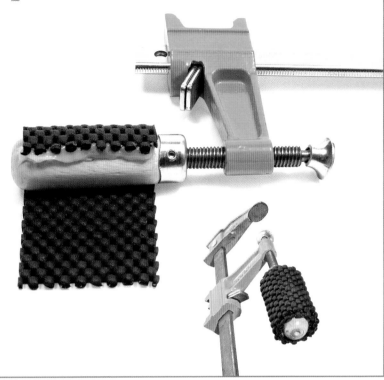

Pressure Spreaders

Getting ready to glue some pre-finished edging on a huge countertop, I realized that I didn't have enough clamps. Rather than buy more clamps, I increased the area each clamp would cover by screwing a 6" long block to its front jaw. I glued cork to the face of each block to protect the edging.

Quick-Release Hose Clamp

I have a couple of tools from which I frequently remove the dust collector hoses. I got tired of getting out my screwdriver and cranking out the adjustment bolt every time. After a bit of experimenting, I came up with this quick-release solution that uses a wire hose clamp and a plastic spring clamp with removable jaws.

First, remove the adjustment bolt from the wire clamp. Then cut about 1 in. from each clamp wire. Next, bend the end of the clamp wires into hook shapes. Drive out the jaw pins from the spring clamp and discard the jaws. Put the pins back into the spring clamp and attach the hooked end of the clamp wires to the pins. Bend the hooks down tight to secure them to the pins.

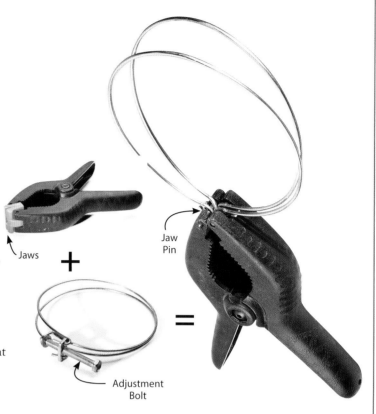

Jaws

Jaw Pin

Adjustment Bolt

Rubber Band Clamping

I've discovered a neat way to clamp solid edgebanding onto almost any contoured edge. I made a pair of jigs with holes drilled to fit removable dowels. I firmly clamp these jigs on both sides of the contoured edge. I apply glue and position the thin edgeband. Then I clamp it down with rubber bands.

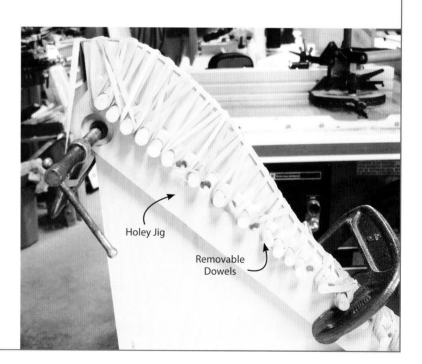

Holey Jig

Removable Dowels

A Press to Laminate Curved Parts

Curved, laminated parts are stronger than parts sawn from solid wood. This press makes laminating easy. The press is made of layers of plywood or particleboard that are glued together. This sandwich is cut into two parts on the bandsaw. The alignment boards (which keep the press and the wood strips lined up) are screwed onto one half. During clamping, some glue squeeze out will occur, so apply plastic packing tape to the clamping press and alignment boards to keep them from sticking to each other and your workpiece.

The strips of wood should be milled to between ¹⁄₁₆-in. and ⅛-in. thick. (Sawing them to thickness on a tablesaw works, but planing them to thickness will produce a better glue joint.) Apply glue evenly to the strips. A small paint roller works great for this. Then place your parts in the press and clamp. Leave the clamps on for at least eight hours. Now you've got a board that's both curved and strong.

Pattern Line

Remove This Part

Plastic Packing Tape

Wood Strip

Alignment Board

Glue Roller

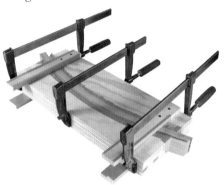

Spacers Center Clamping Pressure

Use a couple strips of wood under your pipe clamps to put the clamp's screw directly in line with your work. This helps center the clamping force, which reduces the possibility of the boards buckling and helps keep the joints tight on both sides of the boards. For ¾-in. stock, a ⅜-in.-thick strip of wood will work with most clamps.

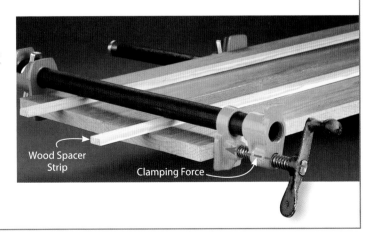

Wood Spacer Strip

Clamping Force

Spring Clamp for Miters

Spring clamps are easily converted to miter clamps by adding swivel jaws. Remove the vinyl tips, then hacksaw a ½" long slot down the center of the metal jaws. Use needle-nose vise-grips to fold down the two halves of each jaw, and then drill a hole for a small bolt or rivet.

To make the swivel jaws, snap off two pieces, ¾"–1" long, from an old hacksaw blade. Drill holes through their centers and fasten them between your spring clamp's folded tips. For extra holding power, double the blades at each tip. Make sure the teeth point towards the clamp's mouth for maximum gripping power.

Shop-Made Edging Clamp

Edging clamps are very useful, but they're a bit pricey. I prefer to make my own. Face-glue two pieces of ¾" plywood together and then bandsaw the "U" shape. Drill holes for the three ⁵⁄₁₆" T-nuts, and then make up the ⁵⁄₁₆" clamp screws using ⁵⁄₁₆" threaded rod, ⁵⁄₁₆" jam nuts, and plastic or rubber caps from the hardware store's plumbing department.

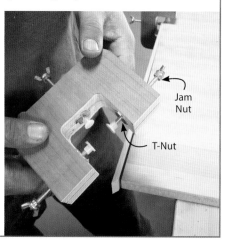

Jam Nut

T-Nut

Short of Hands? Use Feet

To hold a workpiece on its edge for mounting hinges, gluing on edge banding and similar tasks, simply clamp handscrews to the bottom.

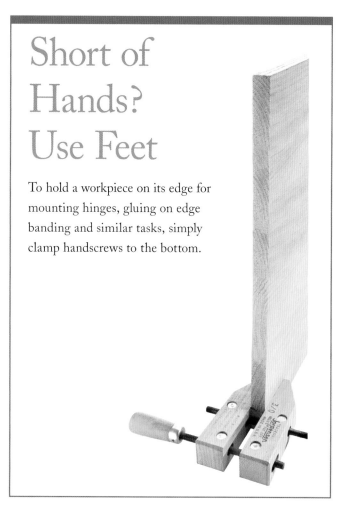

Small Offcut Holding Spring

Often the hardest pieces to cut in quantity are small ones. They're hard to keep from binding against the saw blade and shooting out like missiles. This simple spring clamp, made from a 3/4-in. pipe hanger and a scrap of wood, will hold the buggers down. The U-shape of the pipe hanger provides enough flexibility to hold the piece down and bending the tab up allows the next piece to slide in freely. Bend the pipe hanger so the end is just slightly below the height of your workpiece. After the cut, you still need to turn off the saw to rescue the little piece, but at least it's still there!

Part To Be Cut

Pipe Hanger

Quick Clamp Stands

These clamp stands are quick to make, set up and store away. Plus, they work great. Make them out of 2x4s and use a 1⅛ in. Forstner bit for the notches. These stands keep your pipe clamps from tipping and there's plenty of clearance for turning the cranks.

1⅛" Dia. Notch

2x4

¾" Dia. Black Pipe

Spring Clamps Keep Boards Aligned

Keeping the joints flush during glue-up can be challenging, because boards can slide every direction when you start applying clamp pressure. Spring clamps help to keep adjacent boards from creeping up or down.

Square a Crooked Frame

Experts recommend "checking diagonal measurements" to make sure your glued-up frames are square. So what do you do when the measurements don't match? Reposition the clamps to apply uneven pressure across the joints. Watch the change in dimension of one diagonal as you tighten the angled clamps. The goal is to split the difference between the two original measurements. For example, diagonals off by ⅛-in. require a 1/16-in. change. If the dimensional difference grows when you apply pressure instead of shrinking, the clamps are angled the wrong way.

Spring Clamps Reduce Glue-Up Stress

Gluing up a cabinet in a one-person shop can be stressful. Thankfully, I found a simple cure. A pair of 3-in. spring clamps make sturdy tripod supports on the ends of cabinet parts. They hold everything up while you fit the parts together. Now I don't break out in a cold sweat when it comes time to dry fit or glue up a cabinet. After all, woodworking is supposed to be relaxing, right?

Dado

Cabinet Side

3" Spring Clamp

Squaring Blocks for Precise Corners

Here's a surefire way to keep drawers and boxes square during clamping. Cut some perfectly square blocks of solid wood (or glued-up layers of plywood) about 4-in. square by 1½-in. thick. Drill a 2-in. hole in the middle of each block with a holesaw. Use spring clamps to hold the squaring blocks in place. Add bar clamps and leave the squaring blocks in place until the glue is set.

Squaring Block

String Band Clamp

While making a base for a wooden vase, I had to glue up a small octagonal shape. I made this simple band clamp from a piece of string and a rubber band. Here's how it works: first, tie one end of the string to the rubber band and loop the string around the workpiece; next, run the string through the other end of the rubber band and pull it tight. When you get the right amount of tension, clamp the loose end of the string. For more clamping pressure, use more rubber bands

Rubber Band

Super-Long-Reach Clamps

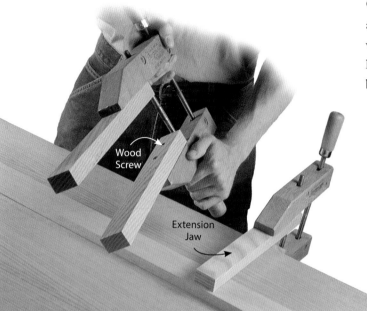

Get at that hard-to-reach project part by adding some long extension jaws to your wood handscrew clamps. Use a hard wood like maple or oak. These species work best because they resist flexing.

Wood Screw

Extension Jaw

Wide Cauls Require Fewer Clamps

Cauls distribute clamp pressure, which radiates from the jaws up to 45 degrees from center. When you locate the clamps, simply make sure the pressure from adjacent clamps overlaps at the outside glue joints. The wider the cauls, the fewer the clamps you'll need. Wide cauls are especially useful when you glue numerous thin boards—butcherblock tops, for example.

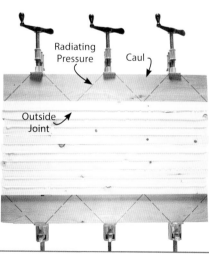

Radiating Pressure

Caul

Outside Joint

Support Clamp

To support a large panel while I drilled holes in the edge for dowels, I added a second sliding clamp jaw to a pipe clamp and clamped it to the edge of my workbench.

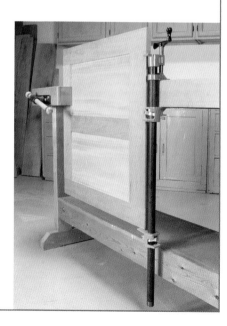

Toggle Clamps: Fast And Versatile

Available in all shapes and sizes, toggle clamps are invaluable for jigs and fixtures. By firmly holding workpieces during difficult operations, they make woodworking safer and more enjoyable.

Toggle Clamp

Trouble-Free Dovetail Clamp

Dovetails are popular because they're strong and self-locking from one side. But you need to clamp the other side with the pressure directly over the joint, if possible. And when the dovetails protrude a bit, that's tough. This unique clamping block solves the problem. You can make one of these blocks with a bandsaw or a dado blade on your tablesaw. You want the feet of the clamping block to be spaced and sized so they fit between the pins of the joint. For assembly, tap the box together and position the clamping blocks. A little masking tape works wonders to hold them in place while the clamps are added. Check your box for squareness and let it dry.

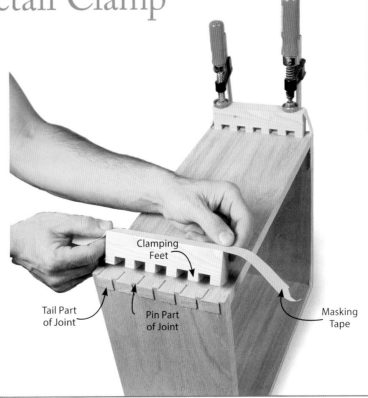

Clamping Feet

Tail Part of Joint

Pin Part of Joint

Masking Tape

Drill Press

Big Holes Without Big Bits

Recently, I needed to drill a couple of 2¼-in.-dia. holes. But instead of buying an expensive bit that I would rarely use, I created these holes with a 1½-in. Forstner bit and a ⅜-in. rabbeting bit that I already own.

Lay out the hole locations on your workpiece. Using the Forstner bit, drill holes in the workpiece and in a template. Attach the template to the workpiece with screws or double-sided tape. Make sure the holes are aligned. Then use the rabbeting bit to rout the workpiece to the larger diameter. Make several passes, raising the bit after each pass. The template allows you to complete the cut.

To create different-sized holes, start with a different Forstner bit or install larger or smaller bearings on the router bit.

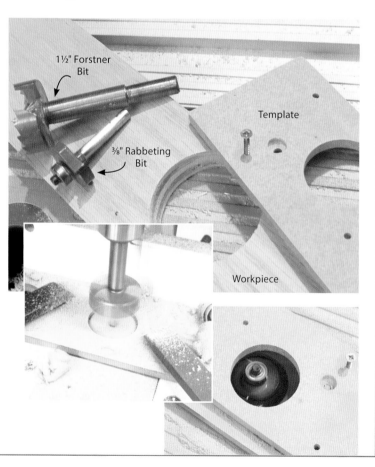

1½" Forstner Bit

⅜" Rabbeting Bit

Template

Workpiece

My Drill Can't Hold a Small Bit

I've found ¹⁄₁₆-in. pilot holes are too big for 18-gauge brads. I bought a set of those tiny wire gauge bits only to find my drill chuck can't tighten down far enough to grab them. Now what?

What you need is a micro-chuck designed to hold miniature drill bits. We tried a number of these little bits. The one we liked best sells for under $7. It held the bits firmly and it had a large chuck with a knurled surface that was easy to tighten by hand.

For $7 you're not going to get precision machining. All the chucks had some wobble yet we didn't break a single bit, even when we drilled the almost-invisible No. 80 into solid oak. Just take it easy; it takes almost no pressure to drive these bits.

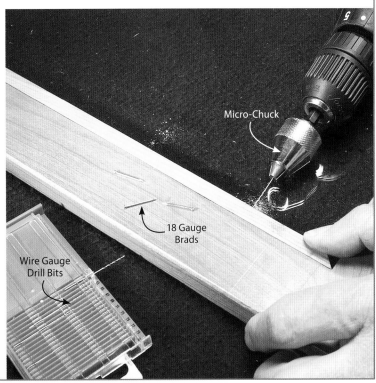

Micro-Chuck

18 Gauge Brads

Wire Gauge Drill Bits

Grain Direction on Plugs

When using wood plugs, I like to keep track of which way the grain runs. This can be tough with some woods once the plugs are cut. To keep track of the grain direction, I draw lines on the board before cutting the plugs. After the plugs have been cut away from the board I can tell at a glance which way the grain runs.

How Fast Should a Forstner Bit Spin?

I just bought a set of Forstner bits for my drill press. The first time I used one I made more smoke than sawdust! How do I figure out the right spindle speed for these bits?

To find the fastest maximum speed for any size Forstner bit, do a little experimenting. Start at a fairly slow speed (800 rpm for 1- to 1⅜-in. bits, 600 rpm for larger ones). If you make chips, fine. Bump up the speed one setting and try again. If you make more sawdust than chips, you're going too fast.

The right speed will vary with the density and moisture content of the wood. You should be making long strings of chips rather than smoke or sawdust. Both smoke and sawdust are warning signs that the bit is turning too fast or you're pushing down too hard.

So what's wrong with a little smoke? If the bit turns too fast, it'll overheat and turn blue around the rim, indicating that it's lost its temper (!). That's not good. The bit will dull much faster and won't make a correctly sized hole.

Forstner Bit

Chips

Drill Bits for Pennies

I've always had bad luck with really small drill bits— if I don't break them, I lose them. I've stopped buying new ones, and now clip the heads off finish nails and use the nails as bits. Smooth nails—not galvanized— work best. To improve its cutting ability, file or grind the end of the nail to a chisel point.

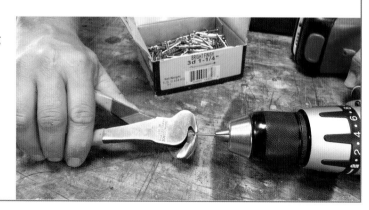

Sliding Drill Press Table

Why doesn't a drill press come with an adjustable fence? My solution is essentially a two-part table. The fence (C) is attached to the top part, which slides on the runners (F) of the bottom part, which is fastened to the drill press table. Setscrews thread through T-nuts mounted inside the side rails (D) to lock the top in position. The bottom holds an insert (E) that can easily be replaced whenever it starts to look like Swiss cheese.

Replaceable Insert

Cutting List
Overall Dimensions* 4⅞" x 14¾" x 20¹⁄₁₆"

Part	Name	Qty.	Dimension
A	Front Rail	1	¾" x 2½" x 20¹⁄₁₆"
B	Table	2	¾" x 7¾" x 14"
C	Fence	1	¾" x 2⅜" x 20¹⁄₁₆"
D	Side Rail	2	¾" x 1¾" x 14"
E	Replaceable Insert	1	¾" x 4½" x 14"
F	Runners	6	¾" x 1" x 14"
G	Base	1	¾" x 14" x 18½"

*Sized for use with 14" drill press

Setscrew

Disposable Drill Press Table

Instead of making disposable inserts for my drill press table, I found that it's faster and cheaper to make disposable fence/table assemblies. I can use the entire surface of my disposable tables, so I get more life from them.

First, make a ¾" x 16" x 20" base for your drill press table and bolt it in place. Epoxy a 3" ¼-20 bolt through one corner of the base. Then cut a fence ¾" x 2" x 18". Drill ¼" holes 2" apart along the ¾" surface of the fence's length. Screw the fence to an MDF or plywood off-cut. Slip the fence/table assembly onto the bolt through the fence's first hole, and secure it with a cam clamp or jig knob. Pivot the other end to position the fence and clamp it in place.

When the first area of the disposable table is full of holes, loosen the clamp and move the fence to the next hole. When you've moved the fence through all of the holes, unscrew the fence and screw it to the opposite edge of the disposable table and start over. When the whole board is used up, salvage the fence for the next disposable table.

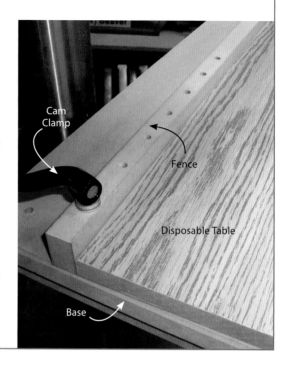

Cam Clamp

Fence

Disposable Table

Base

Drill Centering Jig

There are many times when you need to drill holes down the center of a board. This drill-press jig automatically centers the bit. With some imagination, this design could also be used to center your piece to a saw blade or a router bit. The jig is made of two wooden side bars and two metal end pieces. These are joined to form a rectangle that pivots into a parallelogram. The rectangle is elevated above a piece of MDF with washers and joined to it by screws running through the center of the metal ends. A sacrificial backer board is placed underneath the rectangle.

To set up the jig, lower the bit so the tip is trapped between the wooden sides. "Squeeze" the rectangle onto the drill bit and clamp the MDF board to the drill press table. The drill bit will be centered on any piece held by the jig.

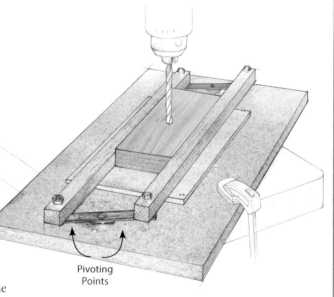

Pivoting Points

Hole-Saw Helper

Hole saws can be frustrating tools. They stop cutting when their teeth fill with sawdust, and that causes the teeth to heat up and dull. If this happens to you, too, try this trick. Drill down just far enough with the hole saw to scribe a shallow circle. Then drill a few ⅜" holes around the circle's circumference. When you return to cutting with the hole saw, sawdust will exit out these holes, allowing the saw to cut cooler and more efficiently.

Sawdust
Exit Hole

Mark-Free Drilling

Sometimes drilling a hole in a finished or ready-to-be finished piece of wood is unavoidable. I keep a pad of sticky notes nearby for this purpose. I put the sticky note roughly over the area where the hole is to go. Then I can mark the location of the hole without making any marks directly on the wood. Paper is easier to write on than either tape or finished wood. A sticky note doesn't harm finishes or leave a residue.

Sticky
Note

Go-Anywhere Drill Guide

When I need holes drilled too far from the edge of a board to use my drill press, I reach for this handy drilling guide. It allows me to position the bit exactly and assures that I'll drill a perpendicular hole, as long as I hold the guide firmly on the workpiece. I can also drill to an accurate depth by chucking the drill bit so it protrudes beyond the guide by the depth of the hole I want to drill. Unlike stop collars that mount on the drill bit, this stop never mars the workpiece's surface.

These guides are so handy, I've made them for many of my bits. First, using my drill press, I drill a perpendicular hole through the block. Then I cut the arch on my bandsaw.

Drill-Press Speed

Do I really need to change my drill-press speed for small-diameter bits? They seem to drill OK at a slow speed and it's kind of a hassle changing the belt all the time.

On the road or in the shop, it's best to obey the speed limit. In the case of twist bits, the small-diameter bits rely on high rpm rates to clear the flutes of wood chips. At high speeds, the flutes are better able to carry the chips up and out of the hole. At slow speeds, the flutes tend to jam up with material, which leads to slow cutting and high temperatures that will dull bits prematurely. There's also a tendency to push harder to overcome the jammed bit, which can result in a broken bit.

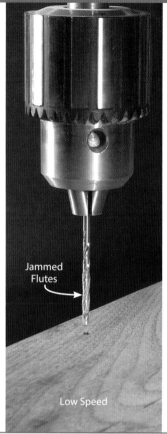

Jammed Flutes

Low Speed

Clear Flutes

Correct Speed

Is My Forstner Bit Ruined?

While drilling hardwood, the rim of my high-speed steel Forstner bit turned blue. Doesn't blueing indicate that the steel has lost its temper? Did I ruin my bit?

Your Forstner bit should be fine, for a couple of reasons. First, blueing on a bit made of high-speed steel (HSS) doesn't indicate a loss of temper. (Tempering is a heating process used to make metal tougher and less brittle.) HSS is tempered at temperatures higher than 1,100 degrees Fahrenheit. To lose its temper, and its hardness, your bit would have to reach the same incredible temperature during use, which is highly unlikely. At 1,100 degrees Fahrenheit, your bit would turn a dull red, as in red-hot, and the wood you're drilling would probably catch fire.

Second, the rim on a Forstner bit doesn't actually drill the hole. The cutting flute does that job by shaving wood from the surface as the bit spins. The rim scores the wood and guides the bit. Turning blue is normal, the result of friction generated from constantly rubbing against the side of the hole. To reduce friction, make sure your bit's cutting flute is sharp, operate your drill press at slow speed and use a steady feed rate.

Rim

Cutting Flute

How Should I Hold a Tap?

I tried threading holes in metal for a woodworking jig, but I can't figure out how to hold the tap vertical. How do you do that?

Use the same tool you drilled a vertical pilot hole with: the drill press. The machine doesn't actually turn the tap, but it will hold it perfectly plumb.

First, lightly chamfer the hole with a countersink. Leave the countersink in the chuck, but unplug your drill press. Tighten the tap in a T-handle tap wrench. This kind of wrench has a hole or dimple on its top for just this operation. Lower the drill press table. Stand the tap in the pilot hole and lower the chuck until the countersink engages the hole in the top of the wrench. Lock the chuck in place and make sure the tap is vertical.

Lubricate the tap with oil. (Machinists use special cutting oil, but ordinary household oil works fine.) Turn the tap with one hand and apply downward pressure through the drill press with the other. After a few revolutions, or if turning becomes difficult, back the tap out one-half turn to break up metal chips. Then continue tapping until the tap spins freely in the hole.

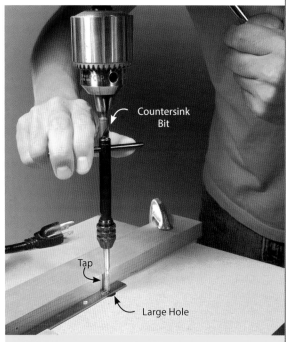

Countersink Bit

Tap

Large Hole

Caution: Unplug your drill press for this operation.

Simple Dowel Drilling

I needed a way to hold dowels steady so that I could drill pilot holes in them. After a little head scratching, I cut a V-notch in a small piece of 2x4. I clamped a second piece of 2x4 against the piece of dowel as a brace.

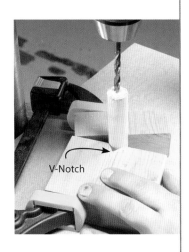

V-Notch

Straight-Shooting Drill Jig

You may not face this problem often, but when you need to drill a hole nice and straight but the part is too big to fit on the drill press, here's what to do: Make this nifty little jig. It's about 1½-in. tall by 2-in wide. Line up your drill bit in the corner of the jig and get a perfectly straight hole every time.

Vertical Drilling Jig

I came up with this slick way to drill a large, straight hole in the end of a post. It works great and makes good use of my tall floor-mounted drill press.

To make the jig, I first swung my metal drill table to the side and clamped on an auxiliary table. I made the table out of two ¾-in. thick by 16-in. wide by 32-in.-long boards, glued and screwed together. The double thickness is required for strength because the drilling action puts a lot of pressure on the table. Then I built the jig and screwed it to the auxiliary table. The 16-in.-long side support board keeps the workpiece vertical in the left-to-right position. The front support board keeps the workpiece vertical in the front-to-back position.

To drill a hole with this setup, I clamp my workpiece to the jig. Then I loosen the clamps holding the auxiliary table in place and adjust the whole setup until the drill bit is correctly positioned over the center mark. If the jig setup flexes while drilling, add some additional support under the bottom of the workpiece, between it and the base of the drill press.

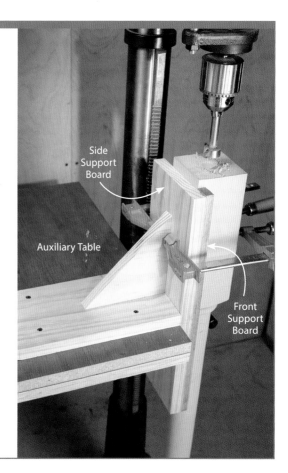

Side Support Board

Auxiliary Table

Front Support Board

Smooth-as-Silk Countersink

Countersink first, drill the pilot hole second. That may sound backward, but it's the easiest way to ensure a perfectly smooth countersink. I used to drill the pilot hole first on the drill press, but if that hole was relatively large or the wood quite dense, the countersink bit would inevitably chatter and make an ugly, rough surface.

One day I tried the countersink bit first with no pilot hole. What a difference! It made a perfect conical depression. It's easy to locate the hole because a countersink bit has a sharp tip. Centering the pilot hole is easy, too. A twist bit practically positions itself in the hole's bottom.

Wow!

Spacious Drill Press Table

I built this auxiliary drill press table to give me the extra support and room I need when drilling cabinet doors and sides. The core is MDF but particleboard would also work fine. I edged my table with oak to make the edges more durable. The plastic laminate provides a smooth surface to work on and should last a long time. Having plastic laminate on both sides keeps the table stiff and stable. The table insert is replaceable and the fence is quick and simple to adjust. The T-slot tracks make it easy to add other jigs and fixtures. My table measures 18 in. by 35½ in. and has proved to be a good size for most work. I bought all the parts at my local home center and woodworking store.

Replaceable Table Insert

Ratchet Knob

Aluminum Angle Fence

¾" Spacer Block

2 Washers

T-Slot Track

Replaceable Table Insert

Plastic Laminate

T-Slot Track

Plastic Laminate Shim

¾" MDF

½" MDF

Oak

Plastic Laminate

Electricity & Batteries

Battery Health Checkup

The battery on my cordless drill runs down quickly, although I haven't had this tool for very long. How can I tell for sure whether my battery is shot?

Run a simple test. First, make sure your battery is fully charged. Then set an electronic multimeter to a 24-volt range and touch the two battery terminals with the probes. A good battery should test 1 to 2 volts over the voltage listed on the battery. A 14.4-volt battery, for example, should read 14.4 to 16.4 volts. If it doesn't, you need a new battery.

The biggest cause of premature battery failure is running it down too far before it's recharged. Unlike a cell-phone battery, a power-tool battery should be charged as soon as it begins to slow. When you detect a loss of power, let the battery cool to room temperature and then put it in a charger.

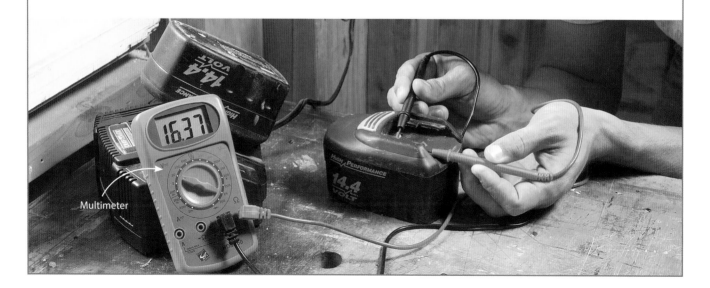

Multimeter

Don't Do This!

When I bought my first cordless drill, I was told to drain the battery all the way down before recharging to prolong the life of the battery. I used to clamp the switch until the drill quit running. Now I hear this is a bad practice. What gives?

Don't drain your battery! Actually, you can stick your battery in the charger anytime you like. Draining the battery all the way down is a bad idea, for any drill, whether it has a NiCd or NiMH battery. The practice will cause heat to build up in the battery. This can actually shorten its life, just the opposite of what you intend. A good rule of thumb is to recharge the battery at the first sign of power loss. Let the battery rest and cool for 10 minutes or so before plunking it in the charger.

Don't Do This!

Recycling Cordless Tool Batteries

How do I properly dispose of my worn-out cordless tool batteries?

We wrote about this question a few years back but it is such an important topic, and with the flood of cordless tools on the market, we feel it's well worth revisiting. Recycling worn-out batteries is hassle-free, thanks to the Rechargeable Battery Recycling Corp. (RBRC). Just go to the Web site, www.rbrc. org, click on "Find a Drop-Off Site Near You," enter your zip code and a list of nearby sites will appear. I tried it and I was amazed; even though I live in a small town, there were three sites a few blocks from my home. Another way to find a drop-off site is to call (800) 822-8837 (1-800-8-BATTERY). These centers will take all your rechargeable batteries, including nickel-cadmium (Ni-Cd), nickel metal hydride

(Ni-MH), lithium-ion (Li-ion) and small sealed lead (Pb) batteries weighing up to 2 lbs. (1kg).

In an effort to increase public awareness, most manufacturers affix RBRC's updated recycle seal onto their battery packs. The new seal gives the RBRC toll-free number.

In addition to battery recycling, the retail drop-off sites will soon accept discarded cellphones. Now I know what to do with my old cellphone collection, too.

Breaker-Popping Tablesaw

I keep popping a circuit breaker with my contractor's saw, and it's driving me nuts. Would changing to a 240-volt circuit solve the problem?

In a perfect world, a 120-volt circuit should handle the 1½-hp motor on your contractor's saw without tripping the breaker. In reality, your circuit may not be delivering the full 120 volts to your saw. This is commonly referred to as voltage drop. Your saw's motor is rated for 120 volts. If it's getting less than that, it will pull more current to make up the difference and that will cause the breaker to trip.

Here's what you can do: First make sure there is no other electrical draw on the circuit. Then, look at how far the outlet is from the service panel. If your panel is in the garage and your shop is on the opposite side of the house in the basement, you're essentially running your saw on a very long "extension cord." The longer the distance, the greater the voltage drop.

To measure the actual voltage being delivered to your saw, have a friend cut some wood on your saw while you take a reading with a voltmeter (available at hardware stores for around $20). A voltage drop in excess of 5 percent can lead to breaker trips. Running the saw on

240 volts would solve this problem. That's because a 240-volt circuit will have one-quarter the voltage drop over a given distance than a 120-volt circuit will have. (This difference is what leads people to swear they get more power from 240 volts than 120 volts.) Instead of about a 16-volt drop (13 percent) shown on the voltmeter in the photo, you would have a 4-volt (2 percent) drop in a 240-volt circuit.

Switch Safety

Sliding switches on some of my older power tools make it difficult to tell whether they're switched on or off. I didn't think much about it until the time my router started right up when I plugged it in—I had unknowingly switched it on while I was changing bits. Before I could pull the plug, the runaway router had jumped right off my bench.

To easily tell whether my tools are on or off, I slide the switches to the on position—with the tool unplugged, of course—and apply a little bright-colored paint on the portion of the housing exposed by moving the switch. Now, bright paint warns that the power is on.

Converting a
Motor's Voltage

I need to change the wiring on an 8-in. jointer from 240 volts to 120 volts. How do I do it?

Motors that can be wired for either 240 volts or 120 volts should have a wiring diagram on the motor or on the inside of the wire junction box cover. The motor will have either numbered wires or color-coded wires. Rewiring you motor is a simple matter of rearranging the connections. To make the change, just match the numbers or colors to the diagram on the motor. Use new wire nuts, and make sure they are twisted on all the way. You'll know you're there when a wire nut no longer turns without twisting the whole wire bundle.

An often overlooked but important factor when going from a higher voltage to a lower voltage is the cord's wire gauge. Motors wired for 240 volts will have 14-gauge or 16-gauge wire. This wire is too small for the increased amperage draw required by a motor wired for 120 volts. Use 12-gauge wire for motors rated at or above 12 amps at 120 volts.

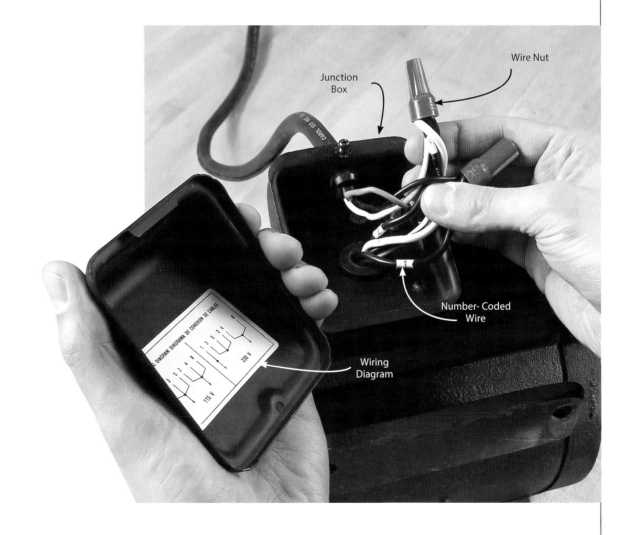

Wire Nut

Junction Box

Number-Coded Wire

Wiring Diagram

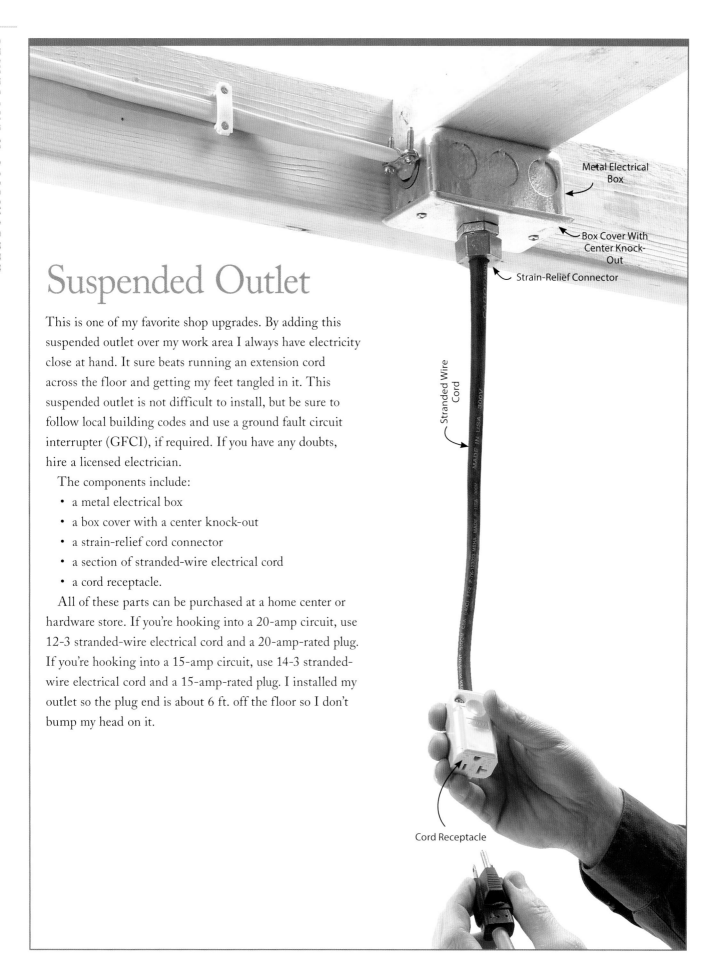

Metal Electrical
Box

Box Cover With
Center Knock-
Out

Strain-Relief Connector

Stranded Wire
Cord

Cord Receptacle

Suspended Outlet

This is one of my favorite shop upgrades. By adding this
suspended outlet over my work area I always have electricity
close at hand. It sure beats running an extension cord
across the floor and getting my feet tangled in it. This
suspended outlet is not difficult to install, but be sure to
follow local building codes and use a ground fault circuit
interrupter (GFCI), if required. If you have any doubts,
hire a licensed electrician.

The components include:

- a metal electrical box
- a box cover with a center knock-out
- a strain-relief cord connector
- a section of stranded-wire electrical cord
- a cord receptacle.

All of these parts can be purchased at a home center or
hardware store. If you're hooking into a 20-amp circuit, use
12-3 stranded-wire electrical cord and a 20-amp-rated plug.
If you're hooking into a 15-amp circuit, use 14-3 stranded-
wire electrical cord and a 15-amp-rated plug. I installed my
outlet so the plug end is about 6 ft. off the floor so I don't
bump my head on it.

Overhead Extension Cord

I have a love-hate relationship with my extension cords. I love how they bring power where I need it. But I hate tripping over the cords or trying to wheel carts over them.

One day while tying up an extension cord for storage with one of those hook-and-loop wraps, I got an idea. I installed a handful of eye-hooks and hook-and-loop fasteners in the ceiling joists. Whenever I need power in a remote spot now, I run my extension cord overhead.

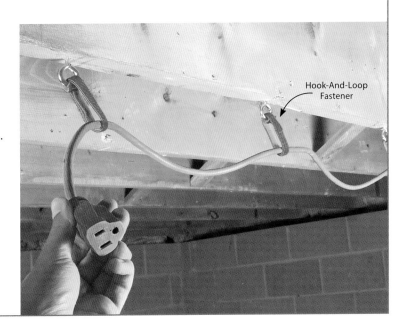

Hook-And-Loop Fastener

Why Do Plugs Vary?

Components

15 Amp   20 Amp   30 Amp

I'm confused by the variety of 240-volt plugs and outlets. Does it matter what type I use with my machines?

Sure does. Each type is designed for a different amp load. To protect your machine's motor, you must match the amp ratings of the motor, plug, outlet and circuit breaker.

Most 240-volt woodworking machines designed for small shops run on 15, 20 or 30-amp circuits. There's a unique plug and outlet configuration for each circuit. Amperage ratings are always printed or stamped on the plugs. If your machine already has a 240-volt plug on it, install the appropriate outlet in your wall and the same size breaker in your fuse box. If your machine doesn't come with a plug, consult the owner's manual and install the appropriate plug, outlet and breaker.

Allowing too many amps to be delivered to a motor may damage or destroy it. You shouldn't plug a motor that's rated at 12 amps into a 30-amp circuit, for example. During a heavy cut, a motor calls for more amperage to maintain torque. A 15-amp circuit breaker would trip in time to protect the motor from overheating. A 30-amp circuit breaker wouldn't offer the same protection. It would continue to provide amperage well past the motor's rating and lead to excessive heating, a motor's biggest enemy.

Finishing

Filling Nail Holes

I am making an oak bookcase as a built-in for our living room. What's the best way to fill the nail holes and finish the trim pieces once they're in place?

Don't try to finish the trim in place. It's best to have all of your finish work done before you install the built-in.

As you install your trim, be careful about where you nail. For example, it's harder to see nail holes in the dark, coarse earlywood of oak than in the smoother latewood (photos below).

After the trim is installed, fill the nail holes with one of the numerous fillers designed to be applied to finished wood. Minwax makes Blend-Fil pencils (available wherever Minwax products are sold); Behlens Fill Sticks

(Constantine's 800-223-8087) and similar products are all available from mail order catalogs that carry finish supplies. These fillers are crayon-like in texture and come in a variety of shades to match most finishes.

These fillers are easy to apply. Simply rub the stick over the hole until it's full, then wipe off the excess with a clean rag. If you goof and the color is off, just take a wire nail, gently dig out the filler and try a different shade. You can also blend colors. For example, if the color from a stick is a little light, score the surface of the filler and rub in a darker color. The two colors will blend in the hole and produce a new shade.

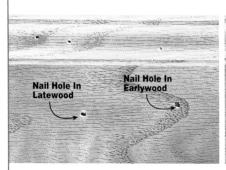

Nail Hole In Latewood

Nail Hole In Earlywood

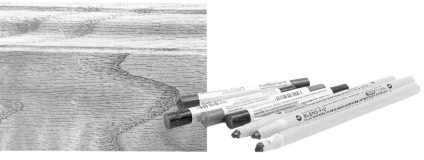

Custom Varnish Sheen

The polyurethane varnish I like comes in gloss and semi-gloss. Is there any way to create a flatter, less glossy look than what comes straight out of the can?

Yes there is, and it doesn't involve sanding or rubbing to alter the sheen. Varnish manufacturers create a semi-gloss or satin sheen by adding flattening agents like silica to their formulas. You've probably noticed it as a layer of sludge that settles out when your varnish sits for a long time. To flatten the sheen you need to concentrate the flattening agents already in your semi-gloss. Here's how:

Let the varnish settle and pour off about half the clear varnish into a second container. Stir up the concentrated mix and try it on a sample board. Keep adding the gloss from the second container until you achieve the desired sheen.

FLATTENING AGENTS

Does Polyurethane Need Sanding?

I've used solvent-based polyurethane for years, and have always been careful to sand between coats. I have been told sanding isn't necessary. Is that true?

Polyurethanes for floors or woodwork are often formulated so they don't have to be sanded, but polyurethanes for furniture generally should be sanded.

Sanding removes unevenness and dust in a brushed surface. If you want a silky, smooth feel to your finish, you must sand between coats no matter what kind of poly you use.

By abrading the surface, sanding also improves the mechanical bond between coats. Sanding scratches effectively increase the surface area, so one coat adheres better to another. Some kinds of polyurethane don't need to be sanded to bond well, but only if you re-coat before the finish hardens too much. The window is usually about 12 hours. If you wait longer, you should always sand.

Bathroom-Cup Mixers

I always mix my own stain because I rarely find the color I want right out of the can. After the many hours of careful planning and execution that go into building a piece of furniture, I just can't open a can of stain and take my chances with the finish.

For mixing small color samples I use those little 3-oz.-disposable plastic cups. The plastic cups work much better than paper cups, which can leak with some finishes. You can buy them at any grocery store. For a few bucks more you can even buy the dispenser, hang it on your shop wall and have them right at hand.

Final Rubout

I always have problems getting a smooth finish. I sand the wood with 220 paper, wipe it with a tack cloth, apply three coats of high-quality varnish, and still get a rough surface! What can I do to get that "professional" look?

You've got dust problems, like everybody else. Even if you carefully tack the wood prior to finishing, the air (and you!) are full of small dust particles that settle on your finish right after you've laid it down. To get rid of the "nibs," rub out the last dried coat with a dab of wax and extra-fine steel wool. This will polish the last coat and scrape off the nibs leaving a silky smooth finish.

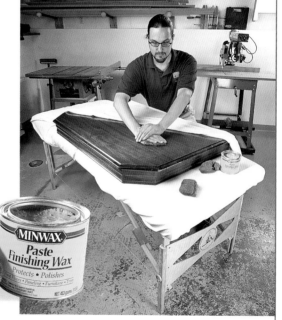

Give your work a final rubdown with wax and extra-fine steel wool.

Better Brush Cleaning

I bought an expensive natural-bristle brush for varnishing, but I can't seem to get it completely clean. The bristles are stiff after the brush dries. What can I do?

Pros clean their brushes in stages, often with special solvents and conditioners. This technique will keep your brush soft for years.

Along with mineral spirits or paint thinner, you'll use a solvent called "brush cleaner" or lacquer thinner. You'll also use "brush conditioner." Ordinary mineral oil works as well. Finally, you'll need a special brush comb. All are available at paint stores.

1

Caution: Wear gloves and goggles.

Rinse your brush in mineral spirits until most traces of varnish are gone. Pour the mineral spirits back into the original container. You can reuse it several times, because the varnish solids will sink to the bottom. Dry the bristles thoroughly with a rag.

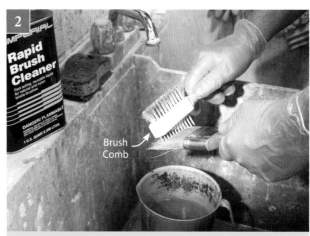

2

Brush Comb

Caution: Wear a respirator with an organic vapor cartridge when using brush cleaner or lacquer thinner.

Repeat the same process with brush cleaner or lacquer thinner. Comb the brush to straighten the bristles and remove all varnish residue. Let the brush soak for 15 to 20 minutes, if time permits.

3

Vigorously clean the brush with dishwashing liquid and hot water. Go through at least four to five wash cycles. Turn the brush upward each time so water runs directly into the bristles. Comb the brush when you're done.

4

Wipe the brush dry with a lint-free rag and apply a small dab of brush conditioner or mineral oil. Work it in, then straighten the bristles once more with the comb. Wrap the brush in its original container and hang it to dry.

Collapsible Drying Rack

Sturdy yet collapsible is easier said than done, but this drying rack is both. It folds flat against the wall to save space until I need it. I made my rack 36 in. tall, with 8 in. between levels. Each side of the rack is made by sandwiching hardwood support arms between plywood uprights.

Each arm measures $^{13}/_{16}$ in. x 1$^{1}/_{8}$ in. x 28 in. The uprights and spacers are 2$^{1}/_{2}$ in. wide. The uprights hinge on horizontal rails fastened to the wall. When open, $^{3}/_{4}$ in. x 1 in. hardwood runners lay across the arms. Blocks attached to the runners keep the arms spread.

The runners' top edges are beveled to minimize the amount of surface contacting the finished pieces to be laid on them. When not in use, the runners store on dowels attached to the rack's hinged uprights.

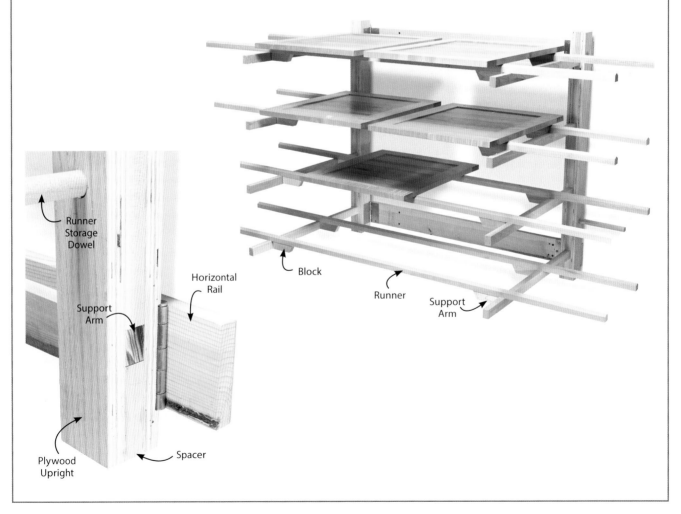

Runner Storage Dowel

Support Arm

Horizontal Rail

Block

Runner

Support Arm

Plywood Upright

Spacer

Freshness Date for Finish

I never thought about the risks of using finish from an old, previously opened can until I had to entirely strip a project because the ancient varnish I used didn't dry properly.

Now I play it safe. I date every can when I first open it, so I know at a glance how long the remaining finish has aged. If the date shows the can has been sitting for a year, I test the finish it contains on a sample. Before I use any old finish on a project, I want to make sure it dries hard.

After two years, my freshness date expires. Using vintage finish may be appealing because it doesn't cost anything, but buying a fresh can is a much better idea.

Getting Stain Out of Corners

I like using gel stain on difficult to stain woods such as birch because it doesn't leave a blotchy look. But man, the stuff is a pain to get out of corners. No matter how hard I push, I can't force the rag deep enough into the corner to clean up the excess stain. Got any neat tricks?

It's no picnic to get any kind of stain out of a corner, and the thick consistency of gel stain makes it especially tough. Here's our suggestion: Use a dry brush to whisk away the excess gel stain. Unlike a rag, the bristles of the brush are easy to get into corners. Use a rag to wipe excess stain off the brush and to keep it dry. It works great! Be sure to clean the brush after you're done so it's ready to come to the rescue the next time you stain yourself into a corner.

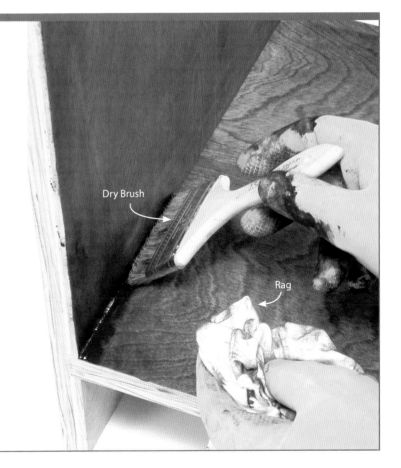

Dry Brush

Rag

Finish on Tap

I buy varnish by the gallon because it's more economical, but after a few uses, the rim fills with gunk and the finish begins to skin over inside the can. As a result, I usually have to throw the can away before it's empty.

I solved this problem by recycling a 5-liter wine box into an airtight varnish dispenser. Choose a box with a twist-open spout. After enjoying the wine (and a good night's sleep!), remove the empty bag and carefully pry the spout out of its fitting. Rinse the bag and let it dry.

Filling the bag with varnish is a two-person job: One person holds a funnel and the bag while the other person pours. Stir the varnish thoroughly before pouring it. After pouring, remove any air that remains inside the bag by carefully compressing it on a table, fitting side up. While the bag is compressed, open the spout and press it back into the fitting. Make sure the spout is oriented to operate correctly when the bag is back inside the box.

Because the bag is air-free, once it's reinstalled, you'll be able to stir the varnish by simply shaking the box. A classy label ensures that no one mistakes your polyurethane for pinot noir.

Is Polyurethane Food-Safe?

I'm planning on finishing a set of wooden plates with polyurethane. Is this finish safe for food?

According to finishing expert Bob Flexner, all finishes are food-safe once they have cured. Polyurethane varnish does not present any known hazard. However, no finish is food safe until it has fully cured. The rule of thumb for full curing is 30 days at room temperature (65- to 75-degrees F).

The question of food safety in finishes revolves around the metallic driers added to oils and varnishes to speed the curing process. Lead was used as a drier many years ago, but now lead is banned.

There is no evidence that today's driers are unsafe. No case of poisoning from finishes containing these driers has ever been reported. The Food and Drug Administration approves the use of these driers in

coatings, and no warnings are required on cans or Material Data Safety Sheets.

Several oil and varnish products are marketed as "food or salad-bowl safe." This implies that other finishes may not be safe, but that's simply not true. Some of these specially labeled products have no driers added to them (and they take quite a long time to dry!), but the rest actually contain the same kinds of driers as other oils and varnishes.

Hanging Racks For Finishing

In my crowded shop, I needed room to finish the doors and shelves of a large cabinet while leaving enough space to continue building the case. So, I built three inexpensive racks to hang them.

The racks are made from electrical conduit. To build one rack, you'll need two screw-in J-hooks, a 10' section of electrical conduit, and two 2-screw conduit connectors. Screw the J-hooks into the ceiling rafters 10' apart. Install a connector on each end of the conduit. Fasten one of the connector's screws to the conduit and run a wire through the other screw hole to hang the unit from the J-hooks.

To use the rack, run an eye screw into the part being finished. Put the eye screw in an area that's hidden after assembly, and loop a wire through the eye. Hang the part from the conduit.

Finishing Rack

While doing the dishes the other night, I looked at the drying rack and thought, "Wow! I need one of these in my shop."

First I drilled centered ⅝-in.-dia. holes every 3 in. along both edges of a 1-in. x 6-in.-wide board. After mitering both edges to a point, I ripped off the two triangular rails. This shape minimizes contact with the finished parts as they dry. To complete the rack, I glued 14-in.-long dowels in the holes and connected the rails by screwing on two ¾-in. x 1-in. pieces. The rails pivot on the screws, so when I'm not using the rack, it folds up flat and hangs on the wall.

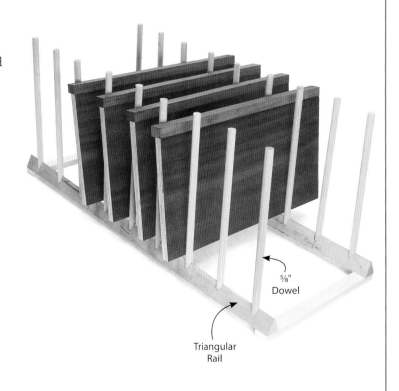

⅝" Dowel

Triangular Rail

Don't Toss Old Varnish—Use It

How do I properly dispose of leftover finishes?

The very best way to dispose of old finish materials is to use them. Several hazardous-waste recycling agencies contacted about this question agreed that this is not only the best practice for the environment but for your wallet as well. Use old finish to seal the inside drawers or the interior of a cabinet where it won't be easily seen. You can thin old varnish and use it as a seal coat on bare wood. Old stain can be spread on scrap wood and allowed to dry before disposal.

If the finish has turned to a gelatin or is otherwise unusable, let the remaining varnish dry in the can. A water-based finish can be put it in the garbage after it has dried into a solid chunk.

Usable solvent-based finishes should be taken to your community's hazardous-waste facility, so they can be disposed of in a way that minimizes their negative environmental effects.

Contamination from a Tack Cloth?

Are oil-based tack cloths compatible with water-borne polyurethane finishes?

Yes. You can wipe off dust with a standard tack cloth without fear of contaminating the surface if you follow two simple directions. One, open up the tack cloth before you use it and form it into a loose bunch. Two, wipe very gently. If you press hard you might transfer some of the oil from the tack cloth to the finish. That would be bad, because the next coat of finish may not adhere to the contaminated area.

Longer-Lasting Steel Wool

It's always bugged me that steel wool pads don't last longer. Each pad is made of thousands of sharp-edged steel strands. The problem is, they're packed together so tightly they clog up right away and most of them never get used.

I'm a die-hard tightwad, so I came up with this trick to extend the life of my steel wool. I unroll each pad and shape it into a fluffy ball before I use it. As the ball gets flattened, I stop and gently pull it back apart. Re-fluffing exposes new sharp edges and releases wood dust and broken-off bits of worn-out steel wool.

Re-Usable Tack Cloth

Microfiber cloth picks up tiny dust particles as well as, if not better than, a tack cloth. Unlike a tack cloth, micro fiber cloths are washable and reusable. Any microfiber cloth will work as long as it has hemmed edges.

No-Stick Caps

It had been a couple of months since I last used my oil finish and when I went to use it the cap was a bear to get off. Drips of finish around the spout had dried like glue. My neighbor suggested that next time I try putting Teflon plumbing tape (available at home centers) around the spout before closing it up. Sure enough, a few months later when I needed more oil finish, the cap came right off.

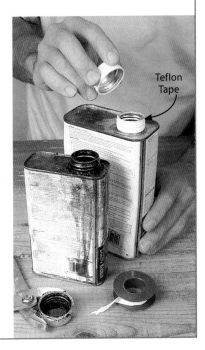

Teflon Tape

Knot Repair

I'm working on an oak table with a top made from three 12-in. wide, ¾-in. thick boards. One of the boards has a tight knot that's about 1½ in. across. There are some small voids around the knot that need to be filled, and I'm concerned about it loosening over time. I considered cutting an inlay, but I'd rather find some way to stabilize the knot. Do you have any recommendations? I'm planning to apply a gel stain, followed by a tung oil finish.

I'm glad you've realized that knots aren't necessarily defects; in many cases, they're marks of character. My standard technique for knot repairs is to fill the voids with a mixture of clear epoxy and fine sawdust.

Make your sawdust by sanding a scrap piece of oak with 220-grit sandpaper. Make plenty because there won't be time to create more once you mix the epoxy.

Apply masking tape to the underside of the knot to prevent epoxy from leaking out. Place the board on your workbench, good side up. Put on protective gloves and mix the epoxy according to the manufacturer's instructions. Blend in oak sawdust gradually until you have a creamy mixture. Push this mixture into and around the knot. Use a flexible palette knife (available from an art supply store) or you could use an old, bent, table knife. Confine the epoxy to the repair area, but mound it slightly. Stir the filled-in area with a pin to eliminate air bubbles. When the epoxy is dry, level it with a plane or scraper, and sand with at least 220-grit sandpaper before applying your finish.

Quick Cure for Sand-Through Woes

Aaaargh! It's so easy to sand through the finish on an edge and it always seems to happen when I'm ready for the last coat of varnish. Here's a quick and easy fix. Grab a touch-up marker and run it along the sand-through. It'll make your mistake virtually invisible. The marker dries instantly so you can put that final coat on right away. Available in a wide variety of shades and colors, these markers are designed to blend scratches and minor sand-throughs into the finish.

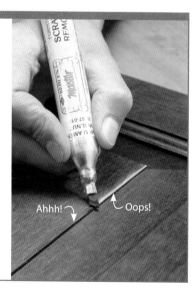

Ahhh! ⤹   ⤸ Oops!

Old Brass From New

How can I get new brass hardware to look old?

Fuming brass hardware with strong ammonium hydroxide (26 to 30 percent), is a tried and true method. Strong ammonia is a hazardous material and has become harder to obtain. We found ours at a laboratory and chemical supply company; commercial printer suppliers are another good source.

Use ammonium hydroxide only in a well-ventilated area. Wear eye protection, rubber gloves and a respirator with cartridges designed specifically for ammonia fumes.

First, remove any lacquer that may be on the hardware by soaking it in lacquer thinner and rinsing with water. Next, suspend the hardware over a small amount of ammonium hydroxide in a glass jar with a tight fitting lid. Attach string to the underside of the lid with duct tape. After about an hour the brass will turn a beautiful coppery brown color. For a darker color, fume the hardware longer.

We tried this process using household ammonia which is approximately one-fifth the strength of ammonium hydroxide and is readily available wherever cleaning supplies are sold. The weaker solution turned the brass a greenish yellow color, much different than the full-strength ammonia.

We also tried a brass antiquing solution sold through craft and specialty stores. Immerse the hardware in the antiquing solution (a mild acid) until the desired color is achieved (half an hour in this case). This solution left a shiny, black chrome appearance on the hardware. Not exactly an antique look, to our eyes.

For highlights you can burnish the hardware with a little 0000 steel wool after fuming.

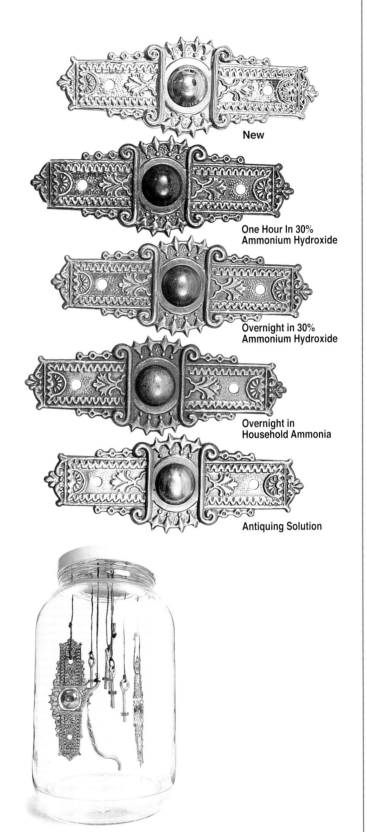

New

One Hour In 30% Ammonium Hydroxide

Overnight in 30% Ammonium Hydroxide

Overnight in Household Ammonia

Antiquing Solution

Finishing Bath

For all you scrollsawers out there, here's a slick finishing tip. You know how tough it can be to brush or spray finish into all those tiny sawed-out areas? Well, give your handiwork a bath instead! The finish will get into all those little areas and seal the wood nicely. Wipe off drips and excess finish with a clean shop cloth and set your project aside to dry. Then, brush or spray the final coats on the faces and sides only. Trying to build up the finish on the inside areas is unnecessary.

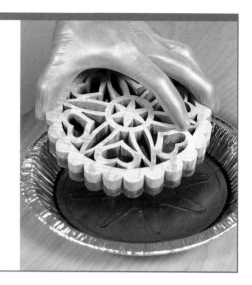

Matching Old Stains

I have to match an old stain. I've come pretty close with a new stain I bought at the hardware store, but it's not good enough. Is there a way I can tint the stain?

There are several fairly simple ways to alter the color of commercial stain. Probably the easiest is to mix two or more colors of the same type and brand of stain to match what you need. This guarantees that the components and drying times are compatible and consistent.

You can also alter a stain with small amounts of concentrated pigment pastes called "universal tinting colors." They are compatible with both oil-based and water-based stains and are available from most home stores and many craft stores. Because the universals, called UTCs, are so concentrated, you probably won't be adding enough to substantially change the drying time of the stain you started with.

If you are certain that the stain is oil based, you can also tint it with artist's oil colors or Japan colors. Both are available from most craft and art supply stores. Again, the small amounts you are likely to add probably won't affect the drying time much, but as a rule of thumb, oil colors will typically slow down the drying time while Japan colors will not.

Proper Varnish Storage

Does varnish go bad sitting on the shelf?

Unopened varnish should last for years on the shelf when kept away from excessive heat. When a can is opened and the finish exposed to oxygen, curing can begin. If the finish skins over, remove the skin and add mineral spirits to restore the original consistency. Water-based finishes have less tendency to skin over. If they do, add a bit of water to restore the original consistency. It's always best to test old varnish on a piece of scrap to make sure it's drying properly before you apply it to a project.

To maximize your varnish's shelf life after it has been opened, transfer any remaining finish to a smaller container. This will minimize the amount of oxygen in the container and preserve the varnish (see photo, right). Be sure to date and label the container. If you're using a glass jar to store the old varnish, be sure to keep it out of direct sunlight to prevent damage from UV radiation.

You can also try Bloxygen, a product that is sprayed into a partially used can and forms a gaseous barrier to protect the varnish. It also protects other solvent-based products, such as wood filler and paint, although it will not protect lacquer or water-based finishes. One can is good for approximately 75 applications.

Make New Varnish Look Old

I built my own kitchen cabinets a few years back. One drawer was damaged, so I stripped the finish from the drawer front, made the repair and applied a fresh coat of polyurethane. The new finish is noticeably lighter than the old one. I sure don't want to refinish the entire kitchen. Is there a way to match the aged finish?

The solution is to tint the new finish with dye. Varnish yellows with age and that's the reason your newly finished drawer doesn't match the old. I recommend using orange shellac. Don't let the name fool you; it's just a color and has nothing to do with real orange shellac. It's best to keep the tinting very light so two or three coats of the polyurethane give you the color that matches your old finish.

For one drawer, pour a small amount of polyurethane into a container. Add a few drops of the dye concentrate, mixing it in well. It'll look like a dark olive oil, which seems weird, but the color looks a whole lot different on the wood. It will take some experimentation to get the dye-to-polyurethane ratio correct. Brush a couple

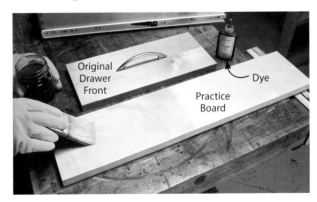

Original Drawer Front

Dye

Practice Board

of coats of the tinted poly on a test board. If the color matches, your formulating is done. If not, adjust the number of coats or the amount of dye until you get a good match.

Repair a Sand-Through

I went right through the veneer when I was sanding solid-wood edging flush on some plywood shelves. How can I fix it?

Sanding through a veneer happens to everyone sooner or later. Here's an old cabinetmaker's trick that will salvage what looks to be a hopeless situation. First, remove the damaged veneer using a router and a straight cutting bit (see photo, below left). Then, select a piece of hardwood whose color and grain resemble those of your veneer stock and cut a strip to fit the groove (see photo, below right).

Veneer seems to be getting thinner every day. To avoid future sand-throughs, make a squiggly line with a pencil along the hardwood-veneer joint. It will help you keep track of how much material you're removing.

Sand-Through

Sand-Through

1.5 PEAK HP

⅛" Deep Groove

Straight Edge Guide

Hardwood Strip

Cut a ⅛-in.-deep groove wide enough to remove the sand-through area. Use a straight edge to guide the router. Cut the groove along the full length of the cabinet side or shelf.

Glue a strip of hardwood into the groove. The strip should be just a hair thicker than the groove is deep, so it can be carefully sanded down flush.

Silky-Smooth Polyurethane

Every woodworker I know uses water-borne polyurethane. Of all the ways I've seen to get a silky-smooth finish, abrasive, steel-wool substitute pads are by far the best. The coarseness of the pad determines the final sheen. A green pad (0) leaves a dull luster, gray (00) leaves satin and white (0000), gloss. I start with a pad that's coarse enough to remove imperfections. Then I work through the different pads until I get the luster I want. I made a cork-faced block (¼-in. cork glued onto a wooden block) for flat surfaces. For edge profiles and other contoured surfaces, I just fold the pad over and go. After a final buffing with a soft, clean cloth I have a flawless finish you just have to run your hand over.

Skinned-Over Varnish

I was all ready to varnish, but when I opened the can, a thick skin covered the top. Is the stuff underneath OK to use?

The varnish underneath the skin should be just fine. Before you use it though, be sure to do two things: First, strain the varnish through one of those paper funnels with a mesh bottom (available at paint stores), some doubled-up cheesecloth or old pantyhose. This will get rid of any small bits of dried varnish that are floating around. Second, try the varnish on a piece of scrap to make sure it dries OK. If you have any doubt, toss the old stuff out and buy new. It's just not worth the risk.

Not So Thick-Skinned

Thick Skin

Storable, Portable Turntable

If you do a lot of spray painting and finishing, but don't have room for a permanent finishing bench, give this turntable a spin. It's surprisingly sturdy and because it rotates, you can get to all sides of your project while standing in one spot. It's lightweight, so it can easily be taken outside. When you're done, just unscrew the pipes from the flanges and store all the parts out of the way in the corner of your shop.

The pipe parts are available at most home centers, hardware stores and plumbing shops. Don't try to use pipes with diameters other then 1 in. and 1¼ in. These are the only pipe diameters that telescope together well. Other pipe diameters either won't fit together at all or will be too loose. The plywood top is 36-in. in diameter and the base is 24-in. in diameter. The total cost of the turntable, including the plywood, is around $40.

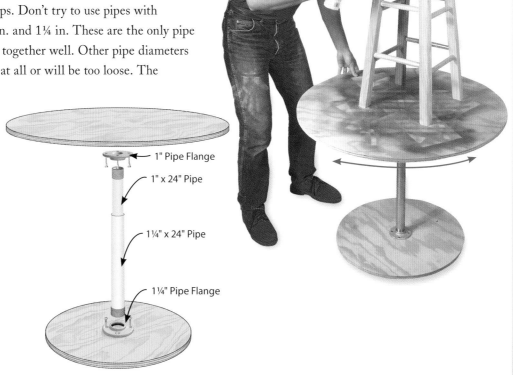

1" Pipe Flange

1" x 24" Pipe

1¼" x 24" Pipe

1¼" Pipe Flange

Small Parts Drying Rack

I made this rack so the finish on my small projects would dry without leaving marks. I cut strips off of a ¾-in. board with my tablesaw's blade tilted 30 degrees. For each new strip, I just flipped the board and moved the fence over ½-in. Then I glued the strips on a piece of plywood, varying the spacing to support different sized items.

Soda-Straw Pipette

I rarely use a stain or dye right out of the can. I make my own custom mixes in small quantities until I get the color just right.

In order to recreate the perfect mix in larger portions, I have to accurately measure the amount of each stain in the mix. Dipping a teaspoon into a can of stain rarely yields an accurate measurement and I always end up with stained hands. Pouring dye from a bottle into a measuring spoon is equally messy.

So now I reach for a plastic straw and dip it into the stain. I block the top with my forefinger and capture some stain in the straw. Then I carefully lift my finger and I can add just the right amount of stain to fill the measuring spoon. Remember the pipettes we used in high school chemistry?!

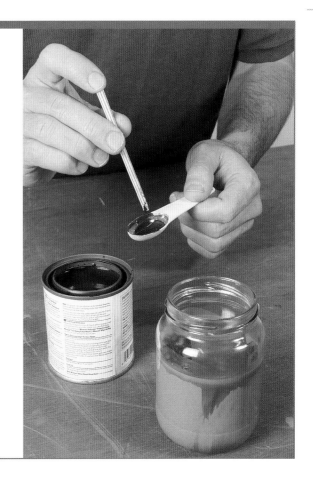

Which Thinner Should I Buy?

I'm confused. My hardware store has a shelf loaded with mineral spirits-based products that all claim to clean brushes and thin paint. What's the best for thinning varnish?

You know, I've wondered the same thing. I've seen a half-dozen different types of thinner, each with a different price, and claiming to thin paint and varnish and clean brushes. Here's the scoop:

The cheapest paint thinner on the shelf works just fine for thinning varnish. If the strong odor bothers you, go ahead and pay a little extra for odorless mineral spirits.

The difference between all of the paint thinner/mineral spirits products is their solvent strength. Turpentine and turpentine-replacement products, such as t.r.p.s., have the highest solvent strength. Some artist's oil paints need that extra solvent strength for thinning and there are a few die-hard users who like the "feel" turpentine gives to the varnish when brushing. Next come regular mineral spirits, often simply sold as "paint thinner." Finally there are the low-odor and odorless mineral spirits. Due to their lower solvent strength, you may find these products less aggressive at cleaning brushes than regular mineral spirits.

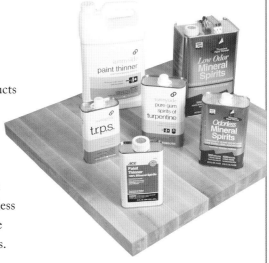

Stripping Options

My grandmother gave me her favorite table, but its top is a mess. Is there an easier way to strip off the old finish than using a messy paint remover?

For surefire success, go straight to a liquid stripper. It will quickly cut through any clear finish and take less time and create less mess than semi-paste strippers. Look for one with methylene chloride, the active ingredient in the fastest working removers.

If you want to do some experimenting, stripper may not be your only answer. Many old finishes will literally melt away with alcohol or lacquer thinner. Alcohol dissolves shellac, and lacquer thinner removes most old lacquer. Furniture refinishers might also be effective. The problem is that one might be more effective than another on a given finish, since their chemical composition varies.

Pour some of the solvent or stripper into a dish. Wipe it over small sections of your piece with steel wool (0 or 00 works well) or a synthetic abrasive pad if you will be finishing the table with a waterborne product. Scrub away, keeping your work area wet by redipping the pad. A gardener's spray bottle is a handy applicator, especially for vertical surfaces.

After the finish begins to break down, wipe away the slurry with paper towels or a rag. Repeat this process until your piece has an even, consistent appearance. Damp rags tossed in a pile are a fire hazard, so hang them outside to dry before you throw them away.

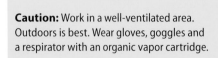

Caution: Work in a well-ventilated area. Outdoors is best. Wear gloves, goggles and a respirator with an organic vapor cartridge.

The Chalk Test

How can I spot flaws in my wood's surface before putting on a finish?

Try this classic method: after jointing or planing, lightly rub the wood with the side of a piece of chalk. Chalk colors all the high spots; low spots remain untouched. You may see flaws that are very hard to spot with the naked eye. Here are some examples:

Planer and jointer snipe. When a planer takes a deeper cut at the beginning or end of a board, it's called snipe. Snipe can be a real pain to sand out because it may be up to a paper-thickness deep. Chalk makes snipe stand out like a sore thumb. Snipe from a jointer indicates that the outfeed table is set too low. Raising the table fixes the problem.

Jointer milling marks. Jointers with three-knife cutterheads always leave a small ripple pattern at right angles to the length of a board. Each knife creates a small crest, like a wave, and a trough. On a final pass, these crests should be fairly close together in order to reduce sanding time, where you have to get down to the bottom of all the troughs. If one of the knives is set too low, some of the crests will be quite prominent; if you've pushed the stock too fast, the crests will be too far apart and the wood's surface will look like a washboard. Chalk quickly reveals improperly set knives and washboarding.

Nicked knives. A nick in a jointer or planer knife creates a long ridge down the length of a board. Chalk highlights the ridge. On most planers and jointers, you can shift one of the knives sideways to temporarily eliminate the ridge, but usually this is a sign that your knives are getting dull.

Hand plane marks. If your hand plane's iron isn't adjusted exactly level with the plane's bottom, it will dig in on one side and leave ridges. Chalk makes these ridges easy to see.

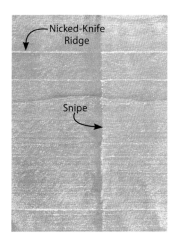

Nicked-Knife Ridge

Snipe

Jointer Washboarding

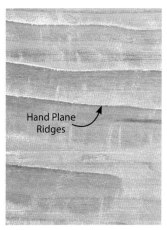

Hand Plane Ridges

Ultra-Smooth MDF Edges

I built some colorful cabinets for our nursery. I like the look of painted MDF, but I can't get the edges as smooth as the faces. Any tips?

I've got just the thing to smooth out those rough edges: spackling compound. First, sand the raw MDF edges with 150- or 180-grit paper. I really like the new sanding sponges for this job. They're stiff enough to get into the corners on a molded edge but soft enough to conform to a rounded edge. Use a putty knife or your fingers to apply the spackling compound (see photo, below left). I used Dap Dry Dex, which goes on pink but turns white when it's ready to be sanded. When it's dry, sand the spackled edge with the 180-grit sponge. It's OK if you sand back down to the MDF a bit. The spackling compound does not have to cover the coarse edge; it just has to fill in the pits. Before you paint, seal the whole piece with a high-quality primer sealer like Zinsser BIN, a shellac-based primer that dries super-fast and sands beautifully. Switch to a 220-grit paper or sponge to sand the primer and the paint. Finally, spray on several coats of color enamel paint. Be sure to lightly sand between coats. The result will be a stunning, glass-smooth surface.

Spread a thin coat of spackling compound onto the edges and sand smooth before painting. Spot-fill any defects on the face of the MDF as well. The result will be ultra-smooth edges and faces on painted MDF.

Spackling Compound

Water-Based vs. Oil-Based Poly

I plan to finish a kitchen table with polyurethane for durability. Should I use water-based or oil-based poly?

If you're looking purely at durability, then an oil-based polyurethane is still superior, but only marginally. There used to be distinct differences between water- and oil-based polyurethanes when it came to durability. Today, the differences are fairly minor.

Oil-based poly will be slightly more resistant to scratches, moisture and heat when compared with water-based poly.

So, why use water-based when oil-based offers improved protection? There are three primary considerations: color, odor and drying time. Some woodworkers dislike the yellow cast oil-based polyurethane puts on white woods, such as maple. In general, a water-based polyurethane will not add color to the wood and will preserve the wood's natural tone. On woods such as cherry or walnut, this can be a disadvantage, because a straight water-based finish

can make the wood look cold and uninviting. That's why finishers often use a seal coat of dewaxed shellac to impart color and warmth before they put on a water-based finish. Another consideration is odor. Water-based polyurethane will give off little if any odor compared to oil-based poly—a real issue if your finish room happens to be in your basement. Finally, water-based poly dries a lot faster, giving dust less time to settle out of the air into your finish.

What Are NGR Stains?

I'm making a Craftsman-style mirror frame from quartersawn white oak, and a friend told me I should check out NGR stains. What are they?

NGR (non grain-raising) stains are actually dyes that color the fibers of the wood. Widely used in the furniture industry, NGR stains give great clarity and a depth of color that's particularly striking on figured woods. Oil-based stains, on the other hand, are often mixtures of dyes and pigments. Pigments act as a semi-transparent layer of color that sits on top of the fibers, obscuring some of the wood's figure.

NGR stains are similar to powdered aniline dyes, but there are some important differences. Water-soluble dyes raise the grain, and alcohol-soluble dyes have a tendency to fade. NGR stains will not raise the grain and are very fade resistant.

NGR stains are usually sprayed on because they dry quickly. If you are going to apply them by hand, it's best

to stay with a small project, such as your mirror frame. It's possible to avoid lap marks, but you must work fast, by hand, over large areas.

NGR stains can be used without a sealer under any waterborne or solvent-based finish. They are available in a wide variety of wood tones premixed and ready to go, but they are expensive (about $9 per pint).

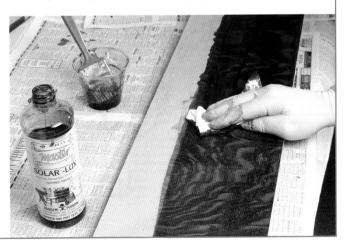

Glue & Gluing

Can I Glue a Month After Machining?

I jointed some boards for a tabletop quite a while ago. When I finally got around to putting the boards together, the glue acted strange. It didn't seem to soak in.

For weekend warriors like us, time in the shop can be hard to come by. It's not unusual for weeks to go by between machining and glue up. The best practice is to glue parts together within a few days of being jointed. The problem you observed wasn't with the glue—it was with the wood. As wood ages, its surface loses some of its ability to soak up glue. If glue can't readily soak in, the bond may be up to 20-percent weaker.

Check your wood's ability to absorb glue with this simple test: Put a drop of water on the surface you're going to glue. If the drop starts to soak into the wood right away, you're fine. If the drop remains intact, however, the surface of the joint should be renewed. One pass with fine sandpaper wrapped around a hard block will do the trick.

Make sure your parts fit tight before gluing, however. Wood moves after it's been machined, and edges that were straight a month ago may now be bowed. If the joints aren't tight under light clamp pressure, re-machine your wood.

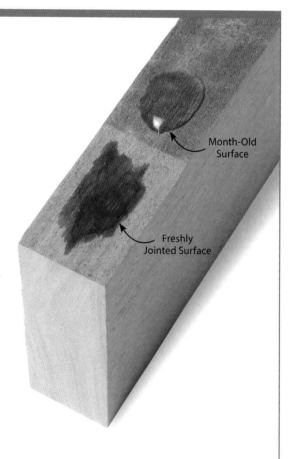

Month-Old Surface

Freshly Jointed Surface

Can I Use White Glue for Woodworking?

In a desperate moment, I grabbed some white glue to finish a glue-up. I've heard white glue works just as well as yellow. Is this true or am I going to regret my rash act?

White glue is plenty strong for woodworking. Yellow glue has certain advantages: It's thicker so it's less messy and it has a higher melting point so sandpaper won't gum up as fast. Also, cured white glue is more flexible than yellow, which can lead to a condition called glue "creep." As solid wood expands and contracts, the flexible white glue can push up in visible ridges. For this reason, white glue is best used where glue creep won't matter, like on interior parts of a cabinet, inside a dado or rabbet or with manufactured sheet stock where wood movement is not an issue.

Avoid using "school" glues, because some brands have about one-third the bond strength of yellow glues.

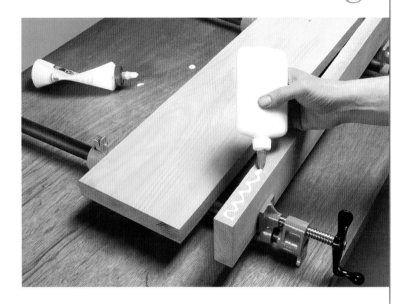

Does Polyurethane Glue Fill Gaps?

I hate it when I slip up and make a joint that doesn't fit tight. I heard that polyurethane glue will fill gaps and hold a loose joint together better than yellow glue. Is that true?

The largest gap that polyurethane glue will adequately bond across is about .005 in. (That's pretty small. The cover of a magazine is .004-in. thick.) The outside limit for yellow glue is about the same. Polyurethane glue will expand in a gap larger than .005 in. It foams and forms very small bubbles of carbon dioxide gas, hardening into the equivalent of styrofoam. These bubbles may "fill" the gap, but *they form a very weak bond*. Filling and bonding aren't the same thing. Polyurethane glue has many good properties, but bonding very loose joints isn't one of them.

Use epoxy when parts don't fit well. It dries by chemical reaction rather than the loss of water, so it doesn't shrink. Neither does it form bond-weakening bubbles. Epoxy will both fill and bond a gap as large as $\frac{1}{16}$ in.

Foam

Polyurethane Glue

Solid

Epoxy Glue

Extend Working Time for Glue-Ups

When it's hot, or when I'm gluing a complex assembly, yellow glue is hard to use, because it sets up too fast.

To slow the drying, I just dampen the wood before I apply the glue. I admit I didn't try this technique until I called a glue company for advice. The company rep said the joints will be plenty strong as long as I don't saturate the wood. A little water goes a long way! Even if the dampened wood appears dry by the time the glue is applied, enough moisture remains to keep the glue moist.

Glue Squeegee

I stack-laminate boards to create turning blanks. Each blank contains numerous laminations, so I have to work fast during assembly. To spread glue quickly and evenly, I use a squeegee designed for silk-screening. You can buy one at an art supply store for about $7. (A regular window-cleaning squeegee from the hardware store would also work.) After squeezing glue onto the surface, I spread it with the squeegee. The amount of pressure I put on the squeegee determines how much glue remains on the surface—I like to leave an even, semi-transparent layer. It's easy to transfer excess glue to a glue-starved area or to the next piece, and cleaning the plastic squeegee is a snap.

Eliminate Clogged Caps

Is your glue bottle half empty or half full? Either way, you're sure to become an optimist after trying this glue-bottle storage block. By storing the bottle upside down, you eliminate the half-dried glue that's forever plugging up the nozzle. Plus, there's no more waiting for the glue to run down the sides and into the tip.

Here's what to do: Take a block of wood about 3 in. x 3 in. and drill a 1¼-in.-dia. hole for the cap of the bottle followed by a ⅝-in.-dia. hole for the neck. Make the hole just deep enough to hold the cap onto the upside down glue bottle. Store the glue bottle in the block and your glue is ready to run right when you need it and because there's no air in the cap, there's never any crusty buildup to clean out.

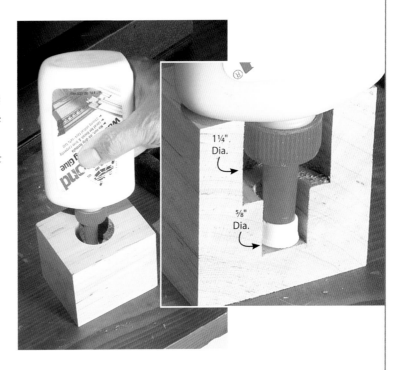

End Gluing Time Trials

Yellow wood glues typically have about five minutes of open time—that's how long you have to assemble the joint after you've applied glue. Five minutes is sufficient for simple glue-ups, but this short window puts a real squeeze on a solo woodworker facing an assembly with numerous joints.

One way to beat the clock is to buy wood glue with a longer open time, from a couple extra minutes to half an hour, depending on the formulation. The only trade-off is longer clamp time, because these slow-setting formulations take longer to dry.

Another clock-beating method is to spread glue with a trim roller. It's amazingly fast and the roller leaves a nice even layer of glue. Trim rollers, packaged in a small plastic tray, cost about $4 in a home center's paint department. The rollers are reusable; just rinse them out. Short-nap rollers produce the best results.

Slow-Setting Glue

Check the Glue

If you're uncertain about your glue's age, test its bond strength. Glue together two small scraps that are each about 1 in. wide, clamp and let dry 24 hours. Hit one piece with a hammer. If the two pieces shear apart with no fibers from one piece stuck to the other, your glue is probably too old. Replace it.

Clean Your Bottle's Applicator

If your glue bottle's cap is clogged with congealed glue, soak it in a jar of very hot water for 15 minutes or so. This softens hardened glue, making it easier to remove.

Longer Lasting CA Glue

CA glue is terrific for quickly bonding small pieces without clamps, but how do you make it last longer? My bottles clog up and the glue hardens way too soon.

Once opened, the shelf life of cyanoacrylate (CA) glue is a short three to six months. But if you zip it into an air-tight plastic bag and store it in your refrigerator (out of the reach of children), the glue will last indefinitely. Cold doesn't affect the bonding properties of the glue, but you should allow the bottle to reach room temperature before using it.

To keep your nozzle from clogging, "burp" your CA bottle after each use. Set the bottle upright and squeeze it until the glue reaches the top of the nozzle. When you let go, you'll create a vacuum that will suck the glue back into the bottle. Next, tap the bottom of the bottle on your workbench several times to force the last drop or two of glue to fall back into the bottle. Then put the cap back on.

If your tip gets clogged anyway, unscrew it from the bottle and soak it in acetone. Use an awl or needle to pry off loosened pieces of glue.

Glue Complex Assemblies in Stages

There's no rule that says you have to glue together a tabletop or a cabinet all in one shot. When you work alone, it's easier—and a lot smarter—to glue in stages, tackling only as many joints as you can safely manage. (Here, for example, the left side joints are being glued first.) Then you won't risk having the glue dry before you can assemble and clamp the joints. To ensure everything stays square and properly aligned when you use this method, always clamp the entire assembly together, even though you're only gluing a portion of it.

Get Ready for a Mess

A cotton rag and a jug of warm water are handy for wiping up spilled glue or lots of squeeze-out. I cut out the side of a plastic jug to make a convenient, disposable container.

Glue Caddy

Being an impatient sort, waiting for glue to reach the bottle's spout became a pet peeve of mine. To put an end to this, I made a stand with a hole in the top matching the diameter of the bottle's lid. It allows the bottle to stand upside down so the glue is always ready to use. For stability, I made the base slightly larger than the top.

Heavy-Duty Glue Scraper

It's best to remove glue before it hardens, but sometimes that's not possible. When I face cement-hard glue, I pull out this robust scraper to bull my way through it. The blade is ⅛-in.-thick tempered steel, as tough as a chisel. There's no chatter, because the tool's long body is made from heavy iron pipe. Extra weight and leverage really count!

I ordered the blade through a catalog for about $8 and bought the rest of the parts from the hardware store for about $10. The pipe is a prethreaded nipple. The blade comes with a predrilled ¼-in. hole, but I had to drill holes through a dowel and the end cap for the threaded rod. The rubber washers dampen vibration. To remove old, dried glue from the blade, I scrape it with a chisel or soak it in hot water.

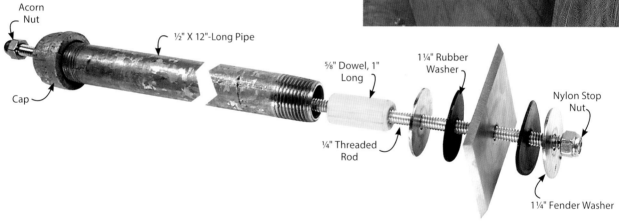

Acorn Nut

½" X 12"-Long Pipe

Cap

⅝" Dowel, 1" Long

¼" Threaded Rod

1¼" Rubber Washer

Nylon Stop Nut

1¼" Fender Washer

Glue-Free Clamps

Dried glue used to make my pipe clamps hard to handle and use. Now I give the pipes a light coat of paste wax from time to time. The wax makes dried glue pop right off. The bottom jaw slides more easily, too.

How Do I Keep Glued Boards From Slipping?

Whenever I glue two boards face to face, they slip and slide out of alignment as soon as I clamp them. I suppose I could add a dozen clamps across their width and length, but isn't there an easier way?

Yes. The trick is to apply just the right amount of glue and pressure.

First, use a squeeze bottle to make a long zigzag or spiral pattern of glue over the bottom piece. Then place the other piece of wood on top and rub the two together, pressing fairly hard. This spreads out the glue to cover the whole surface. Rubbing also squeezes out the excess glue so what remains absorbs into the wood and gets tacky faster. After a minute or so, the glue will begin to grip. Now slide the boards into alignment.

Put on your clamps, but only apply enough pressure to keep the clamps upright. Then tighten each clamp a little bit at a time, like putting lug nuts on a wheel. The glue tack and the gradual tightening will keep the pieces just where you want them.

First, rub boards together under pressure.

Next, tighten each clamp a little bit at a time.

Perfect Glue Bottle

I buy glue in gallon jugs and, having tried about every glue bottle on the market, I thought I would never find the perfect one. My search ended while washing dishes with my wife one evening. The dish-soap bottle was empty so I rinsed it out thoroughly and filled it with glue. Just the ticket!

Moisture-Starved Glue Joint

I built a project with MDF and polyurethane glue, but now it's coming apart. I thought this kind of glue was super strong. What did I do wrong?

Polyurethane glue is plenty strong for woodworking, but it can't be applied like good old yellow glue. Pete Ragland, head of the technical department at Gorilla Glue, recognized your problem immediately. Polyurethane glues need moisture to form a strong bond and MDF can be dry as dust. When you're gluing man-made materials or kiln-dried wood with polyurethane glue, Ragland says you must introduce moisture to the joint. He says the best way is to dampen one surface of the joint with a moist sponge. A single swipe is sufficient; too much moisture can cause MDF to swell. Apply polyurethane glue to the other surface and clamp the joint for three to four hours.

Rub-Joint Gluing

My panel glue ups drive me nuts because the boards slide around whenever I clamp them together. Then I end up beating them back into position. What's going on?

Most likely you're putting too much glue on the joints and your boards are simply "swimming" around on the excess glue. Try the rub-joint gluing method instead.

Apply glue to only one edge of the joint, slide the two boards back and forth until the glue becomes tacky, and then clamp the boards. Bonus: rubbing the boards together distributes the glue evenly and produces a strong, thin glue line.

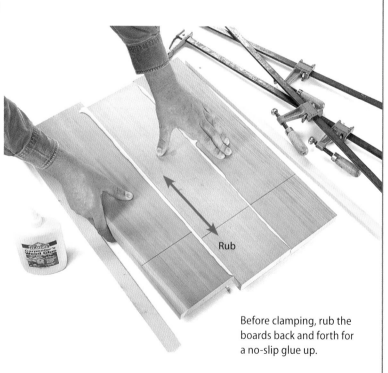

Before clamping, rub the boards back and forth for a no-slip glue up.

Using Wet Wood

I'm building outdoor furniture from rough cedar. When I cut the wood, it's soaking wet on the inside. Should I use polyurethane glue since it's a moisture-cure glue?

Not when the wood is that wet. Polyurethane glue uses moisture to cure, but too much moisture will cause the glue to cure before it gets a chance to soak into the wood fibers and create a bond. You need to get the moisture content (MC) near the surface of the wood down to 10 to 25 percent before you use polyurethane glue (6 to 15 percent if you use a water-based Type II or Type III glue).

Rough cedar from the lumberyard is often very wet, but it loses that water rapidly. The best thing to do is cut your lumber into rough sizes and then stack the wood indoors with stickers between each board so all four surfaces of each board are exposed to the air. Cedar dries rapidly; leave it for a week or two and you should be good to glue.

Visible Moisture

Soaking Wet Cedar

Saw Kerf Stops Glue Squeeze-Out

When gluing trim or other surface-applied pieces of wood, cut a shallow saw kerf near the edge of the piece being glued down. The glue will get trapped in the groove instead of squeezing out onto the other piece of wood.

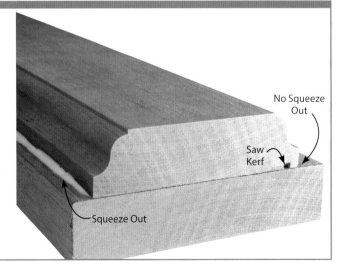

No Squeeze Out

Saw Kerf

Squeeze Out

Which Glue for Bent Lamination?

A chair design I'm working on requires bent laminations for the back spindles. I'm using maple and am having a hard time keeping the glue lines from jumping out. Any suggestions?

Because bent laminations are under constant stress, they require glue that sets hard. Epoxy, urea resin, resorcinol and polyurethane are all good choices for bent laminations. Of these four glues, urea resin and resorcinol achieve the most rigid glue line when cured. While resorcinol has a Type I rating (a good choice for outdoor applications) its color is very dark, making it unsuitable for lighter woods like maple. Consider using a urea resin glue with a light catalyst specifically designed for blonde woods. (It's also available with a medium or dark catalyst.)

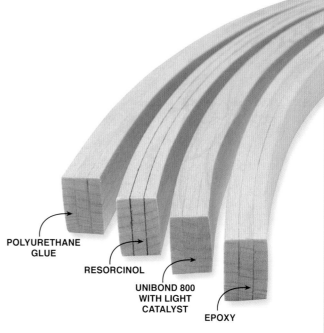

POLYURETHANE GLUE

RESORCINOL

UNIBOND 800 WITH LIGHT CATALYST

EPOXY

Tip: You can also minimize glue lines by selecting straight-grained stock to cut your laminations from and assembling the laminations in their original order.

Taping Joints To Control Glue Squeeze-Out

Check For Flush Fit

Masking Tape

Prevent ugly glue marks by taping the joint before you glue.

Glue has the annoying habit of getting into wood grain and not showing up until you stain. To avoid the disappointment of these ugly glue marks, apply tape along the joints prior to gluing and clamping. As the glue squeeze-out starts to dry and turns waxy, scrape it off with a putty knife and remove the tape. The only glue that should be left is a thin strip right along the joint. Sand it off when it has completely dried.

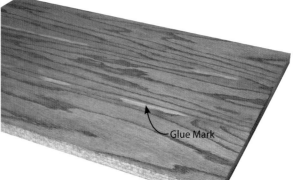

Glue Mark

Virtual Gluing

I've got three unusual boards to glue together, but I'm having a hard time visualizing all the combinations of which board should go next to which. Any tips?

Here's one idea: make "virtual" tops. Take photos of the boards, cut up the pictures, and tape them together in different arrangements. Make copies of the arrangements you like, so you can directly compare one with another.

Let's assume that you've got three boards and both sides of each board are good enough to face up in your top. Pick one side of each board and mark it as A1, B1 or C1. Lay the boards together, in any order, and take a photo. Turn the boards over, mark the opposite faces as A2, B2 and C2, and take another photo. Print several copies of both photos and you've got your virtual boards.

Cut up the photos and arrange the pieces as you wish. You can even "rip" a board with a pair of scissors to see how the figure in one board may best blend with the figure in another.

Stronger Miters

When I put glue on end-grain miters, it soaks in too fast, so I don't get a strong joint. How can I prevent that?

Seal the miters first with glue size, which you make by mixing equal parts water and glue. Test the size by brushing it on a scrap miter. Let it sit for a minute, then lightly wipe off the excess with your finger. Let the size dry for a few hours. It should leave a smooth surface, ready for gluing. If the miter is rough, which would prevent the joint from closing tight, add more water to the size mixture. On thirsty open-grained woods, such as oak, you may need to increase the proportion of glue in the size mixture.

Hardware

Brad Nailer vs. Finish Nailer

I'm ready to buy my first pneumatic nailer. I'm not sure which size gun will suit me better: an 18-gauge brad nailer or a 16-gauge finish nailer. Any advantages to one over the other?

An 18-gauge brad nailer is the best all-around nailer for cabinet work. Brad nailers leave smaller holes and are less prone to split wood than finish nailers are. In making cabinets and furniture, you'll usually depend on glue and clamps to form a structurally sound bond, so finer gauge nails will be strong enough to hold the parts together until the glue sets. These thinner brads are also great for applying trim to cabinets and tacking jigs together. The brads' small size makes them more versatile in the shop.

The 18-gauge brads come in a variety of lengths from ⅝ in. to 2 in. The narrow gauge and head on a brad make a small hole that's easily filled. In contrast, 16-gauge finish nails are longer at 1¼ in. to 2½ in., are thicker and have larger heads that provide more holding power. They are better suited for carpentry projects, such as putting moldings up on a wall.

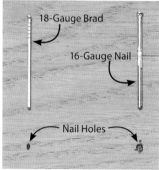

Brad Driver in Reverse

My pneumatic nailer makes quick work of assembling cabinets, but if a nail blows out the side, it can be a real mess. Those power-driven nails often bend or break if you try to pound them back with a hammer or pull them through with a pliers.

Faced with this problem, I discovered a new use for my old, hand-pushed brad setter. It works great to push the errant nail back so I can get ahold of the nail's head with a pliers. The hollow barrel of the setter goes over the end of the nail and keeps it from bending. There's a metal plunger inside the barrel that pushes the nail back up. I sometimes have to tap on the setter with a hammer to get the nail moving.

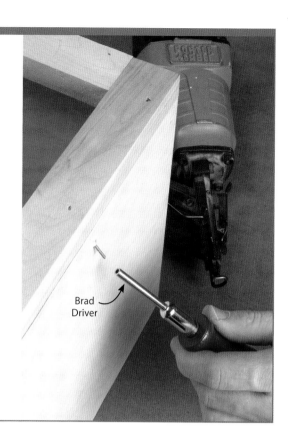

Brad Driver

Bargain Screw Lube

A toilet bowl floor gasket is an excellent lubricant for screws—it's much more slippery than paraffin, soap, or all of the other materials I've tried. It's very soft, so all you have to do to coat a screw is to push it into the ring. One gasket lasts for years. You'll find them in hardware stores and home centers.

Convenient Screw Holder

I epoxied a rare earth magnet on my drill to keep screws and drill bits close at hand.

Magnetic Nail Starter

Over the years I've built dozens of cabinets. Installing the little nails for the shelf standards was the worst part of this job until I discovered this little device called a magnetizer. It's commonly used to magnetize screwdrivers for picking up screws. I used it to magnetize my nail set and now I can pick up and start the little nails with ease.

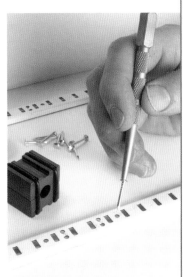

Phillips Tip Repair

When your Phillips tip gets beat up, don't throw it away. Make a stop at your bench grinder first, and grind about 1⁄16" off the tip's end. This allows it to sink deeper into a screw's head, so you can get a little more use out of the tip before tossing it.

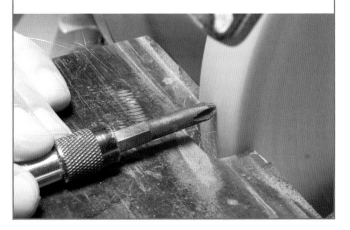

Rectangular Nail Setter

Sometimes my pneumatic brad nailer fails to set the nail head fully beneath the surface of the wood. The brads I use have rectangular-shaped heads and a regular nail set makes a round hole that's too big.

I solved this problem with a custom punch. Using my benchtop grinder, I ground down the tip of a punch to match the size and rectangular shape of my brads. This modified punch works just like a regular nail set but the rectangular shape blends better with the wood's grain and is less visible when finished.

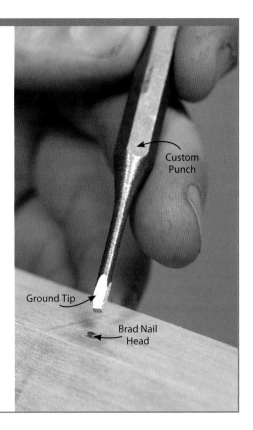

Custom Punch

Ground Tip

Brad Nail Head

New Road for Old Drivers

I use lots of Phillips-head sheetrock screws, which are made of hardened steel. They're tough on bits. A worn-out bit can't be renewed, so I reshape it to fit a slotted screw using a small diameter sanding drum. I place the bit in a magnetic holder and slide the holder into a wooden block that has a kerf cut in one end. Tightening a screw squeezes the ends of the block around the holder. Using the block, I can precisely position the bit in order to grind perfectly parallel sides.

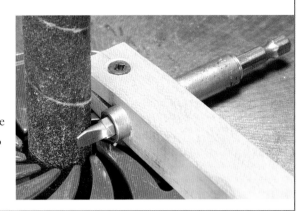

Nail Size Equivalents

I see plans calling for 6d nails, but when I want to use my pneumatic nail gun, the nail sizes are in inches. How do I convert from one to the other?

The *d* in 6d is the symbol for a penny in the English monetary system. Some believe that the use of the term *penny* to describe nail size evolved from the old English custom of selling nails 100 at a time. Thus, 100 small nails might cost 4d while 100 larger nails might cost 8d. Today, the designation refers to the nail's length. The length of pneumatic nails and brads, however, is given in inches. Check the photos below for a quick conversion.

Even though the lengths are equivalent, you'll find a conventional nail is thicker than a pneumatic nail of equal length. The conventional nail needs the extra girth to resist bending under repeated hammer blows. (In my case, they need to be as thick as railroad spikes.)

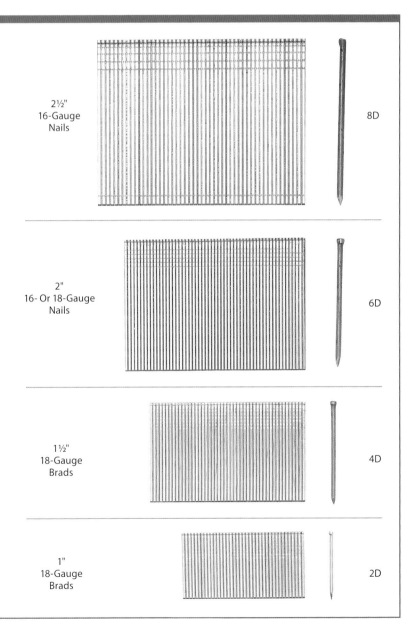

2½"
16-Gauge
Nails — 8D

2"
16- Or 18-Gauge
Nails — 6D

1½"
18-Gauge
Brads — 4D

1"
18-Gauge
Brads — 2D

No Trace Screw Removal

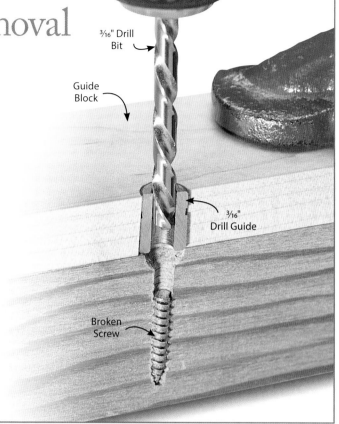

Last summer I built some outdoor furniture and used brass screws. Geez, it's a pain when those screws break off.

After I snapped a couple I couldn't find my screw extractor so I had to get creative!

I've got a set of steel drill guides that I use to make custom drilling jigs for shelf pegs and dowel holes. I discovered that if I put the 3/16-in. drill guide into a block of wood and clamped this assembly over the broken screw, I was able to drill it out. Then I plugged the hole with a piece of wood and some glue. Once I inserted a new screw, the fix was invisible. I've tried this with brass and mild-steel type screws but it doesn't work with hard drywall-type screws.

3/16" Drill Bit

Guide Block

3/16" Drill Guide

Broken Screw

Rusting Screws

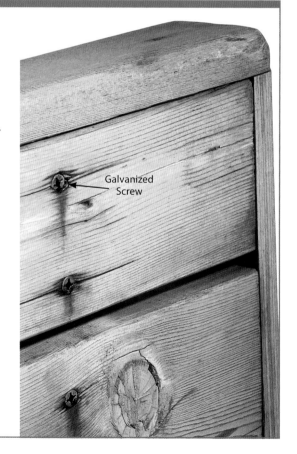

I built some outdoor furniture a few years ago. I used galvanized screws and cedar, thinking they would stand up to the elements. The wood has done fine, but from each screw, there's a black stain running down the wood. I thought galvanized screws didn't corrode.

The best way to prevent this from happening is to use stainless steel screws. Stainless steel screws cost a little more than plated, corrosion-resistant screws. For example, a 100-count box of 2½-in. No. 8 stainless steel screws costs about $3 more than a box of plated screws. Stainless steel is well worth the extra cost.

The galvanized screws you used in your project were most likely damaged during installation. Phillips drive screws are notorious for causing the bit to jump, or cam out, as the screw is driven. This often damages the rust-resistant coating (whether galvanized or epoxy), which exposes the steel to water and oxygen, resulting in corrosion. The iron in the screw reacts with the tannin in the cedar and any environmental moisture to produce those black streaks on your furniture. A stainless steel screw will resist corrosion no matter how mangled it gets.

Galvanized Screw

Shop-Made Wing Nuts

Wooden wing nuts are easier on your hands than metal ones. Making them is a great way to use up shop scraps and leftover hex nuts. When you need a wing nut, you won't have to go to the hardware store.

Start with a strip of wood that's about ¾" thick, at least ¼" wider than the hex nuts, and long enough to work with safely. Using a Forstner bit, drill holes the exact depth of the hex nuts. Size the holes so that the nuts fit snug. Drill a hole sized for a bolt the rest of the way through. Dab some petroleum jelly on the nuts' threads with a cotton swab, then apply epoxy around the holes' shoulders and insert the nuts. The

petroleum jelly keeps the epoxy from sticking to the threads. To make sure each nut is level, thread in a bolt. It should stand straight up. When the epoxy has cured, cut and shape the wing nuts for a comfortable grip.

Square Drive vs. Phillips-Head Screws

The primary advantage to square-drive screws is they are much less prone to "cam-out." Cam-out refers to the slipping of the bit in the screw head as the screw is driven.

The square-head screw was invented by P. I. Robertson, a Canadian, in 1908. It offered a big advantage over the slotted screw head because it was self-centering and not prone to slipping when driven. But, an early attempt to market these screws in the United States failed. This left the Robertson screw confined to the Canadian market.

The Phillips-head screw was initially developed in the 1930s for industrial use. It offered the same self-centering advantage as the square drive but was designed to cam out. Cam-out was considered an advantage in the industrial assembly line, preventing screws from being overtightened and giving a little cushion to the furious power drivers

of the day. But the advantage for industry was the bane of woodworkers. Cam-out for them meant marred finishes and scarred wood.

Eventually, the Robertson-head or square-drive screw migrated across the border and, by the 1970s, was making strong inroads in the furniture and woodworking trades.

A new hybrid screw-head design is a square-drive screw that, in a pinch, allows you to use a Phillips driver.

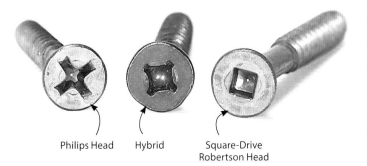

Philips Head   Hybrid   Square-Drive
Robertson Head

Reinforce Plywood for Hinge Screws

Plywood edges don't provide a very good anchor for hinge screws. So while building a wooden toy box that had a piano-hinged lid, I reinforced the plywood edge by routing a groove and gluing in a strip of solid wood. This provides a strong place for the hinge screws, and should hold tight for many years.

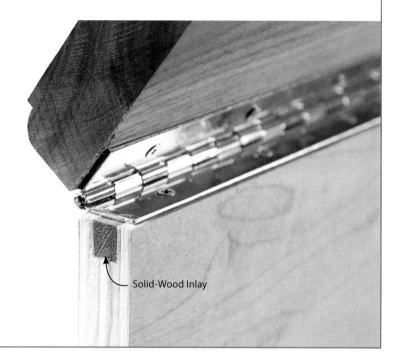

Solid-Wood Inlay

Are Broken Screws Removable?

Argh! I broke off a brass screw while installing a small hinge. Can I get it out?

Join the club! Every woodworker has faced this problem. The best answer is to drill around the screw with a hollow bit, an unusual device with reverse teeth. Furniture repair guys used to painstakingly make these screw-extracting bits themselves, but now we can buy three sizes from a mail-order catalog or on the Internet.

Here's what you do: Buy a hollow bit with an inside diameter that's larger than the screw. Use a drill press to make a perpendicular hole in a piece of scrap that's the outside diameter of the hollow bit. This guide block keeps the bit from wandering. Clamp the guide block over the broken screw. Then chuck the hollow bit in a portable drill set to "reverse." Drill around the screw. When you get near the bottom of the screw, it will unthread itself from the wood. (The hollow bit's teeth are backward so they cut when the drill is in reverse.) Sounds too good to be true, but it really works! Plug the hole with a dowel.

Next time you use brass screws, drill a pilot hole first, then screw in a steel screw to thread the wood. Replace the steel screw with a brass one and lubricate it with a toilet wax ring or moist soap shavings.

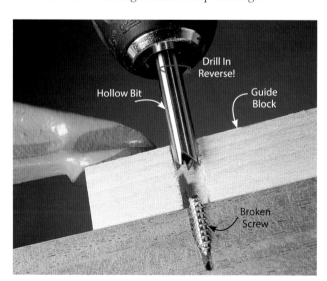

Drill In Reverse!

Hollow Bit

Guide Block

Broken Screw

Stripped-Out Allen Head

**Do you have a fix for a stripped-out
Allen head on a setscrew?**

Fortunately, there *is* a simple solution to this
aggravating problem. Put a little 5-minute epoxy
on the end of an Allen wrench and set it in the
stripped out hole. Let the epoxy cure over night,
so it's good and hard, then turn the screw out
as you normally would. You can toss the fused
wrench and nut or, if you're cheap like me, take
a blowtorch to the nut. The heat will soften the
epoxy and release the damaged nut, leaving your
wrench ready for use.

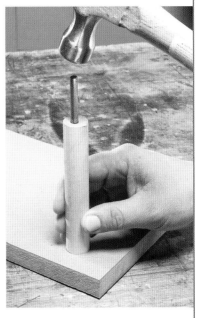

Staple Set

Pneumatic staplers don't always set ¼"
crown staples flush. Driving them the
rest of the way with a hammer causes the
staples to kink, so I designed this easy-to-
make tool, which I call a "staple set."

To make the set, cut a 5" section of dowel
at least 1" in diameter and drill a ¼" hole
down the center. You'll have to drill the
dowel from both ends to reach all the way
through. Insert a 6½" length of ¼" steel rod
into the hole. Place the staple set over the
staple and tap the steel rod. This sets the
staple without bending it.

Joinery Tricks

Board-Stretching Joint

I bought a planer/molder so I could make my own moldings. My living room required one 28-ft.-long molding, but all I had to make it were 12-ft. boards. I didn't want to settle for separate 12-ft. molding sections mitered during installation. I wanted this molding to be one continuous piece. Joining the boards with diagonal scarf joints before molding them was the solution.

To make a scarf joint, lay out the angles using at least a 4-to-1 ratio—4 in. of run for every 1-in. rise. Increasing the ratio strengthens the glue joint. The joint will be inconspicuous if you match the boards' grain direction and patterns. Use your bandsaw or a sabersaw to cut the angles. Then joint the edges by attaching a fence and routing with a flush-trim bit.

Glue the boards together on a flat surface. Install the clamps perpendicular to the joint to keep the pieces from sliding. You may have to notch the edges of the boards to hold the clamps at the proper angle.

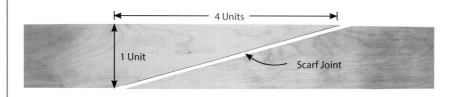

Hand-Split Tenon Jig

Here's a time-tested method for making small tenons on straight-grained stock. It's quick and effective, but not super precise, so I use it when I'm after a simple, rustic look.

Attach a hand plane blade, bevel-side up, to a suitably sized spacer board. Note that the blade splits the waste off the top side of the stock. The thickness of the spacer under the blade is the sum of the thickness of the tenon plus the thickness of the shoulder underneath the tenon.

Screw the spacer to a flat board and clamp the board to your bench. Screw a block of wood behind the blade to keep it from sliding. Saw the tenon shoulders first. Then place the workpiece against the blade and split the waste with a tap from a mallet. Flip the stock over and split the other side to complete the tenon.

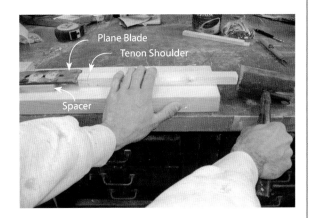

Make Perfect Dadoes With a Router and a Jig

This jig automatically cuts perfectly-sized dados.

Locate the jig so the fixed fence lines up with the bottom of the marked dado. Squeeze a couple plywood offcuts from the shelf stock between the fixed and adjustable fences and tighten. This sets the space between them to perfectly match the material thickness.

Using a ½-in. pattern cutting bit in your router, make one pass with the bearing against the fixed fence and another with the bearing against the adjustable fence. The result is a dado that perfectly matches your material.

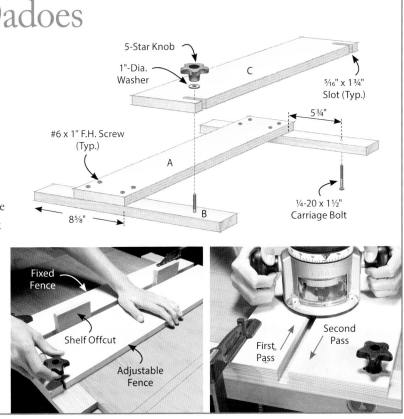

Best Dado Depth

For years, I made all my dadoes ⅜-in. deep in ¾-in. plywood. If I made dadoes on opposite sides of a divider, however, I had to change their depth and recalculate shelf lengths just for that joint.

I've since learned it's a lot easier and just as strong to set the depth of cut for every dado to ¼ in. This makes calculating shelf lengths a whole lot easier, and I never have to make special calculations for a double dado.

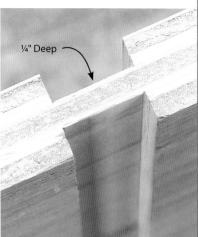

¼" Deep

Cut Rabbets With a Sacrificial Fence

A sacrificial fence protects your stock fence from damage. I make my fence from melamine because its slippery. I cut a ⅜-in. x ¾-in. groove to accept a commercial featherboard. A scallop cut in the face of the sacrificial fence allows me to bury part of the blade.

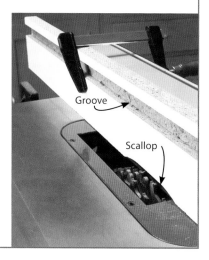

Groove

Scallop

Chair Leg Repair

My kitchen chairs are hardly valuable antiques, so when I broke a rung on one I wanted a strong but simple fix. I drilled out the broken tenon from the mortise and plugged it with a piece of wood. Then I trimmed off the end of the broken tenon on the stretcher and drilled a ¼-in.-dia. by 1-in.-deep hole into the end. I epoxy glued a 1¾-in. piece of threaded rod into this hole. Then I drilled out a corresponding hole into the wood plug and epoxy glued the threaded rod into the wood plug. Epoxy glue is a great gap-filling glue, which means the alignment of the threaded rod doesn't have to be perfect. This fix may seem a bit rough, but it works, and besides—this chair will never be on "Antiques Roadshow."

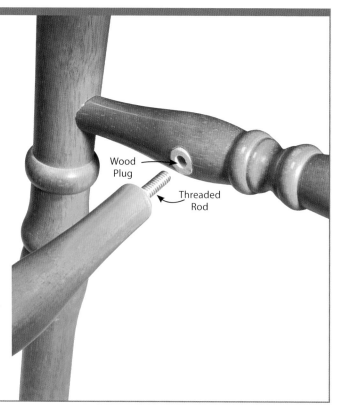

Wood Plug

Threaded Rod

Cut Rabbets Slightly Oversized

I cut the rabbet at the top of cabinet sides slightly wider than the top's thickness. The top is used to set the fence so the dado head projects $\frac{1}{32}$-in. past the plywood. This positions the top just below the cabinet side after assembly. To make the side flush with the top, lay the cabinet on its side and make a quick pass with a flush trim bit.

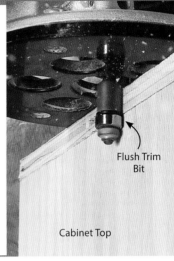

Flush Trim Bit

Cabinet Top

Face Vise Mortising Jig

This simple box-shaped jig replaces one of the face boards in my woodworking vise. During assembly, I made sure the jig's top was dead flat and perpendicular to the face that would fasten to the vise. The jig mounts flush with the bench top, so my router is fully supported. All I have to do is install the workpiece flush with the jig and the bench, adjust the router's edge guide and go.

Edge Guide

Dovetail Gauge Block

It's no secret that setting up your router for a half-blind dovetail jig can be frustrating. Extend the router bit up too far and the joint will be too tight. Lower it down too far and it will be too loose.

I made a gauge block to record the perfect setting, once and for all. To make the block, I first used the standard trial-and-error method to make a tight-fitting dovetail joint. After I figured out how far the bit must extend, I rough-cut a notch in a block of wood using a bandsaw. I made the notch about ⅟₁₆ in. less deep than the bit's height. I turned the router over and used the dovetail bit to recut the notch's bottom. Now when I rout dovetails, I simply raise the bit until it touches the notch, lock the router down and start cutting.

Grain Match Matters

It takes more than a precision fit to make a miter joint look good; the wood's grain and color should match, too. Using a single board to band a tabletop or build a picture frame makes color matching easier. Straight-grained boards are easier to match than those with wavy patterns. When matching wavy grain, try this: Miter one piece and then use it to find a matching area on the piece that will adjoin it.

Don't Over-Glue

Often we tend to think, "If a little is good, a lot has got to be better." During glue-up, this is definitely not the case.

A brush makes it easier to gauge the amount of glue you're putting down and where you're putting it. Spread a uniform film that's just thick enough so you can't see through it. Keep the glue in the bottom of the dado or rabbet but off the sides. I find this technique prevents excess glue from oozing out of the joint during assembly.

Elegant Tabletop Fasteners

On my best work, I want the bottom of my project to look as good as the top. That's when I make an old-fashioned set of wooden tabletop fasteners, or "buttons," rather than use the modern stamped-steel type.

A button allows a solid-wood top to expand and contract through the seasons. When the top's grain runs parallel to the rail, the button slides in and out of the slot as the top slowly moves. When the grain runs at right angles to the rail, the button slides side to side.

To make the buttons, cut dadoes in a long block (see photo, below). Drill and countersink holes for the screws and then chamfer the long edges. Saw apart the blocks and chamfer the ends with a file or disc sander.

Top's Seasonal Movement

Flip Faces To Make a Flat Top

I have a tough time getting my jointer's fence perfectly square. I can't figure out a way to fix it, so I've adopted an old cabinetmaker's trick that cancels out the error.

Here's the deal: I alternate the faces that go against the jointer's fence (see photo, below). Each edge has a slight bevel from the out-of-square fence. Arranged without alternating the faces, the two edges form a V shape. An open joint would result on one side or the other if I were to force the top flat. By alternating the boards, I get a perfectly tight joint and a flat top, even though the edges aren't square. The only trick is to mark the boards beforehand so I place the correct sides against the fence.

Here's an extreme example: Both these boards were jointed with the fence way out of square. Arranged as shown here, the bevels cancel each other, resulting in a tight joint and a flat top.

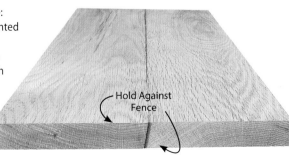

Hold Against Fence

Make Micro Adjustments with a Disc Sander

No tool can tweak a miter's fit as easily as a disc sander can. You can shorten the workpiece a hair with a quick touch of the disc. You can also adjust the angle by a fraction of a degree. Instead of fussing with the miter gauge, make tiny adjustments by sticking a paper shim between the gauge and the workpiece.

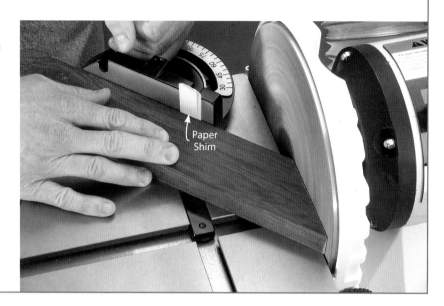

Paper
Shim

Make a Gauge Block

Setting up a stackable dado head to fit your plywood can be fussy and time consuming, but you'll significantly reduce the guesswork by making a dado gauge block.

To make the block, cut a $^{23}/_{32}$-in. wide dado in a board big enough to allow for six more dados with space between. Add a single .005-in. shim to the $^{23}/_{32}$-in. setup and plow a second dado next to the $^{23}/_{32}$-in. one. Continue adding shims and making dados in .005-in. increments until you get to a ¾-in. dado. Mark the dadoes as you go.

To use, slip your plywood into the test dadoes until you find the perfect fit. Then, read the number of shims needed.

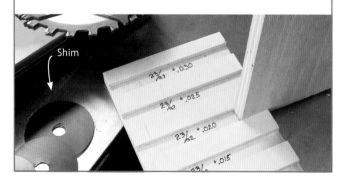

Shim

Lock The Height

Always lock the blade-height handwheel before cutting. Vibration can make the handle turn, changing the depth of cut. This change is often hard to observe until assembly time. A big oops, if you just cut dadoes for a kitchen full of cabinets.

Make More Room in the Mortise

I well remember the day when I couldn't get a mortise-and-tenon joint to come together no matter how hard I tightened the clamp. I had ignored a fundamental rule: Always make mortises $\frac{1}{16}$ to $\frac{1}{8}$ in. deeper than the tenons.

There are two reasons for doing this. First, you don't have to obsess about making a perfectly smooth bottom in the mortise, which saves time. Second, space is needed for excess glue. This was the reason my joint didn't go home. The tenon had a tight fit on all four sides. Too tight, really. It had pushed all the glue to the bottom of the mortise. A deeper mortise would have given the glue space to pool and allowed the tenon to go home.

Space For Glue

Mortising by Machine

I'm having trouble with my mortising machine. I cut mortises by slightly overlapping each hole, but I've broken a few bits and my chisels have overheated and turned blue. Is there a problem with my method?

Yes, there's a better method than overlapping holes. When you overlap, you're essentially cutting a hole with three sides. It's like trying to drill overlapping holes with a twist bit. The bit wants to follow the path of least resistance. It walks into the neighboring hole, bending as it goes. When a mortising bit cuts an overlapping hole, it bends, too, and rubs against the side of the chisel. Both get hot. The chisel turns blue as the temper is drawn out, and the bit eventually snaps.

The solution is to drill four-sided and two-sided holes. Drill the two ends of the mortise first. Because the bit meets equal resistance on all four sides, it goes straight down.

Now, instead of overlapping, leave a space about half the width of the bit, and drill another hole. Keep skipping half a hole like this until you get to the other end of the mortise.

Next, drill two-sided holes in the half spaces. There's equal resistance on opposing sides of the bit, so the bit travels straight down.

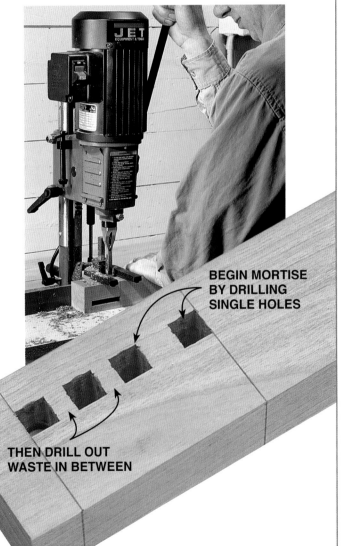

BEGIN MORTISE BY DRILLING SINGLE HOLES

THEN DRILL OUT WASTE IN BETWEEN

Make Tight-Mitered Edging

My father used to tease, "I cut the darn board twice and it's still too short!" Of course he was kidding—or was he? When I make a mitered tabletop, I start with one or two pieces that are "too short" and a bit too wide. Jointing their inside edges effectively lengthens them until I get a perfect fit. This is much easier than trying to cut the boards to exact length.

The center of this top is a piece of plywood. (Solid wood won't work here because the center piece is unable to expand or contract with the seasons.) I often use biscuits or spline to align the edging with the plywood and to reinforce the corner joints.

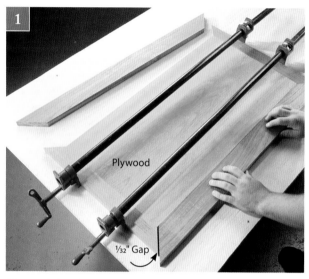

Miter and glue the short pieces first. Rip the long pieces about ¼ in. wider than the short pieces. Cut the long pieces a bit short, so they each have a 1/32-in. or so gap at one end.

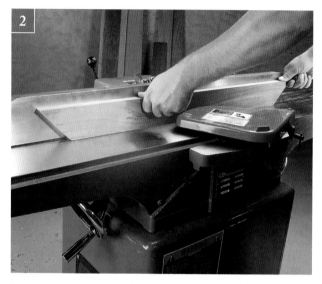

Set your jointer to take a minimal cut, about 1/64 in. Joint the inside edges of the long boards. This lengthens the distance between the miters. In effect, the board becomes longer.

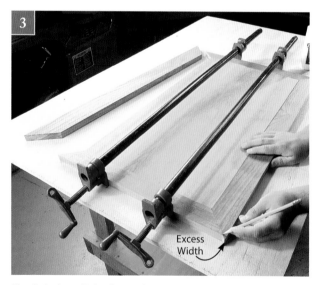

Check the board's fit after each jointer pass. When the miters come tight, mark the excess width, rip the boards and glue them on.

Right-Angle Guide for Jointing

Planing the edge of a long board perpendicular to its face is a real challenge. To make the job easier, I built a guide that attaches to the side of my plane with rare earth magnets. Now jointing an edge is much easier. I simply alter my grip to take full advantage of the square-cornered support that the fence offers.

Rare Earth Magnet

Shoulder

The guide consists of four pieces of ⅛-in. MDF glued so one pair of pieces shoulders the sole of the plane (see photo, above). On the sole, this shoulder must extend slightly beyond the blade. The magnets are epoxied into their predrilled holes.

The Touch Test

When you're building a box or frame, the opposite sides must be precisely the same length. Otherwise, even the most perfect miters won't form a tight joint. To compare lengths, hold the parts together on a flat surface and feel the ends. Your finger can detect differences your eyes can't.

Perfect Tenon Shoulders

I thought I had tenon-making with a dado set figured out, but one day it all went haywire. One side of the joint wouldn't draw tight. The culprit? An inadequate stop-block setup.

I used to grab any old small cutoff for a stop block, holding it to the fence with a spring clamp. Wrong on both counts. The problem with a small stop block chosen willy-nilly is that it's not necessarily square. If the stop block isn't precisely square to the table, the shoulders come out at different heights. The problem with a spring clamp is that it doesn't deliver enough pressure. If the tenon pieces repeatedly bang into the stop block, they can easily knock the block out of square or out of position.

Now I use a big block, dedicated to the purpose, and a strong clamp.

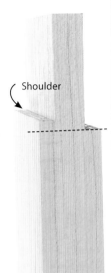

Shoulder

Uneven shoulders make an ugly joint. These shoulders are way off, but even a small error can create an unsightly gap.

Split Dowels for Easier Dry Fitting

Dry fitting dowel joints can be downright aggravating. They fit so tightly, it's next to impossible to disassemble the joint. For an easy solution, use a bandsaw and a block with a hole in it to cut slots in the ends of a few dowels. These dowels are easy to insert and remove, but still hold the joint together well enough to check the fit. For final assembly, don't forget to use normal dowels!

Saw Kerf

Holding Block

Test Long Joints

Hard-won experience has taught me to test edge joints before gluing boards together. The test is simple, but effective.

After jointing, I tighten a clamp across the middle of two neighboring boards. I walk around to both ends and wiggle the boards up and down past one another. If they rub together, great. The joint is tight and good to go.

If they don't rub against each other, I've got a problem. One edge—or both—isn't quite straight, which could result in the joint coming apart after it has been glued together. It may take years to fail, but it's not a risk worth taking. I rejoint both edges, making sure to put all my hand pressure down on the infeed table until halfway through the cut, then gradually switch to putting all the pressure on the outfeed table. That usually does the trick.

If using the right technique doesn't solve your problem, your jointer may need a tuneup.

The Right Mortise/Tenon Fit

What's the right fit between a mortise and a tenon? I'm going crazy trying to measure them with a dial caliper!

You're not alone. This question has bugged just about every woodworker, but the answer doesn't lie with precision instruments.

A crusty woodworker of the old school once said, "If you need your shoe to pound a tenon into a mortise, it's too tight. If it just drops in by itself, it's too loose. If you can tap it in with your hat, it's just right." Well, nobody wears a hat in the shop any more, but you get the idea.

If the fit is too tight, your glue-up will be a nightmare and the joint may actually fail. Water-based glues slightly swell wood, so a joint that's tight when dry becomes even tighter when wet. Way too much pressure is necessary to force out the air trapped in a tight mortise. To make matters worse, you may "starve" the joint of adequate glue if it's scraped off the mating surfaces as the tenon enters the mortise.

If the fit is too loose, the glue won't bond the tenon and the wall of the mortise. White and yellow glues shrink as they dry and at most they can tolerate a gap about the thickness of a sheet of paper. That's more or less the amount of clearance in a joint that slips together easily by hand (or hat!).

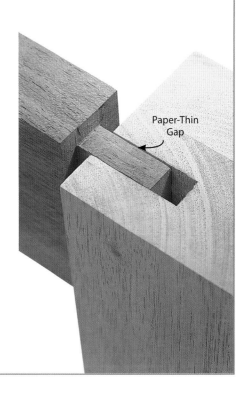

Paper-Thin Gap

Jointer-Planer

Anti-Snipe Solution for Short Boards

I can't stand planer snipe. Especially when I'm planing small (and expensive!) boards of exotic wood for the boxes I build. To prevent planer snipe I send my boards through on a sled. I make the sled at least 6-in. longer than my workpiece. Then I glue a rear stop block and side strips to the sled. The side strips and stop block need to be at least as thick as the final thickness of the board you're planing. This ensures that the side strips and stop block get sniped instead of your good wood.

Safety note: The length of the workpiece that you place on the sled must be as long or longer than the minimum recommended length for your planer or you could experience kick back. Check the owner's manual for your planer or call the manufacturer to find out the minimum length. Never attempt to plane boards shorter than the minimum recommended length.

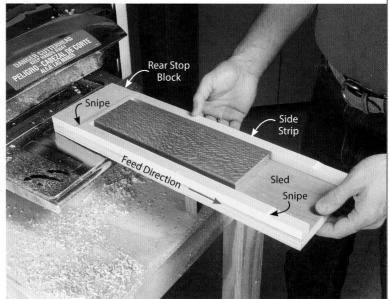

Board Too Wide for Jointer

I've got some beautiful planks that are too wide for my jointer. I really don't want to rip them down to size and risk breaking up the grain pattern. What can I do?

This is a common problem for which there are a number of solutions. You could use a hand plane to joint one face before sending it through the planer. Or, build a carriage to support the uneven board and hope nothing slips. Here's an easier way: use your jointer's rabbeting table, (you'll find it hiding under the guard), and a piece of plastic laminate to joint those boards in two passes.

First, unplug your machine and remove the guard. Don't worry, the board will completely cover the knives. Just be sure to use push blocks and turn the machine off between passes!

Set your fence to cut a little more than half the board's width.

Stick a piece of plastic laminate on the rabbeting table of your jointer with double-stick tape. Then lay a straightedge across the plastic laminate shim so it overhangs the outfeed table. Adjust the infeed table until the shim and the outfeed table are flush (Photo 1).

Remove the shim, plug in your jointer and make your first cut (Photo 2).

Replace the shim, turn the board end for end and joint the other half of the same face. The previously jointed area should ride on the shim and prevent any tipping (Photo 3). Now you're ready for the planer.

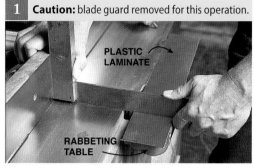

1 **Caution:** blade guard removed for this operation.

PLASTIC LAMINATE

RABBETING TABLE

Set the depth of cut equal to the thickness of the shim.

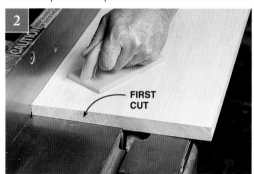

2 FIRST CUT

Remove the shim and make the first cut.

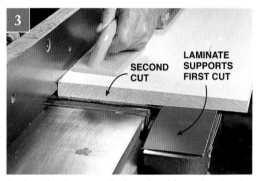

3 SECOND CUT — LAMINATE SUPPORTS FIRST CUT

Replace the shim, turn the board end for end and make the second cut.

Highlight Cast-In Marks on Your Joiner

The cast-in alignment marks on a joiner can be difficult to read. If you're tired of squinting, use a permanent marker to highlight the marks. The difference it makes will amaze you.

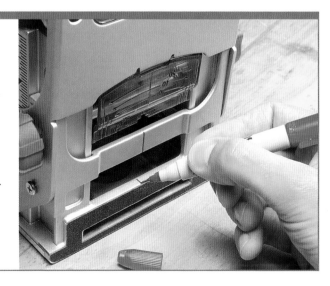

Grind Your Own Knives

With this simple jig, a drill press and a cup grinder, I can sharpen any jointer or planer knife. First I make a hardwood block and cut it to ¹⁄₁₆ in. less than the length of the knives. Then I add a retaining piece at each end, as shown. Install a medium-grit cup grinder in the drill press and set the speed at the high end of its range. Lower the grinding wheel until it just touches the blade, then lock the quill. Continue grinding until all nicks in the knife are removed. Use the same procedure to grind the remaining knives, then hone them on an oil or waterstone in the usual way.

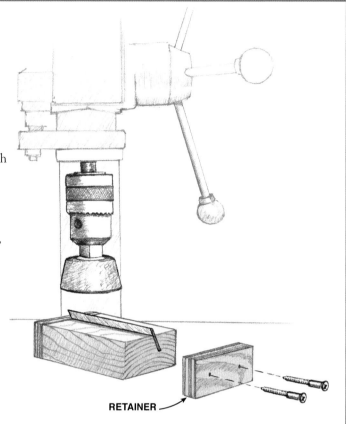

RETAINER

Universal Planer Sled

Let's face it: running a twisted board through the planer doesn't make it flat. The board will still be twisted when it comes out. The trick is to use a sled that prevents the board from rocking as it's being planed. That's not a new idea, but I've made a sled that accommodates a board of almost any size, no matter how twisted.

I made the sled 12" wide and 6' long. It can be glued up from narrow boards, made from MDF, or be a melamine shelf purchased from a home center. Whatever the source, it has to be flat. Glue a ½" thick stop block to the leading edge. Drill holes in the sled wherever needed and insert T-nuts from the bottom. Counterbore the T-nuts so their flanges don't catch on the planer's bed.

Next, mill a bunch of ½" thick hardwood strips. Bevel some of the strips' ends, and leave others square. Bandsaw adjustment slots down the strips' centers. The wedges steady a wobbly board, and the square-ended strips hold it in place. Secure the blocks and wedges by screwing pan-head machine screws and washers into the T-nuts. Make sure the screws don't stand proud of the board you're planing!

Stop

Improved Push Pad

Ordinary push pads tend to slip, I've found, when face-jointing a board. I modified one of mine by cutting ½" of the rubber padding off its back end and then screwing on a ½" x ½" cleat. Now the rear push pad hooks the back end of the board. No more slipping!

Cleat

Jointing with a Planer

I came across some wonderful oak boards for a small table I wanted to build. The problem was the boards were too wide for my jointer and I didn't want to rip them any narrower. I solved my dilemma with this planer sled that allows me to use my planer as a jointer. The trick is to keep the board from rocking during planing. A wood shim under the high corner is all it takes. I add hot-melt glue to the shim and all four corners of the board to keep them from shifting on the sled during planing. Once I have one side planed flat I take the board off the sled, flip it over and plane the other side. The boards for my table were only 4-ft. long and the sled is about 6-in. longer. This technique works equally well for longer boards although you will need a longer sled and you may need additional shims along the sides.

Shim

Hot-Melt Glue Gun

Stop

Sled

High Corner

Jointer Quandary

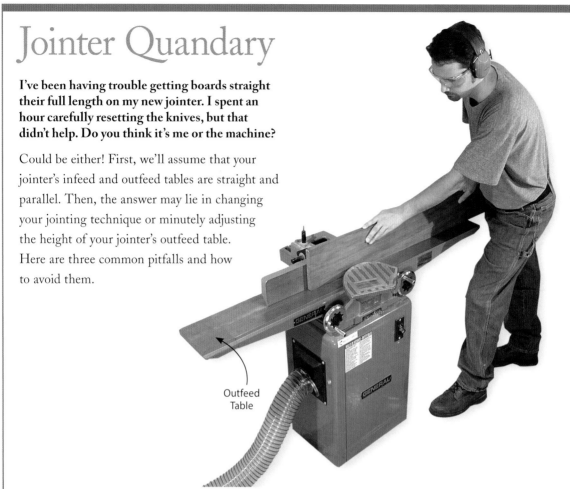

I've been having trouble getting boards straight their full length on my new jointer. I spent an hour carefully resetting the knives, but that didn't help. Do you think it's me or the machine?

Could be either! First, we'll assume that your jointer's infeed and outfeed tables are straight and parallel. Then, the answer may lie in changing your jointing technique or minutely adjusting the height of your jointer's outfeed table. Here are three common pitfalls and how to avoid them.

Outfeed Table

Problems

Persistent Convex Edge
Sometimes an edge remains curved every time you joint it.

A Sniped End
Sometimes a jointer takes a heavy bite at the tail end of a board.

Snipe

A Tapered Cut
Sometimes a cut mysteriously trails off to nothing.

Taper · Uncut Section

Solutions

Joint the Belly First
This is a problem of technique, not an incorrectly adjusted machine. Jointing a long, convex board is difficult because rocking it is so easy. Try this: Joint the center of the board first. Take a few passes to make a solid and true reference surface. Then make longer and longer cuts until you joint the full length of the board.

Raise the Outfeed Table
Although you did your best to set the knives level, it doesn't always work. You'll see the dreaded snipe if the outfeed table is even a tiny bit below the tallest knife. Loosen the gib screws on the back side of your jointer, raise the outfeed table a hair and try jointing again. Keep raising the table by very small amounts until the snipe disappears, then lock down the gib screws.

Lower the Outfeed Table
Rule out the possibility that you're dealing with a slightly convex edge before changing any settings. Start fresh with a 2- to 3-ft.-long board that's been ripped straight on the table saw. Draw a pencil line down the sawn edge and joint the board. If the tail end of the line remains visible, you've got an outfeed table that's too high. Lower the table until you get a sniped cut, then raise the table until the snipe goes away.

Planer Sled

When I run a wide, rough board through my planer, it doesn't come out flat. What should I do?

Build a sled. A planer sled is nothing more than a big board itself–but one that's very stiff and absolutely flat.

Planers aren't meant to make boards flat, though. They make boards thinner. If you run a warped board through a planer, it will come out warped, too. A little bit flatter, perhaps, but it won't have the same degree of flatness you would get from a jointer. It's better to joint the face of a board first, then run it through a planer.

But if you don't have a jointer, or your board is too wide for your jointer, you can still use your planer to flatten a board using a sled. Here's a good way to make one from inexpensive material.

Start with sheet stock that's somewhat flexible, such as ½ in.-thick MDF. (Thicker material may not work because it's harder to force it flat.) Cut the MDF into four pieces about 12 in. wide and 48 in. long. Glue the pieces together on a surface you know is flat, such as a tablesaw or door (Photo 1). The result will be just what you need: a huge board that's both flat and stiff.

Screw a stop to one end to prevent your rough board from kicking back out of the planer (Photo 2). (Caution: don't screw from above. You should totally eliminate any chance that your planer knives could contact the stop's screws.) When you use your sled, the end with the stop should be the trailing end.

Place your rough board on the sled and place shims under areas of the board that don't touch the sled (Photo 3). It's essential that the board doesn't rock or bend as its being planed. Then run both sled and rough board through the planer as if it was one huge piece of wood. Once one side of your rough board is flat, you can set aside the sled and run the other side through the planer.

Make a sled by gluing together pieces of ½ in. MDF placed on top of your tablesaw. Use bricks to force the MDF to lay flat and to apply clamping pressure.

Cut one end of the sled, then attach a stop block.

Place your wide board on the sled, then fill any gaps with shims, such as playing cards. The shims prevent the board from rocking or bending as it's planed.

Simple Sharpening Jig

I've tried several different shop-made jigs for sharpening my jointer and planer knives but this one has proved the simplest to use and make. When making this sharpening jig it's important to make the slots at the correct angle so the bevels of the blades lay perfectly horizontal. This way the sandpaper will have even contact. My jointer blades required a 38-degree angle but check yours because it may be different.

I also had to saw the angled slots with the board on its edge. That's because my tablesaw (like most) tilts to only 45 degrees. This is not far enough for the slot to be cut with the board laying flat. Cutting it on its edge solves this problem. Take a look at your saw and you will see what I mean. Double-check the angle of your jointer knives and saw the slots to match. I added a blade guard to keep things safe.

For the sanding block I used chunks of ¾-in. MDF with sheets of silicon carbide sandpaper attached with spray-on adhesive. I started with 220 grit and worked my way up to 600 grit for a final honing.

Sanding Block

Jointer Blade

Stop Block

Blade Guard

Setting Jointer Knives

How can I set my jointer knives without using a jig?

A wood block and a pencil will do the job on a jointer with an adjustable outfeed table. If the outfeed table on your jointer doesn't adjust, you're better off using a magnetic jig or dial indicator.

Make a maple block about ¾-in. thick, 3-in. wide, and 12-in. long. Unplug the jointer. Remove the pulley guard so you can rotate the cutterhead by hand. Leave the dull knives in place.

You'll use the block to measure the height of the knives above the cutterhead. Set the block on the outfeed table, as in the photo below. Press down lightly on the block and rotate the cutterhead. The knife should tick against the block or lift up the block and carry it a short distance.

Next, lower the outfeed table until the block moves about ¼-in. as you manually turn the cutterhead. Using the edge of the outfeed table as a reference, mark the movement of the block from where the knife picks up the block to where it lets it down. This indicates how high the knife sticks up above the cutterhead. Now you can remove all the dull knives and have them sharpened.

The idea is to set the sharpened knives at the same height as the old ones. Put in a sharp knife. Rotate the cutterhead and raise or lower

the knife until the block travels the distance marked. Check both sides and tighten down the knife, then check again. Set the other two knives the same way, and then raise the outfeed table until each knife barely ticks the block. Make sure all the knives have been tightened down, then plug the machine in and joint a 3-ft. board. Raise the outfeed table if there's snipe at the end of the board. Lower the table if the cut trails off to nothing.

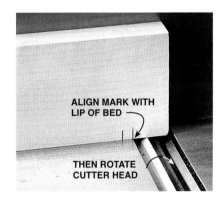

ALIGN MARK WITH
LIP OF BED

THEN ROTATE
CUTTER HEAD

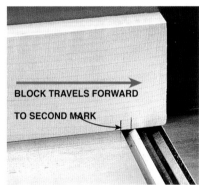

BLOCK TRAVELS FORWARD

TO SECOND MARK

Perfectly Square Edges Using a Planer

I've had trouble making square and smooth edges on face frame parts, but this planer jig solved all my problems. It produces accurate and consistent results. For the jig's base, cut T-slots in a ¾" x 11" board that's a little bit longer than the planer's bed and extension tables. Use T-bolts and wing nuts to fasten two 1½" x 1½" aluminum angles to the jig. Adjust the angles to fit tight around your board. Clamp the jig to the planer's bed, then feed your stock between the angles. Use smaller or larger angles for different widths of stock, being careful to ensure your planer knives come nowhere near the angles' top edges.

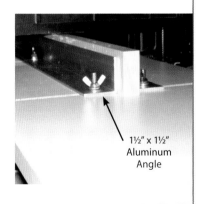

1½" x 1½"
Aluminum
Angle

Turning

Duplicate Spindles with a Semaphore Jig

A semaphore jig performs the same task as a story stick and caliper but it is more automated. With this jig you don't need to place pencil lines on the blank, nor do you need to have a caliper. Each arm of the semaphore jig rides on the surface of the rough spindle. When you part down to the correct diameter at each location, the arm swings all the way through. An adjustable semaphore jig can be reused for other turnings, so spending a little extra time making one can pay off in the long haul.

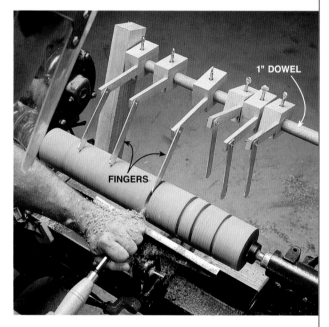

I built this adjustable semaphore jig in about 3 hours and all of the parts were available from my local hardware store for less than $20. The number of arms you make depends on the complexity of your turnings—make as many as you need. To make this jig, first I took a piece of 2-in. wide by 1½-in.-thick maple and dadoed a ¾-in. wide by ⅜-in.-deep groove down the middle. I cut this board into 3-in. lengths. Then I glued the 8-in.-long arms into the dadoes. After the glue was dry, I drilled 1-in.-dia. holes through the blocks for the 1-in.-dia. dowel. Each thumbscrew is screwed into a threaded insert and acts as a clamp against the 1-in. dowel. The fingers are made from ⅛-in. by ¾-in.-aluminum bar stock, and held onto the arms with No. 8 machine screws, nuts and washers.

Bowl-Gouge Sharpening Jigs

Try as I might, I can't seem to get a good edge on my bowl gouges. Are bowl-gouge sharpening jigs worth looking into?

Bowl-gouge sharpening jigs do a great job. The jigs give many turners a higher degree of control and repeatability than they get doing it by hand. But don't kid yourself; using a jig is not like using a pencil sharpener. The technique does involve a learning curve; it's just not as steep as learning to sharpen by hand. You still have to know how to shape the tool and when to stop grinding by observing the sparks.

According to expert turner and instructor Alan Lacer, the motion used to sharpen a gouge on a grinder is very similar to the one used to turn a bowl on the lathe. As you master one skill, you'll be learning the other. However, if you're spending more time on the grinder than on the lathe, a sharpening jig can get you over the hump and allow you to concentrate on developing your skills on the lathe first.

There are a number of jigs on the market and all of them work well. The basic jig usually consists of a mounting plate that holds either an adjustable arm or a tool rest (not shown). (The tool rest, an adjustable platform used for sharpening chisels and plane irons, is far superior to most stock tool rests.) The adjustable arm has a cradle to hold the gouge handle to create a traditional grind (Photo 1). To create a fingernail profile, you need to purchase a tool holder to go with your basic set (Photo 2).

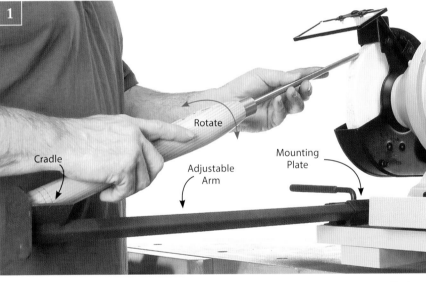

To grind a traditional profile on a bowl gouge, you need a basic jig setup consisting of an adjustable arm with a cradle to hold the gouge and a mounting plate to hold the arm. To use, simply rotate the tool handle in the cradle.

To create a fingernail profile, you need a specialized tool holder. The tool holder pivots in a cradle on an adjustable arm. Rocking the handle back and forth creates the profile.

A Real Swingin' Tool Rack

I try to use every square inch of space in my shop, so I made a storage rack for my turning tools that swings out when I need it. When I'm done turning, it swings back, completely out of the way. Two 5-in. strap hinges mount the rack to a ¾-in. x 8-in. x 24-in. piece of plywood that's screwed to the wall. Plastic shields on the front and sides guard my hands and protect the tools while leaving them easy to identify. The bottom is open, so wood shavings fall right through.

Drawer Slide Tracing Jig

I recently needed a jig to trace lathe turnings. I tried a variety of designs but none produced the accuracy or ease of operation that I wanted.

While rummaging around my shop, I discovered an extra set of 10-in. ball bearing drawer slides left over from another project. I attached a single slide to a bracket and attached a pencil to the slide with a notched wood block and Wing Nut. The bracket fits in a dado in the jig's base. The lathe turning is held between a couple of sharpened machine screws. The right holder is attached to a T-track with a T-bolt and knob so I can move it for different part lengths. To use the jig I move the slide in and out against the turning while I slide the bracket left or right. The pencil does the drawing and I end up with a very accurate tracing of the part.

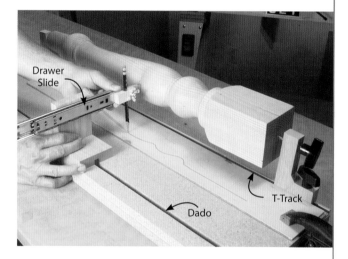

Drawer Slide

T-Track

Dado

PVC Turning-Tool Rack

My growing collection of turning tools was getting out of control. I needed some way to keep them organized and within reach. One Sunday morning while staring at the pipe organ at church, it hit me. Right after services, I went to the home center and bought 10-ft. lengths of 2-in., 1½-in., 1¼-in. and 1-in. PVC for $2 to $3 apiece. I also bought a number of end caps for each-size pipe (35 to 60 cents each). I screwed each end cap down onto a sheet of plywood. Then I used a miter saw to cut lengths of PVC pipe to hold each tool. Cementing the tubes into the caps is optional. When I get a new tool, I just add another tube. I love it!

PVC Tube

PVC End Cap

Plywood Base

No-Wobble Pen Mandrel

While turning wooden pens, students in my woodshop classes kept wearing out the points on the live centers of our mini lathes. The points fit into the hollowed end of the pen mandrel. If the mandrel isn't clamped tight enough between the lathe's head and tailstock, it spins on the point and wears it out (left photo). A worn-out point allows the mandrel to wobble and makes it impossible to turn the pen blanks.

To keep the classes running smoothly, I had to solve the problem right away. So I removed the worn-out points and installed wooden plugs tapered to fit inside the lathes' live centers. Each plug contains a brass pen sleeve that perfectly houses the mandrel (middle photo). These plugs are perfect for occasional use, but I needed a more permanent solution.

I had a machinist friend make these cone-shaped brass nuts that thread onto the mandrel (right photo). The cone shape matches the live center's large tapered opening. This nut installs easily and centers itself every single time.

Stock Mandrel Nut

Worn Center Point

Hollowed End

Tapered Plug

Brass Pen Sleeve

Cone-Shaped Nut

Tapered Opening

What's all that Chatter?

I'm having a hard time turning smooth spindles on my lathe, even though my tools are sharp. Near the tailstock, my turnings always look like they've been whittled. What do you suggest?

Your problems are caused by vibration, and the faceted result is called chatter. Most often, chatter-producing vibration is indicated by a telltale audible hum that occurs while you cut. Chatter can be the result of your cutting technique, flex in the turning blank, or worn-out bearings in your lathe.

You'll get chatter if:

- the tool extends too far beyond the tool rest
- you hold the tool at the wrong angle
- you push the tool too hard
- you hold the tool too lightly
- you don't hold the tool firmly enough against the tool rest
- you use tools that aren't sharp

If you can stop the hum by supporting the blank with your free hand while making a light cut, the blank is flexing. To be safe, support the blank on its back side, opposite the tool rest.

A "steady rest" (an accessory that mounts to the lathe bed) stops this vibration by supporting the blank near the cutting action.

If the problem isn't cutting technique or flex in the blank, it's your lathe. Because chatter only occurs near the tailstock end of your machine, the most likely culprit is your live center. Be suspicious if it doesn't spin freely or if you can detect play between the tip and the shaft. For a conclusive test, install a different center. A "dead" center (no moving parts) is best. If the hum disappears, your old live center was the problem.

Many inexpensive lathes come equipped with live centers of dubious quality. A better-quality replacement is a worthwhile upgrade. I discovered the hard way that sanding on a lathe can be hard on the fingers. Now, to protect my fingers, I cut the fingertips off a latex-dipped work glove and wear one or two of the fingertips while sanding. Not only does this protect my fingertips, it also makes it much easier to hold onto the sandpaper.

I found a pair of these gloves at a hardware store for about $4, or you can order them. Caution: Don't wear the whole glove while working on your lathe. You could be seriously injured if the glove got caught on your turning project or lathe.

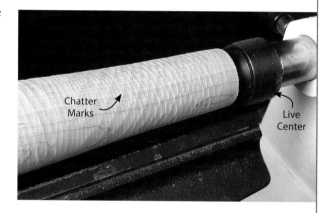

Chatter Marks

Live Center

Instant Rosewood

I like to use purpleheart pen blanks because they're less expensive than other exotic hardwoods. Recently, I stumbled on a cool trick. I discovered that I could cause the wood to overheat and turn dark by using the back side of the sandpaper while the wood is turning. Light overheating makes purpleheart look like rosewood; further overheating makes it look like ebony. Heating alternating sections creates light and dark contrasts as if the pen was made of multiple pieces of wood.

Turning Duplicates With a Story Stick

The most common way to make duplicate turned spindles is to use a story stick and calipers. The story stick has marks to indicate where transition points are, such as the valley of a curve, or a shoulder between two shapes. With the lathe spinning, transfer these marks to the rough spindle with a pencil. Then cut down to the correct diameter for that location with your parting tool. Once you have all of your transition points parted to diameter, shape the profiles in between.

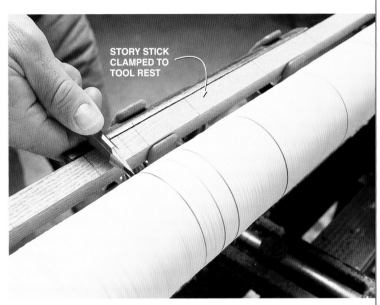

STORY STICK CLAMPED TO TOOL REST

Wedged Lathe Tool Rack

My lathe tool rack is based on a fishing rod rack that I made some time ago. Made from 3/4-in.-thick walnut, it measures 3⅛-in. by 10-in. by 30-in. I made the front and back tool supports by ripping a 3⅛-in.-wide board in half after drilling centered 1½-in.-dia. holes on 1⅞-in. centers. I installed the 2¾-in.-wide bottom board at a 45-degree angle to gently wedge the long handles between the bottom and the two supports. This system accommodates different handle styles by allowing each tool to find it's natural resting point. Now my lathe tools rest firmly in place, yet are easy to remove and replace.

Tool Supports

45° Angle

Measuring & Marking

Freehand S-Curve

You don't need complicated geometry to draw one of the most beautiful lines in furnituremaking, the reverse curve, or ogee. All it takes is a pencil with an eraser, a straightedge and confidence in your ability to freehand a series of very short curves.

The idea is to break up the large task of drawing the entire curve into smaller tasks. There's a lot of symmetry in an ogee, so it's easy to lay out a few points that the curve will pass through and connect the dots. Follow these three easy steps to draw a graceful reverse curve:

1. Connect the endpoints of the curve with a straight line. Divide the line into four equal parts.
2. Mark an equal rise and fall to the curve. Connect the dots with straight lines.
3. Bend each straight line into a freehand curve.

Take It Further

Once you get the hang of it, you can use the same strategy to draw a more dynamic reverse curve with unequal sides. Simply set the midpoint of the curve off center in Step 1, then mark two different sizes of rise and fall in Step 2.

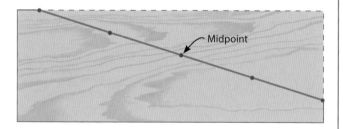

Midpoint

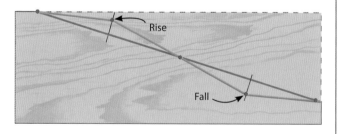

Rise

Fall

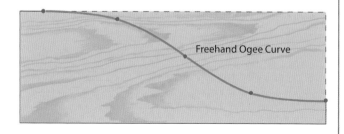

Freehand Ogee Curve

30-Minute Marking Gauge

Make this handy little gem for less than $5. You'll need one piece of hardwood for the beam and another for the fence. You'll also need two ¼-20 threaded inserts and a thumbscrew. Drill a hole through the fence for the thumbscrew, 1½-in. from one end. Then rip the fence into two pieces. Cut a dado for the beam in the center of the top piece. Enlarge the drilled hole in the bottom piece and install one threaded insert. Glue the pieces back together and bandsaw a kerf up to the beam opening. Install the other threaded insert

Fence ¾" x 1⅞" x 7"

Bandsawn Kerf

Beam ⅜" x 1" x 11"

in the beam, ¾-in. from the end. The pencil threads into this insert, so it really stays put. On the beam's other end, I installed a hardened screw after grinding the point sharp, to use for scribing.

3-4-5 Square

If you want to check something for square, try using the carpenter's 3-4-5 Method. If one leg of a triangle measures 3 in., and the second measures 4 in., the hypotenuse must be 5 in. if the corner is square. This also works with 6, 8, 10; 12, 16, 20; and so on. Any units of measurement will do, as long as you use multiples of 3-4-5.

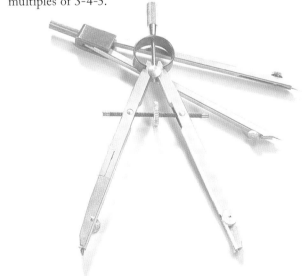

Bent-Stick Arcs

Bending a thin stick is a quick way to lay out an arc. Trouble is, it takes two hands to bend the stick. How are you going to draw a line around it?

The answer is to use two thin sticks, taped together at the ends. (My sticks are ⅛-in. thick and ¾-in. wide.) Place a spacer of any length between the sticks at their centerpoints. Now your hands are free to draw the arc. Adjust the spacer's length to make arcs of different curvature. Shifting the spacer off the centerpoints creates asymmetrical arcs.

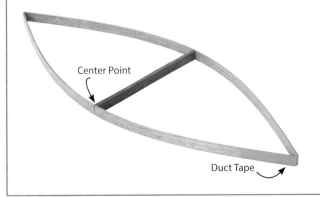

Center Point

Duct Tape

Circle Center

Use a framing square to find the center of a circle by placing the corner of the square on the circle, and marking where the legs meet the circumference. Draw a line from one mark to the other. Do this a second time. These lines intersect at the center.

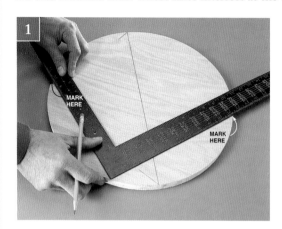

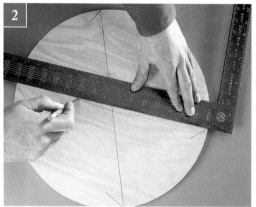

Big Stamps Prevent Little Mix-Ups

You know this is the left side of the front right leg. Or is it? After dry-fitting your project for the umpteenth time, have you ever caught yourself trying to figure out which two parts go together? You can write notes on the parts themselves until you're blue in the face, but no marking system beats stamping a number right on the joint, especially for complex jobs in dark wood.

Most steel stamps are so tiny that they're not legible in wood, but these jumbo stamps work fine. When you finally get around to gluing your project, there'll be no doubt about which parts belong together.

Better Templates

If you want to make templates that will last a long time, try the following materials; Plexiglas, tempered hardboard, Baltic birch or ApplePly plywood. Vinyl flooring and contact paper also work well for patterns.

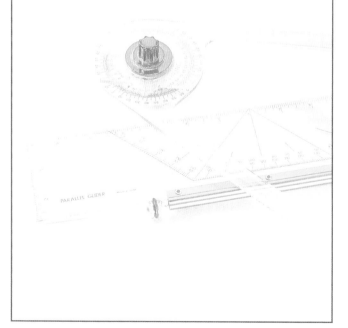

Accurate Squares

To check a square for accuracy, place the head on the edge of a board and draw a line along the blade. Flip the square and do the same on the other side. If the lines are parallel, all is well. If they are not, your square is not square. If you have a framing square that tests out of square, you can adjust it. Lay the corner of the square on an anvil, and tap the face with a hammer. Hitting it close to the outside reduces the angle, tapping near the inside increases it.

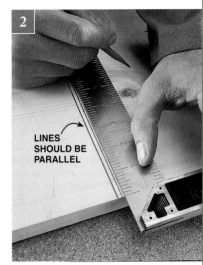

LINES SHOULD BE PARALLEL

Adjustable Curves

Laying out a large curve with a cobbled-together, oversize compass is a pain in the neck. Instead I use a bowed slat that can be adjusted to any curve. I used to bend the slat with my hands and drew the curve with a pencil in my mouth. That didn't work very well! The solution came to me in the bathroom when I looked up and saw that little chain hanging from the ceiling light.

Here's what I did: First I ripped a thin, ⅛-in. slat, 1½-in. wide and 36-in. long. In the middle of each end I cut a ½-in.-long slot on the bandsaw. I slipped in the end of a 40-in.-long beaded chain (available at most hardware stores) through one slot. While holding the free end of the slat and pulling on the chain, I create a curve in the slat. Slipping the free end of the chain into the other slot locks the slat into the curve. By shortening or lengthening the chain I can make subtle changes in the curve.

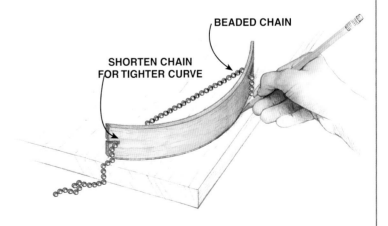

BEADED CHAIN

SHORTEN CHAIN FOR TIGHTER CURVE

Customize a Drafting Square

Drafting squares are inexpensive, accurate and great for tool or jig setup. Because they're plastic, you can easily customize them to suit the job. We filed notches in this square to keep the saw teeth from interfering with setup. Drafting squares are available in various sizes at art and office supply stores.

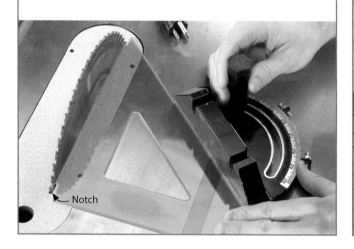

← Notch

Dividing a Board

This one is a chestnut, but everyone ought to know it: You can quickly divide a board into equal widths without complex fractions. Place a ruler diagonally across the surface so you can mark off the number of segments in whole numbers. For example, to divide a board into seven equal parts, place the zero mark on one edge, and place the 7 in. mark on the other edge. Make a pencil mark at each 1 in. mark to divide the board.

FOR SEVENTHS
PLACE 7 ON EDGE

Divide the Circumference

To divide the circumference of a round spindle, wrap masking tape around it so it overlaps itself, and make two aligned marks, one on each part of the overlap. Remove the tape, measure between the marks, and divide as needed. Reapply the tape to transfer the layout to the cylinder.

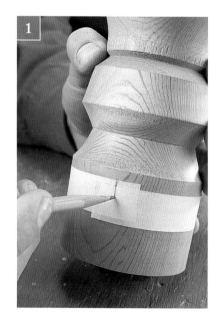

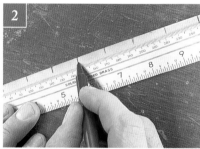

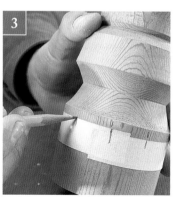

Freebie Marking Knife

I get a kick out of making new tools from old parts. I keep all my old files and chisels to turn them into something useful around the shop. The same goes for hacksaw blades. I turned a dull one into an excellent single-bevel marking knife.

I prefer a single-bevel to a double-bevel marking knife for accurately drawing a square line. (If you lean a double-bevel knife the wrong way, the line wanders away from the square.) To make this single-bevel knife, I clamped the old hacksaw blade in my metal-working vise, snapped off a 6-in.-long section and ground down the teeth. I flattened one side of the working end on sandpaper taped to my tablesaw, then curved and sharpened it with a 100-grit wheel on my grinder. A curved end with a long, continuous edge stays sharp longer than a pointed end. I attached the handles with epoxy.

Hacksaw Blade

¼" x ½" x 4¾" Handle

Lay Out An Oval

Way back in junior high school, my shop teacher showed us a simple method for laying out an oval. All he used was a ruler and a strip of paper. I can't remember how it worked. Can you help?

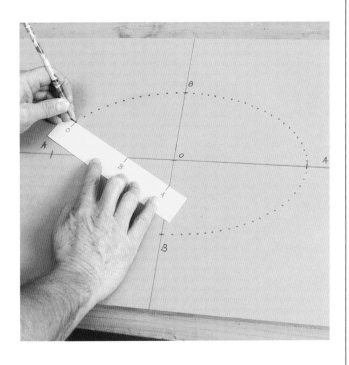

Sure, here goes: Draw horizontal and vertical lines that intersect at point 0. Mark half the oval's length (A) on the horizontal axis. Mark half the oval's width (B) on the vertical axis. On a strip of paper, mark a 0 on one end and distances 0 to A and 0 to B.

Place the strip of paper so that mark A falls anywhere on the vertical line and mark B falls on the horizontal line. Mark a dot on the board next to the strip's 0 point.

Reposition the strip and make another mark where the 0 point lands. Continue making these tick marks all the way around. Drawing the oval is just a matter of connecting the dots.

Look Ma, No Compass!

All you need to draw a perfect arc of any diameter is three small nails, a piece of thin plywood and this old boatbuilder's trick.

Why use this weird geometry? Other methods have their drawbacks. A curve drawn around a bent stick flattens out at the ends. A curve drawn with a trammel or giant compass requires you to know the exact radius of the circle and its center point, and both may be difficult to figure out.

This method is easy. You can work directly on a board or make a template. First, figure out where the arc begins and ends. Nail two brads at those spots. Then decide how high the arc will be. Nail another brad in the center and top of the arc.

Now make the jig, as shown below, left. Draw one half of the arc at a time. Start by removing one of the end brads. Butt the jig against the two remaining brads, as shown. Slide the jig back and forth along the brads. A pencil placed in the notch will mark a perfect arc. Replace the brad you removed and repeat the operation to make the other half of the arc.

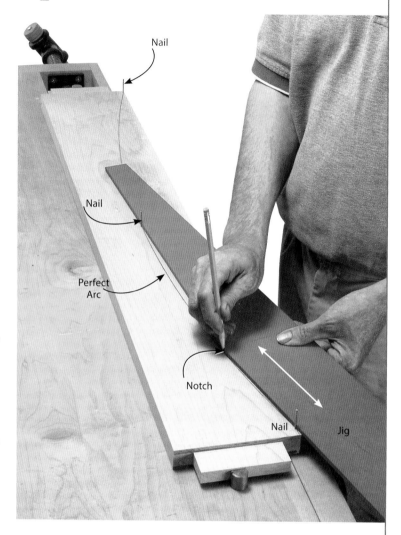

How to Make the Jig

1. Make three marks on your board, two at the ends of the arc and one at the highest point in the middle.
2. Transfer these measurements to a thin piece of plywood that's a little longer and wider than the arc. Taper one end of the plywood to match the triangle made by the marks. Then, cut a small notch for the pencil.

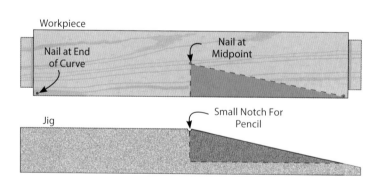

Make Crisper Gauge Lines

I love a wheel-type marking gauge for laying out tenons and dovetails. Its round cutting wheel must be super-sharp to make fine lines across the grain. Sharpening this tiny object looks nearly impossible, but it's really quite easy.

First, unscrew the cutter from the gauge. Place a piece of 320-grit or finer sandpaper on a flat surface, such as ¼-in. thick glass. Place the cutter on the sandpaper, flat side down, and push it around in circles. This is hard to do with your finger, but it's a cinch when you use the eraser end of a pencil. Don't mess with the cutter's bevel side. Install the cutter in the gauge and make a line across the grain. It should be as crisp as one made by a razor-sharp knife or chisel.

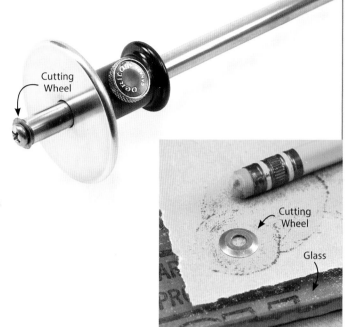

Cutting Wheel

Cutting Wheel

Glass

Make Accurate Inside Measurements

Every woodworker knows not to rely on inside measurements made with a tape measure. Instead, I use two steel rules with dimensions that run to the edges. I butt one rule at each end, so the graduations overlap. To calculate the exact inside measurement, I read one ruler from the 10-in. mark on the other and add 10 inches. Using this method, the inside measurement above is exactly 15½-in.

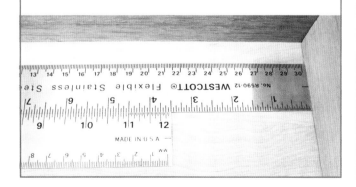

Make Your Marks On Painter's Tape

Instead of writing directly on a project's parts, I stick a piece of painter's tape on each part, and put identifying marks on the tape. Now I don't have to sand off pencil marks or stop during assembly to measure and make sure I'm using the right part.

Mark With A Chisel

A sharp chisel makes an excellent marking knife because it has a single bevel. Double-beveled knives have to be held just so in order for one bevel to snug up against a square. A chisel has to be handled the right way, though. Pull the chisel toward you, with the handle leaning away. If the handle leans toward you, you'll get a ragged line.

Marking Dark Wood

I often use dark, exotic wood for turning pens. It's difficult to see center marks on these species, so I paint the ends of my pen blanks with liquid paper. After it dries in a few seconds, I can easily mark the center with a pencil.

No-Math Saw Setup

So, you've got a big, square hunk of wood that you want to turn on the lathe. You figure sawing off the corners first will save a lot of work. How do you correctly position the saw's fence?

It's simple. Unplug the saw and tilt the blade 45 degrees. On a left-tilt saw, move the fence well to the right, away from the blade. On a right-tilt saw, remove the fence and put it on the left side of the blade.

Next, lean the blank against the blade. Move the fence to touch the blank's opposite corner (photo, above right). Plug in the saw, place the blank flat on the table and rip each corner (photo, below right).

One Step at a Time

ARGH! I cut all the parts according to the cutting list and my face-frame came up short! I worked out the math and the cutting list was correct. What went wrong?

Oops

Rule number one when building complex projects directly from a set of plans: Don't cut every part at once! If you cut and fit as you go, your project is bound to work out. Also, if there is an error in a plan, you'll likely spot it before it's too late.

The problem with completely trusting a cutting list has to do with the fact that one small discrepancy affects the dimensions of subsequent parts. Maybe the fence on your tablesaw was off by a hair and your shelves were a bit long or maybe your ¼-in.-deep dadoes were a little shallow. These small differences can add up to a carcass that's too wide for the face frame dimension that's specified in the plan. The solution is to build complex projects as a series of components and to cut and fit the rest of the project to what's already been built. In your case, cutting and dry fitting the plywood box first, then measuring to see what size the face frame really needed to be would've saved you time, material and aggravation.

Pattern Transfer Tool

When faced with copying a curved leg for a broken chair, I had a hard time making a pattern. I tried guiding a pencil against the leg, but the pencil wobbled and I couldn't keep it upright. I solved my tracing problem by making a jig to transfer the profile.

In the end of a piece of 2x4 scrap I cut a (tight) slot for a flat carpenter's pencil. I cut away the pencil's edge to expose the lead. Then I sharpened the pencil, beveling only one side. Finally, I added a strip of masking tape to protect the leg. With the pencil in the block and pressed against the leg I can trace any profile onto paper.

2x4 Block

Chair Leg

Tight Fit on Pencil

Masking Tape

Remove Corners to Trace Tight Inside Curves

Cut Chisel-Edge on Pencil

Precision Depth Gauge

My dovetail jig doesn't have a depth gauge, and with my engineering background, I like things to be precise. This depth gauge allows me to set my router bits to within .001 of an inch. I also use it to set saw blade heights and check the depth of rabbets and dadoes. Start with a 4-in.-square piece of 1-in. thick hardwood. Drill a 2¼-in.-dia. hole in the center, then cut the piece in half to create the arched legs. Next, drill a hole through the top, the same diameter as the stem of your dial indicator. A brass threaded insert with a setscrew locks the indicator in place.

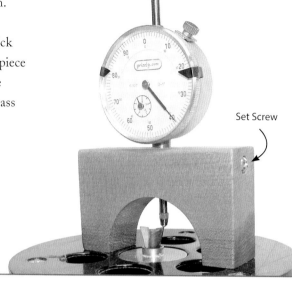

Set Screw

Perfect Shelf Pin Spacing

This is an incredibly easy way to drill evenly-spaced ¼" holes for shelf pins. Just cut a strip of perf-board 1½" wide and trim it to the length of the panel. Cover the holes you're not using with masking tape, and then position the strip on the panel's side. Clamp or tape the jig in place. Flip the jig over to drill the other edge of the panel.

Photocopy Template

I used to hate hanging objects, like power strips, that have hidden T-slots on the back. No matter how carefully I measured, I could never get the mounting screws in the right place on the wall.

Then I realized that I could make a perfect full-size copy of the pattern on standard 8½ by 11-in. paper using my scanner and printer (a copier would work, too).

I taped the pattern where I wanted to mount the power strip, drilled the holes and set the screws. Shazam! It worked perfectly.

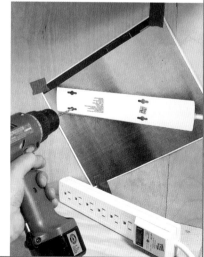

Precision Gauge Lines

Draw a cutting gauge across a board and you should get a razor-sharp line that will become the precise shoulder of a handmade dovetail or tenon. But that's not the kind of line you get with a new gauge, right out of the box. A new gauge makes a pretty wretched line that skips and jumps, with fuzzy, torn edges.

An effective marking gauge knife should have a single bevel and a slightly rounded tip. A single-bevel edge starts the joint off on the right foot. It cuts a groove with one vertical wall and one sloped wall. The vertical wall is the beginning of the joint's square shoulder. The sloped wall goes on the waste side of the joint. (A double-bevel knife makes two sloped walls.) A rounded, fingernail-shaped tip stays sharp longer than a standard triangular point because there's lots more wear surface. You'll rarely have to resharpen it.

Here's how to reshape a new cutting gauge knife on a grinder or belt sander:

1. Remove the knife from the gauge.
2. Bandsaw a 1-in.-long slot on a 6-in.-long piece of ⅜-in. dowel.
3. Insert the knife in the slot. Wrap masking tape around the dowel to hold the knife in place.
4. Grind the knife past the existing bevels. It's only a thin piece of steel, so quench often to avoid bluing.
5. Rotate the dowel on the tool rest to create a rounded bevel. Remove the burr by honing.

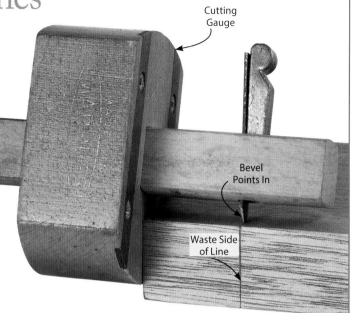

Cutting Gauge

Bevel Points In

Waste Side of Line

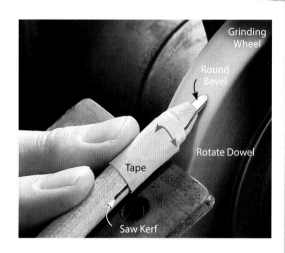

Grinding Wheel

Round Bevel

Rotate Dowel

Tape

Saw Kerf

Quick Marking Gauge

A combination square can easily be used as a marking gauge. Use a fine, triangular file to cut a small V-groove in the center of the end of the sliding rule. Put a pencil or steel scribe in this notch and, using the square's head as a guide, draw your lines.

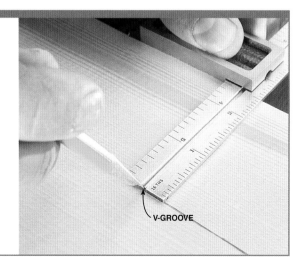

V-GROOVE

Stand Your Rule On Edge

I'm an old fan of folding rules. Unlike tape measures, they don't have a hook at one end that may require you to start at the one-inch mark for an accurate measure. Boy, have I made some embarassing mistakes that way! There's a trick to using folding rules accurately, though. For precise marking, stand the rule on edge rather than laying it flat. This places the division lines right on the wood.

I really like this new-style rule, which is made from plastic. The joints are cleverly constructed so that every division line runs down to the wood, even at the joints. On old-style wooden rules, the metal fittings at each joint prevent many division lines from running to the rule's edge.

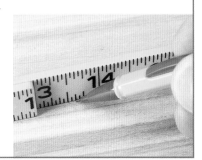

Surefire Marking Gauge

Screwing plywood pieces with drywall-type screws is quick and easy, but drilling holes in a straight line can be tricky. That's why I made this handy little marking gauge that allows me to quickly and accurately mark a line on my plywood for drilling screw holes. To make it, simply cut a ⅜ in. by ⅜-in. rabbet into a board that is about 1-in. wide by 8-in. long. You now have a marking gauge to make a line that will put your screws exactly in the centered edge of your ¾-in. plywood.

Stippling Tool

I came across an old pattern my grandfather drew many years ago on a big sheet of paper. I was itching to build the piece but I couldn't figure out how to transfer the pattern onto boards so I could cut them out on a bandsaw. I didn't want to cut up the paper because of sentimental value and I don't have access to a big copier. Borrowing from my wife's sewing expertise, I made a stippling tool by snipping off the head of a needle and pushing it into the eraser of a wooden pencil, sharp-pointed end out. I taped the pattern on my board and pricked through the paper into the wood. I removed the pattern and connected the prick marks with a pencil line. Slick!

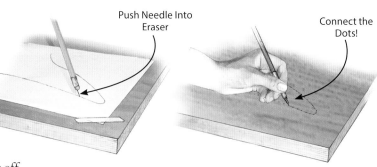

Push Needle Into Eraser

Connect the Dots!

Sliding-Head Beam Compass

My beam compass is perfect for drawing huge arcs. It's super easy to make, and I can adjust it quickly without using screws or clamps. To change the arc's radius, I just slide a saddle-style head along the beam.

Make the beam from a piece of hardwood. Mine is 1" x 1¼" x 36", but you can make it any size you want. Make the sides of the sliding head from ¼" plywood, and the bottom from ½" or ¾" plywood. The head should fit snugly on the beam, but still be able to slide. For the pivot point, I drilled a hole in the head's bottom and inserted a dowel center. (A nail would work just as well.) Drill a hole in the beam's other end to hold the pencil.

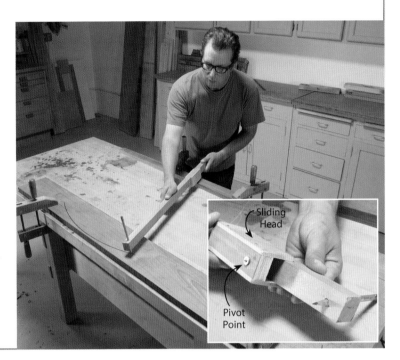

Sliding Head

Pivot Point

Taking Dimensions From Photos

Sometimes a catalog has a piece of furniture that I'd love to build myself. How can I get the dimensions for a piece of furniture off a photograph?

Try this method for scaling from photos:

Start by taping the picture to a large piece of paper. Draw a vertical reference line through the piece so that it crosses the detailing you'd like to dimension, like drawers and doors. Use a triangle to mark out horizontal lines wherever you need dimensions. These lines should be 90 degrees to the vertical reference line (Photo 1).

To determine the scaled dimensions you need an architect's rule. Architect's rules are three sided with a total of six scales starting at 3/32 in. to 3 in. They are

available at most office supply stores and cost only a few dollars. (Here we chose 80-in. for the height of our cabinet. We used the 3/32-in. scale and set the rule at an angle with the 0 on the top line and the 80 on the bottom.) Draw a line along the rule and measure each space along that line to determine the dimensions of each element.

For the horizontal dimensions, just repeat the process with a horizontal reference line and vertical measuring lines.

If the piece is too tall or too wide, simply change the angle of the ruler to correspond with your desired dimensions.

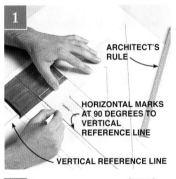

ARCHITECT'S RULE

HORIZONTAL MARKS AT 90 DEGREES TO VERTICAL REFERENCE LINE

VERTICAL REFERENCE LINE

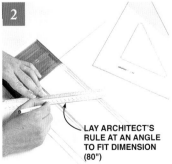

LAY ARCHITECT'S RULE AT AN ANGLE TO FIT DIMENSION (80")

Thickness Gauge

I use this handy device constantly to check and compare thickness on a variety of projects. Slide the gauge over the edge of the stock, keeping the graduated edge flat on the surface of the board, and read the thickness. You'll have to make the graduations yourself, based on a board you gradually plane thinner and thinner. If you want to record some odd size, make a pencil mark on the lower edge. The more gradual the taper of the opening, the more accurate the gauge.

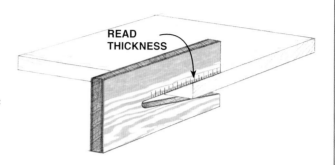

READ THICKNESS

Taping Diagonals

Measuring diagonals with a tape was a pain for me because the hook would always fall off the corner before I could get a reading. Finally I adapted a tape by riveting a small, notched block to the end, as shown. Now I can slip the tape over the corner of the cabinet to be squared with no fear of it slipping off. This is a good use for broken steel tapes missing their first couple of inches.

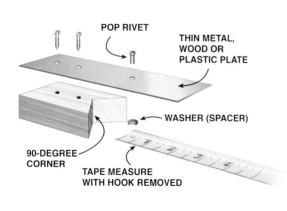

POP RIVET

THIN METAL, WOOD OR PLASTIC PLATE

WASHER (SPACER)

90-DEGREE CORNER

TAPE MEASURE WITH HOOK REMOVED

Tuned-Up Marking Gauge

To make a marking gauge work better, file the tip to a sharper, more knife-like point with a fine-mill file.

TIP

Which Leg Goes Where?

This marking system might look as complicated as ancient hieroglyphics, but its logic is quite simple. Ultimately, it gives you this fair warning, "Don't make a mortise on the wrong side of the leg!"

This is a method of marking four legs to identify once and for all which leg goes where. Indicate the outside faces of your legs by marking them on the top. (The marks are easy to draw. Just hold your pencil like a marking gauge.)You won't touch this surface again, so there's no danger of losing your bearings by removing the marks in tapering or bandsawing the legs. Once you've laid out the marks, you can jumble up the four legs to your heart's content and still be able to return them to their correct positions in seconds.

Stand the legs up on your bench and with a bold, squiggly line, mark where all the mortises go. When it comes time to actually make the mortises, if you're not staring directly at one of those squiggles, something's wrong!

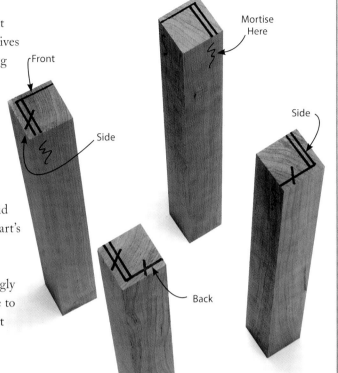

Versatile Center Gauge

I wanted to add accent dowel "dots" down the center of some slightly curved, tapered table legs. Sounds simple, but I nearly pulled my hair out trying to accurately find the center of these legs using a ruler! I was about to tick off the center of the leg every ¼ in. to get the curve I wanted.

Forget it! I came up with a clever, self-centering gauge that works on any board, straight, tapered or curved.

I drilled a snug-fitting hole for a pencil in the middle of a ½ in. by ¼-in. stick. Then I drilled two smaller holes for 10d nails an equal distance from the pencil hole. I spaced these holes so the distance between them was a little larger than the widest section of the leg.

I placed the gauge over the tapered leg and rotated it until the nails contacted the sides. I drew the center line of the board while keeping the nails against the side. Try it, it really works!

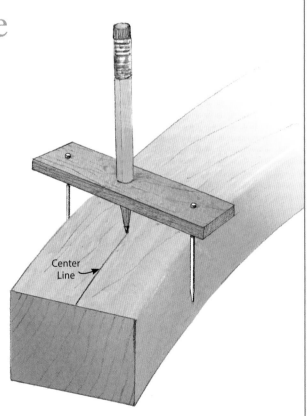

Plate-Joiner

Align Solid Edging to Plywood

Have you ever sanded through a piece of plywood while trying to even up some solid edging that's too low? You can avoid this heartbreak by using biscuits to ensure the entire length of edging is slightly higher than the plywood.

The whole idea is to make a slightly offset joint, with the edging raised up above the plywood by a very small amount, such as the thickness of a playing card. Biscuits are ideal for achieving this precise "misalignment."

To make this offset joint on ¾-in.-thick edging, set your plate joiner to biscuit size #0. Cut slots in the edging (photo, below left). Next, cut slots in the plywood, but this time place a shim under the fence (photo, below). Any kind of thin shim will work, such as plastic laminate, a playing card or a couple of pieces of construction paper.

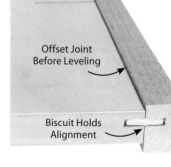

Offset Joint Before Leveling

Biscuit Holds Alignment

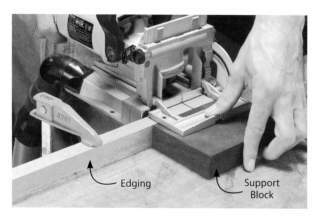

First, cut #0 size slots in the edging. Support the fence with a block that's the same thickness as the edging, so the fence doesn't tip.

Edging — Support Block

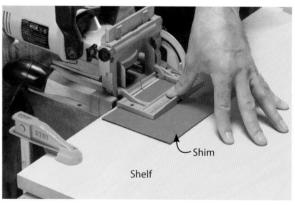

Now cut slots in the plywood. Putting a shim under the fence produces an offset joint that's easy to level successfully.

Shim — Shelf

Cut a Double-Wide Slot for Added Strength

Using two biscuits in a double-wide slot is a great way to increase joint strength when the stock is too thin for two separate slots. This is especially useful when joining a ¾-in.-thick table apron to a leg. Some manufacturers include or offer a 4-mm spacer that fits under the fence for this task, but you can easily make one yourself from scrap wood. Create the double-wide slot by inserting the spacer after the first cut. This will raise the blade just the right amount to create room for a second biscuit.

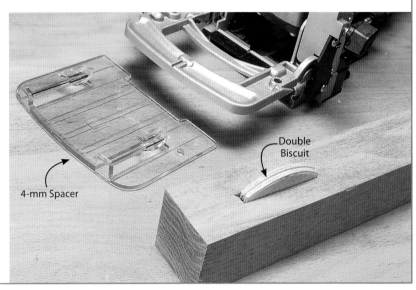

4-mm Spacer

Double Biscuit

Hold the Fence For Accuracy

It's easy to misalign a slot with both your hands on the joiner's handles. Working that way, you can't feel whether the fence is fully in contact with the stock. The slightest shift up or down on the handle can cause the biscuit slot to be cut wrong. Use one hand to hold the fence down onto the board and you'll eliminate errors.

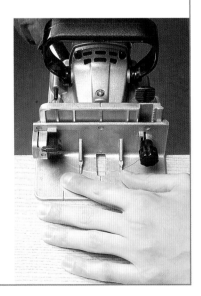

Alternate Grain Direction When Using Double Biscuits

Biscuits are made from compressed beech wood. The grain runs diagonally across the biscuit. The biscuit is weakest along this grain line. When you install two biscuits in a joint, put them in with the grains running in opposite directions. This will counteract the short-grain weakness in each biscuit.

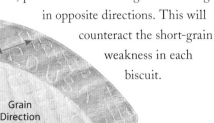

Grain Direction

Align Long Edge Joints

Gluing up long boards can test the nerves of even the most seasoned woodworker. The goal is to get a perfectly flush top right out of the clamps, but all too often you end up with a top that needs a ton of planing or sanding before it's even.

Biscuits make glue-ups go much easier and drastically cut down on the amount of sanding time. Many long boards are slightly bowed, but biscuits help bring bowed boards into alignment.

Here are some tips for cutting the slots:
- Select tight-fitting #20 biscuits.
- Position the centers of the outermost slots at least 3 in. from each end. This allows for you to trim ¾ in. off after gluing without exposing a biscuit slot.
- Cut slots about 8- to 10-in. apart.
- Use the fence of your biscuit joiner, not the base, as the reference surface. Press the fence firmly on the top of the board.
- Spread glue on the edges of your boards, but not in the slots. This speeds your glue up. After all, the biscuits are for alignment only; the joint will be plenty strong without them.

Bowed Board

Reduce sanding time by aligning bowed boards with biscuits. Reference your plate joiner fence from the top of each board.

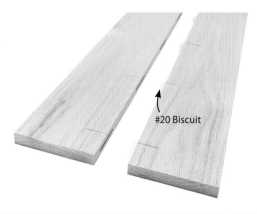

#20 Biscuit

Apply Glue With an Acid Brush

Glue must be evenly applied throughout the biscuit slot to get the strongest joint possible. The easiest way? Squirt some glue into the slot and then run a glue brush, sometimes called an acid brush, through the slot until the glue is evenly coated on both sides and the bottom.

Angled Biscuit-Cutting Jig

We all love biscuit joints, but making them in the angled ends of narrow boards can be a challenge. It's so tricky to balance the biscuit joiner's fence on the end of the small miter. The results can be inaccurate and even dangerous. That's why I built this jig. It not only holds the workpiece but also allows me to use my biscuit joiner in a comfortable horizontal position.

Biscuit Gauge

I use my biscuit joiner all the time to quickly make strong joints. With narrow boards like face frames, I used to spend a lot of time figuring out which biscuit size to use so the slots wouldn't be too wide and show. To avoid all that recalculation, I made a permanent reference block.

I cut slots for No. 0, No. 10 and No. 20 biscuits in a block of wood and recorded all the information I need: the slots' exact widths, depths and centerlines. When locating slots for mitering, I insert a biscuit and note its curvature. This way I avoid cutting slots too close to the miter's tip. I drilled a ½-in. hole through the block to hang it over my bench, but I often keep this handy tool in my apron pocket.

Biscuit Joiner Jig

Cutting slots for biscuits in small or narrow stock, such as when slotting solid-wood edge banding for shelves or cabinets, can be downright dangerous. There's no effective way to hold both the joiner and the stock with your hands. Also, the rotation of the joiner blade can fling a small piece of wood away from you. To avoid this, I devised this jig. Clamp it between bench dogs or clamp it to the benchtop with C-clamps so the plywood base just overhangs the bench. Adjust the fence so the stock you are cutting is flush with the edge of the jig. Clamp the stock down with the toggle clamp and you're ready to cut.

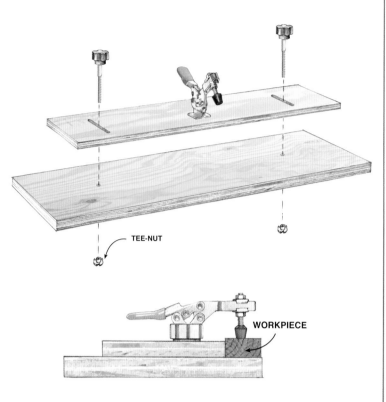

TEE-NUT

WORKPIECE

Fast, Accurate Face Frames

After you've put together a few face frames with dowels or pocket screws and discovered that the pieces don't line up, you may hear a faint inner voice. It will be saying "next time, use biscuits!"

Biscuits align parts far better than dowels or pocket screws, so it's easier to even up rails and stiles after gluing. Even small biscuits (the #0 size) offer enough holding power for any face frame that's glued to a cabinet. If a frame is narrower than a biscuit, don't worry. Simply let the slot and biscuit run out the inside corner.

Build a simple jig (right) to hold narrow pieces. Two toggle clamps secure the workpiece. After gluing the frame together, trim the excess biscuit with a router and flush-trim bit or a sharp chisel.

Toggle Clamp

Adjustable Side

Hook

Hold narrow face-frame pieces with this adjustable jig. It adds extra bearing surface to the end of a rail so your plate joiner won't slip sideways.

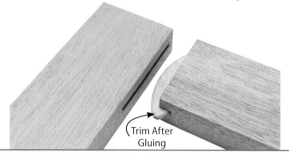

Trim After Gluing

Join Long Miters

Long miter joints look terrific. They make an all-plywood case look seamless at the corners. But getting long miters to look right can drive you nuts.

Let's be realistic; biscuits alone aren't enough. We recommend you add a small piece of hardwood edging to the outside corner as insurance. Here are two reasons to go to this extra trouble.

First, a tiny bit of slippage during glue-up is normal, and when you sand an ordinary mitered corner with tips that don't exactly line up, you're bound to sand through the face veneer on the piece that stands proud. This reveals some of the plywood's core, which is usually a different color.

Second, a sharp mitered edge is easily damaged, so it's best to round off the miter with a ⅛-in., or so, radius. You can't do that on ordinary plywood without going through the face veneer. The solution is to inset a thin strip of solid wood.

To make a long mitered joint, cut the miters on your tablesaw. The bevel should point up in order to minimize tear-out. Then fire up your plate joiner.

Reference from the Outside Edge

Adjust the fence on your plate joiner to wrap over the outside edge of the miter (Photo A). Set the height of the fence so the slot will be a little below the center of the miter. This prevents the biscuit slot from coming through to the outside surface. Insert the biscuits and glue the case together.

Rout the Corner

Add a fence to your router's base and install a ¼-in.-straight bit. Adjust the bit and fence to cut a ⅛-in.-square rabbet (Photo B). Normally, you cut from left to right, but in this situation you should cut the opposite way, from right to left, to minimize tear-out of the thin face veneers.

Add a Hardwood Strip

On a tablesaw, rip strips that are very slightly over ⅛-in. square. Apply glue to the rabbets and clamp the strips in place with masking tape (Photo C). Alternate the direction you pull the tape to draw the edging tight.

Scrape off the excess glue before it hardens and cut the edging to length. Sand it flush to the plywood and round the edge by hand or with a round-over bit.

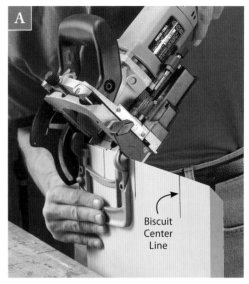

Cut accurate slots by angling your fence over the edge of a long miter.

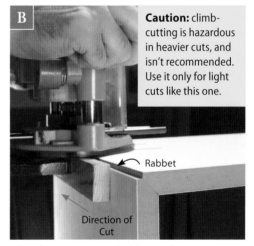

Caution: climb-cutting is hazardous in heavier cuts, and isn't recommended. Use it only for light cuts like this one.

After gluing, rout a small rabbet on the corner of the cabinet. Move the router from right to left (climb-cutting) to minimize tear-out.

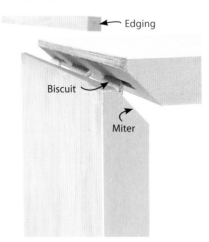

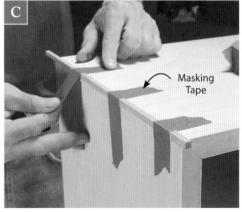

Glue a hardwood strip in the rabbet to make a durable edge. Once rounded over with sandpaper, the strip is practically invisible.

How's Your Depth of Cut?

If you need to crank hard on your clamps to get joints to close up, your slots may not be deep enough. Here's an easy way to set up your machine before you get into trouble.

First, cut a slot in a scrap piece of wood. Then place a biscuit in the slot and draw a line across its face. Remove the biscuit, flip it around and stick it back in the slot. Draw a second line.

Pull the biscuit out and see what you've got. The pencil lines should be about ¹⁄₁₆-in. apart, meaning that each slot is about ¹⁄₃₂-in. deeper than half the width of the biscuit. If your pencil lines are closer together, the slot isn't deep enough. Most plate joiners have an adjustment screw for changing the slot's depth, but you may have to fish out your owner's manual to figure out how it works!

¹⁄₁₆"

Depth of Slot

Join Shelves with Only One Setup

Joining shelves to the sides of a cabinet can eat up a lot of precious shop time. Dadoes work well, but you've got to set up a saw or a router to make a dado exactly the right width, and then you have to worry about whether the dado will show on the front of the case. If you don't want to see it, you've got to make a stopped cut, and that means even more fussing around.

Biscuits get the entire job done quickly, and the joint is very strong. Layout is simple, because there's virtually no setup. Better yet, the joint doesn't show. Reserve dadoes for shelves that need to take a very heavy load. For all other shelves and dividers, use biscuits.

Layout is nothing more than drawing a short line on the edge of your case, indicating where the top of the shelf goes. Clamp the shelf right on the line (Photo A). Draw lines on the shelf to indicate the center of each biscuit slot. Pick up your biscuit joiner, set it to the #20 size and cut slots in the shelf. Stand the machine up on end and cut slots in the case side (Photo B). That's it.

Both slots are registered from the bottom of your machine. When you stand up the shelf and put in biscuits, the shelf will sit exactly on your pencil line. Seems too easy, doesn't it?

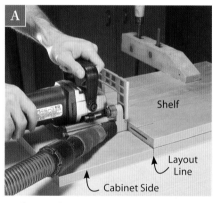

Shelf

Layout Line

Cabinet Side

Cut biscuit slots in the end of the shelf first.

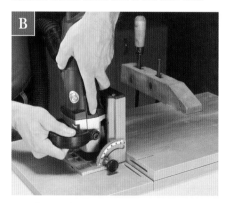

Stand your plate joiner on end to cut slots in the side of the case. The end of the shelf is a built-in straightedge.

Mid-Field Biscuits

Here's a simple jig for accurately cutting biscuit slots on the face of a wide board, such as the sides of a bookcase. The jig is just a large plywood T-square, made from three pieces of ¾" x 3" x 22" plywood. Glue two pieces to make the blade. (The extra thickness provides more surface to register against.) Screw the blade to the third piece at a 90° angle.

To use the jig, mark the location of the shelf's bottom on the workpiece. Slide the jig's fence against the front edge of the workpiece, line up the top of the jig's blade with your mark, and clamp the jig in place. Stand your biscuit joiner on end to cut the slots. Cut the slots in the shelf by laying the shelf on a flat surface, so that the slots are registered from the shelf's bottom.

Perfectly Flush?

I recently bought a plate joiner in hopes that it would help me get perfect alignment when edge-to-edge gluing. I'm still getting some unevenness at the joints. What gives?

Biscuits help considerably with alignment, but getting absolutely perfect alignment is unlikely. Having glued up what seems like acres of tabletops, I find that slight variations in wood thickness, minor warpage or loose-fitting biscuits can all throw off the joint. A slight tipping up or down of the plate joiner can also cause a misaligned joint.

You can overcome some of this misalignment during glue-up by tapping or pressing high spots into place before fully tightening the clamps. Otherwise it's best to accept a slightly uneven joint and then sand or scrape it flush.

Another option is a spline joint. Use a slot cutter in your router. Then mill your own spline to fit. Because the spline joint runs the full length of the board, it offers very consistent alignment.

Preserve Your Biscuits with Kitty Litter

Nothing is more aggravating than a biscuit that won't fit into a slot—except maybe a whole bag of biscuits that won't fit. Biscuits swell as they absorb moisture, whether from glue or the air. To prevent swollen biscuits, store them with a desiccant, such as kitty litter. The kitty litter absorbs moisture and keeps the air inside the container dry. Pour a small amount of kitty litter (the crystalline variety is less messy) onto a cloth, tie it up and toss it into the container. No more fat biscuits and they'll always smell nice.

Quick Case Construction

There's nothing faster than biscuits for assembling a simple case. You can cut slots for one case in about the same time it takes to set up a dado set in a tablesaw. Add a back or a face frame to the case, and you have a very strong unit.

If you've been using pin nails or screws for simple casework, consider this additional benefit: Biscuits are completely invisible; nothing shows on the inside or the outside; there are no nail holes to putty or screws to plug.

When you cut into the side of the plywood, use a thick support board to help balance your plate joiner. A 2x4 milled square works great; it's easy to cut to length as needed, and then toss it when you're done. A 2x4 is just wide enough so your clamps don't interfere with the base of the plate joiner.

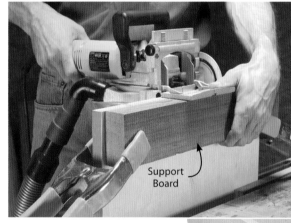

Support Board

Make invisible corner joints super-fast with a plate joiner.

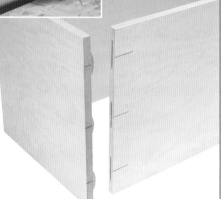

Make Corner Splines

Decorative corner splines sure make an ordinary box look great. But they can be a bit dicey to cut on a tablesaw. Let your plate joiner come to the rescue. A simple jig holds the box and the joiner so you can cut slots quickly with minimal setup hassles. The jig is nothing more than a piece of scrap plywood with two wood strips set at 90 degrees to each other. A cradle fits around the plate joiner base and keeps it from rocking on the box corner. The cradle is indexed to the jig with a couple dowels. Use spacer blocks to adjust the spline spacing. Plunge the joiner into the wood slowly to prevent tear-out where the blade exits the wood. With this box, you only need one spacer block; just flip the box over to cut the upper slot.

Spacer Block

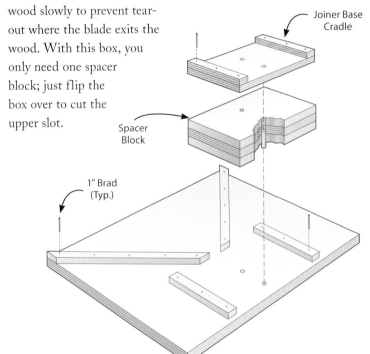

Joiner Base Cradle

Spacer Block

1" Brad (Typ.)

Quick, Accurate Fence Settings

Gauge blocks work great for quick, accurate fence settings. All you do is pinch the block between the fence blades. This technique will also ensure the fence is set parallel to the blade. Joiners with rack-and-pinion fence adjustments automatically set the fence parallel with the blade. For this type of joiner, use spacer blocks between the fence and a flat surface—like your benchtop—for rapid fence settings.

Gauge Block

Prevent Biscuit Pucker

Recently, I joined a frame using double biscuits. As I was finishing the cabinet, I noticed small depressions at some of the joints. What gives?

The depressions you see are a caused by biscuit pucker. This phenomenon usually results from placing a biscuit too close to the board's surface. Biscuits are made from compressed beechwood designed to expand when introduced to moisture from glue. If you use a lot of glue in the slot, the excess moisture may also cause the surrounding wood to swell. As the biscuit and the wood around it expand, a bulge may develop at the surface. When you sand the board, you shave off the bulge. Eventually, however, as the wood dries, it shrinks back to its original size, leaving in the board's face a slight depression called biscuit pucker.

There are a few ways to prevent this from happening:

1. Make sure your biscuit slots are at least ¼ in. from the surface. Double biscuits do make a joint strong, but take care when using them in ¾-in. material. You should stack the biscuits close together in the center of a ¾-in. board.

2. Let the joint completely dry—usually two or three days—before you sand or plane it.

3. If you are using the biscuits primarily to keep the joint in alignment, use single biscuits. Apply glue only to the surfaces to be joined, not to the biscuits.

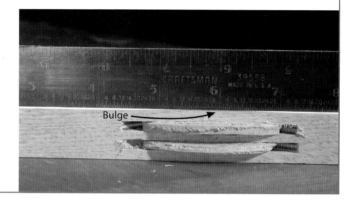

Bulge

Run Biscuits Long in Narrow Frames

You don't have to own a mini-biscuit joiner to assemble narrow frames. If possible, simply shift the slots so the larger biscuit extends into areas where it won't be seen, for example, the top or bottom of a face frame. After the glue has dried, cut the protruding biscuit with a handsaw. Then flush-trim with a router or sander.

Gauge Block

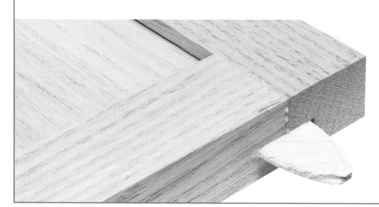

Reinforce Short Miters

To strengthen miter joints in narrow stock, use face frame biscuits. They're like standard biscuits but smaller (about 1³⁄₁₆ in. long), so you can use them in stock as narrow as 1 inch. To cut the slots, use a ⁵⁄₃₂-in.-thick slot cutter in your router table. Set the router fence so the bit cuts a ⁵⁄₁₆-in.-deep slot. Then clamp 45-degree guides to your router table. The guides make it easy to feed the workpiece into the slot cutter. Use one guide (A) for one end (A) and the other guide (B) for the other end (B). Test your setup before cutting actual parts of your project.

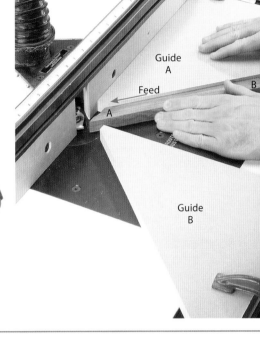

Slot
Cutter

Simplify Drawer Making

Why bother with fancy joinery when biscuits will hold together a drawer box just fine? Save the dovetails for show pieces, or for when a large drawer rides on wooden supports and must be super-strong. If you're using metal slides and a false front, biscuits are perfect. The joint doesn't show, and has enough strength for many years of use.

Half-inch Baltic birch plywood and #0 biscuits are a good combination for making drawers. This plywood has very few voids, so its edges generally look good. The slot for a #0 biscuit goes into ½-in.-thick stock without coming through the other side.

To make the drawers, draw layout lines down the center of each piece. Cut slots in the ends of the front and back pieces. Cut slots in the faces of the side pieces. It's tricky to balance a plate joiner on the end of ½-in. stock, though. To make it easier, simply clamp two pieces together. You can cut slots in two pieces with one setup.

Two slots are easier to cut than one. Clamp thin boards together to make a wider bearing surface for your plate joiner.

Slot Cutter vs. Plate Joiner

I saw an ad for a slot-cutting router bit. I have a router and buying the bit instead of a plate joiner would save me a lot of money. Is there a downside to this cheaper option?

It depends on what kind of joints you plan to make. A slot cutter does a good job with flat edge-to-edge or end-to-end joints (Photos 1, 2 and 3). Other joints can present some problems:

- A butt-corner joint (Photo 4) can be made, but requires the extra step of clamping a support board to the piece with the face slot. This gives your router a broader surface to rest on.
- On a tee-butt joint (Photo 5) you can rout the end slot but it is impossible to cut the face slot in the other board.
- A corner miter (Photo 6) is best handled using the slot cutter in the router table with an angled jig to hold the work. If your pieces are very big this can get quite cumbersome.

A plate joiner (photo at right), on the other hand, will make all of these joints with ease. It also has built-in dust collection.

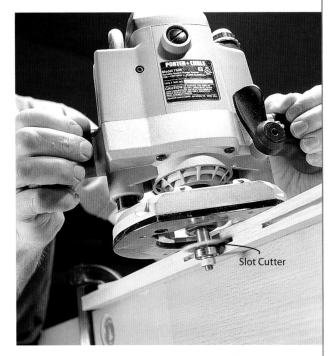

Slot Cutter

Cutting biscuit slots with a slot cutter is easy on flat work.

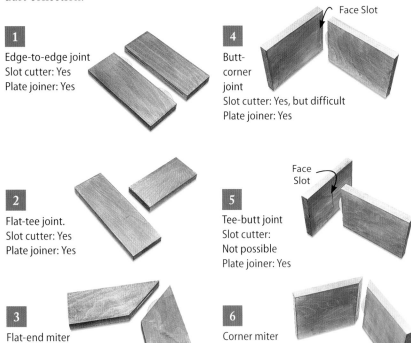

Face Slot

1
Edge-to-edge joint
Slot cutter: Yes
Plate joiner: Yes

2
Flat-tee joint.
Slot cutter: Yes
Plate joiner: Yes

3
Flat-end miter
Slot cutter: Yes
Plate joiner: Yes

4
Butt-corner joint
Slot cutter: Yes, but difficult
Plate joiner: Yes

Face Slot

5
Tee-butt joint
Slot cutter: Not possible
Plate joiner: Yes

6
Corner miter
Slot cutter: Yes, but difficult
Plate joiner: Yes

Cutting angle joints with a plate joiner is quick and easy. It's possible, but awkward, to do this with a router.

The Mysterious Misfit

I was cutting slots for a long edge joint the other day, and everything was humming right along. But, when I put the boards together, they didn't line up worth a darn!

Turns out I made a very simple mistake. All along I thought my plate joiner's fence was sitting on top of the board (Photo A). Nope. On some cuts, the bottom of the plate joiner must have been sitting on the bench instead. The board was a bit bowed, so I ended up making slots at different heights. That's why the boards weren't flush.

To fix this, I glued biscuits in the bad slots, cut off the excess and started over. This time I made sure the board hung over the edge of the bench when I cut each and every slot (Photo B).

Slots may not line up if your plate joiner sits on the benchtop. There may be a small gap under the fence.

Hang your boards over the edge of the bench to make consistent slots every time.

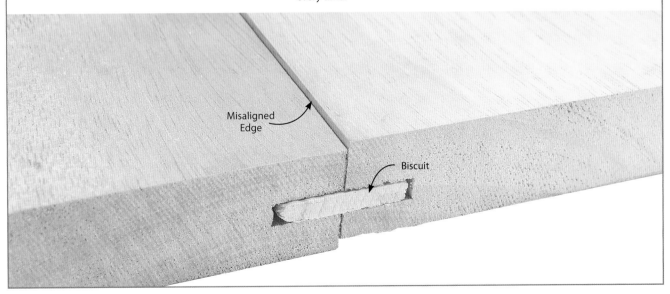

Router

Cut Dadoes with a Router

Here's the scene: You're building an entertainment center and the sides are 7-ft. high and almost 3-ft. deep (big enough for that big-screen TV you've always wanted). But the sides have to be dadoed for shelves. Forget trying to use a dado head on the tablesaw, unless you happen to have 8-ft. rails on your saw! Instead, use a router and this easily made jig:

Make the jig from a straight board and a piece of ⅛- or ¼-in. plywood or hardboard wide enough to extend 4 in. on either side of the board. Glue and screw together, then trim the bottom board using your router and a straight bit. The diameter of the bit should be whatever size you plan to use for the dado. I trim one side with a ½-in. bit and the other side with a ¾-in. bit.

To cut the dado, simply line up the edge of the jig with wherever you want the dado.

Glue and screw together, then trim the bottom board using your router and a straight bit. The diameter of the bit should be whatever size you plan to use for the dado. I trim one side with

a ½-in. bit and the other side with a ¾-in. bit.

To cut the dado, simply line up the edge of the jig with wherever you want the dado.

Making The Jig

STRAIGHT-EDGED BOARD

Benchtop Router Table Cabinet

My first router table was a simple benchtop model. It was convenient to park on a shelf, but not convenient to use on an actual bench—that put the router table's surface too high. To place the table at the right height, I built a small cabinet to go underneath it, and added a mobile base sized for a drill press. I stored my wrenches, extra collet, starting pin, featherboards and coping sled in the cabinet, away from all the dust.

Better Joints

I like the clean look of thin, solid-wood edge banding on plywood. But, without a jointer to remove the saw marks, I'm unable to get an invisible joint. Any suggestions for a guy without a jointer?

Instead of a jointer, you can use a router table. An up-cut spiral bit does the best job, but a straight cutter will do.

For the board to have continuous support before and after the cut, you'll need to create an offset on the outfeed side of the fence that's equal to the amount of wood removed. A strip of self-stick ultra-high molecular weight (UHMW) tape on an auxiliary fence does the trick. UHMW is a special plastic that wears forever and provides a slick surface for the wood to glide on. Using a straightedge, set the fence so the cutter is exactly flush with the taped side.

To make the narrow strips for your invisible joint, start with a wide board and clean up one edge on the router table. Then rip the ¼-in. strip from the clean edge of the board. Repeat for as many strips as you need.

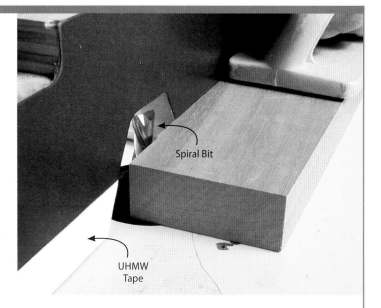

Spiral Bit

UHMW Tape

Cutting Dovetail Slots

Some tables, such as the classic Shaker style, have a turned center column with three dovetail slots to hold the legs. I make these slots with the spindle still in the lathe. That way I can use the lathe's indexing pin to accurately space the slots.

First I make an open box, with a tongue below, that engages the lathe bed. The top of the box is open and the router slides in rabbets cut in the sides, as shown.

After turning and finishing the spindle, I lock the index pin at zero. Then I clamp the box to the lathe bed, position the router and adjust the depth of cut.

After making the first cut I mark the position of the router plate on the carriage with a pencil. Then I rotate the spindle 120 degrees (for a three-legged table), reset the index pin and make the next cut.

I advise making a trial cut in a piece of scrap first. To reduce the chances of breaking your dovetail bit, remove most of the waste with a straight bit before cutting the dovetail slot.

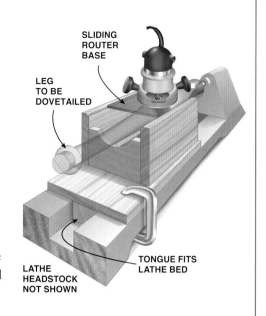

SLIDING ROUTER BASE

LEG TO BE DOVETAILED

LATHE HEADSTOCK NOT SHOWN

TONGUE FITS LATHE BED

No-Fuss Flush Trimming

My flush-trimming setup allows trimming veneer and solid wood edging up to ⅜-in. thick. It consists of a router with a ½-in. straight bit, a table and a perpendicular fence. A 1-in.-thick spacer separates the fence and table. The router mounts to the fence so the bit is flush with the tabletop. I attach my shop vacuum's hose to a hole drilled through the cleat, under the bit. I size the edging so it overhangs by ¹⁄₁₆-in. or less.

Get the Burn Out

Arrgh, another burned cut! Don't you hate it when this happens? Here's a fix. Shim out the workpiece with thin cardboard and take a second light cut. Burning most commonly occurs on end grain or when you use a dull bit. Feeding the workpiece too slowly also can cause burning.

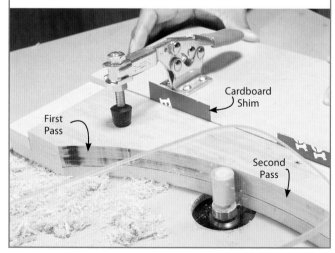

First Pass

Cardboard Shim

Second Pass

Help! My Router Makes Huge Sparks!

When I run my router I see lots of small, blue sparks inside. Recently the sparks have grown larger. Is this OK?

Nope. Small sparks are normal, but large sparks are an indication that your brushes are wearing short. That means your router is running inefficiently. It's time to remove the brushes and possibly replace them.

The sparks are the electrical arcing of current from the brushes to the motor's commutator (the large cylinder inside the housing). Large sparks mean the brushes are too short to be adequately held tight to the commutator by their springs. As a result, the motor has to work harder to make the electricity jump the gap between the brushes and commutator.

Every router has two brushes. To service them, unplug the router, remove the caps and pull out the brushes. If they are chipped, cracked or shorter than ¼ in., replace them with ones made specifically for your router. To remove any carbon dust, use an air compressor or a can of compressed air to blow out the holes that house the brushes. Look into the holes with a flashlight. If

the commutator is pitted or severely worn, it will need professional servicing. If the brushes are in good shape put them back in the same holes, in the same orientation and replace the caps. If you have installed new brushes, run your router for two to three minutes to fully seat them. Your router may "cough" and sputter a bit until it comes up to full speed, but that's normal.

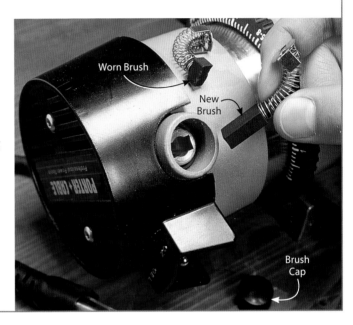

Worn Brush

New Brush

Brush Cap

Drill Bit Depth Gauge

Did you know that a simple drill bit is also an extremely accurate measuring tool? Let the light bulb go off in your head and you'll probably think of dozens of ways to measure with your bits. Here's an old favorite.

Setting the height of a router bit with a ruler can drive you nuts. Where, oh where, should the end of the ruler stand? You can't put it next to the bit because there's a huge hole in the base of the router.

Span the hole with a drill bit that's the same diameter as the depth of the groove you want to cut. Lay a small block of wood across the tips of the router bit, then adjust the router until you can just slide the drill bit under the wood block, like a feeler gauge.

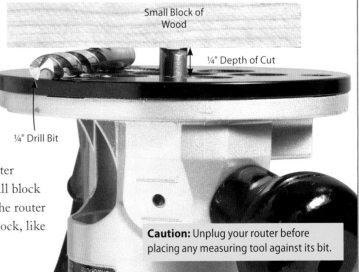

Small Block of Wood

¼" Depth of Cut

¼" Drill Bit

Caution: Unplug your router before placing any measuring tool against its bit.

Do Router Speed Controls Actually Work?

I have a single-speed router and want to use a large panel-raising bit in it. I know that I need to slow down the rpm. Will a router speed control work?

Yes. A router speed control will certainly slow your router to a safe speed. And you're right to be concerned about doing so. Your router wasn't designed to handle a large bit spinning at its single high speed. In addition, you may burn your panels because the tips of the bit are turning too fast. When you feed the wood by hand, it's impossible to keep up with the bit.

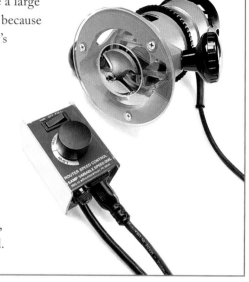

A speed control is a reasonable solution for occasional use, but you may run into a problem with your router's warranty if you use the control frequently. The cooling fans in single-speed routers are generally designed to cool only at maximum speed. Slowing the router with a speed control also slows the fan. There's a possibility that the router could overheat and become damaged. Most router manufacturers will not warranty their tools when used with a speed control.

For heavy-duty and frequent use, replace your large diameter bit with a vertical panel-raising bit (which can be run safely at full speed) or buy a big, 3-hp variable-speed router and run your large diameter bit at a slower speed.

Dovetail Jig Support Fence

I love my dovetail jig except for one thing: If I forget to hold the router flat, it can tip backward off the front of the jig and ruin the job.

To solve the problem, I made my own L-shaped support fence that sits flush with the top of the jig. A ⅞-in.-wide ledge glued to the fence's ⅜-in.-thick face creates the "L" shape. Slots in the face allow slipping the fence over the two knob-capped bolts that secure some of the jig's templates. To lock the fence in position, I just tighten the knobs. Alignment blocks make installation easy and prevent accidental nicking of the jig's brackets.

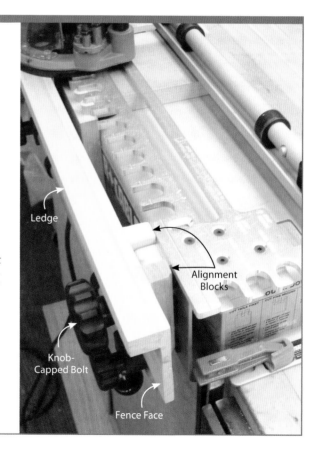

Ledge

Alignment Blocks

Knob-Capped Bolt

Fence Face

Fence Face

Edge Banding Leveler

Leveling edge banding is easy with my router, a ½-in. straight bit and a simple jig. The jig has a groove to house the edge banding, a fence to ensure the bit can't accidentally cut into the plywood top and a handle for two-handed control. I remove the router's baseplate and mount the router directly to the jig. Then I set the bit to cut just above the plywood.

The fence determines the cut's width: The distance between the fence and the bit's far edge must be the same as the edge banding's thickness. On my jig, the fence registers against the groove, so I have to plane it to the proper thickness. By changing fences, I can trim edge banding of any thickness. To edge-band a panel on all four sides, I glue and level the side bandings first and then band the ends.

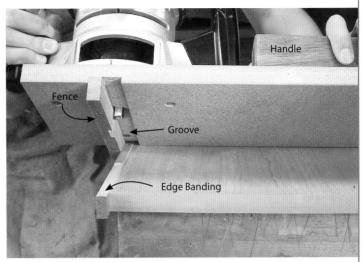

Flattening End Grain with a Router

My favorite woodworking projects are clocks—big ones or little ones. If it ticks, I'll make it.

My latest venture provided me with the challenge of flattening the face of some log sections that I wanted to make into clocks. Belt sanding was too slow and using a thickness planer is unsafe. In the planer, a log section, which is end grain, can break apart and shoot out at you, with results that are better imagined than experienced.

I devised this simple routing jig. I attached a sled to the bottom of my router that rides on the two side rails. If the log section rocks because it is uneven, add a shim until it's steady. When one side is done, flip it over and do the other. I do a final sanding on the surfaces with an orbital sander.

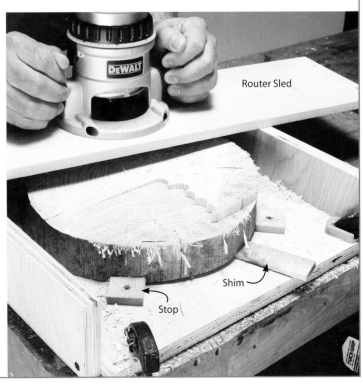

Lock Miter Joint

How do you set up a lock miter bit?

There are two critical adjustments (Fig. A). First, you set the bit's height; second, you position the fence. Once that's done, you can rout both sides of a lock miter joint without changing anything.

To get started, you must use a variable-speed router set at 10,000 rpm to slow down this large-diameter bit to a safe speed. Make some test pieces that are exactly the same thickness as the parts you'll join together.

Then adjust the bit's height by eye until it looks like it's centered on the workpiece. Position the fence by eye, too.

Make test cuts on two pieces (Photo 1). Put the pieces together and see whether their outside edges are flush. Raise or lower the bit as needed, without moving the fence, and make more test cuts until you've got the bit exactly centered on the thickness of your material.

Next, tweak the fence's position in or out and make some more test cuts. Your goal is to make a sharp edge on top of the workpiece, leaving just a whisker of its original edge. If the fence is too far out, you'll make a blunt edge on the workpiece, and the joint won't have a sharp outside corner. If the fence is too far in, you'll get a jog along the workpiece's edge, and the board will snipe at the end of the cut.

Once you've set the fence, machine half of your pieces flat on the table. Cut the other half by holding them vertically against the fence (Photo 2).

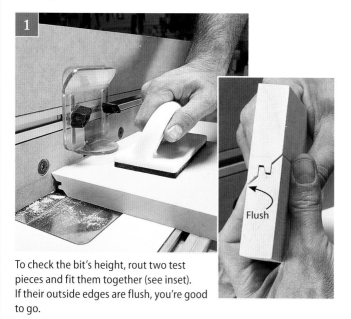

To check the bit's height, rout two test pieces and fit them together (see inset). If their outside edges are flush, you're good to go.

Flush

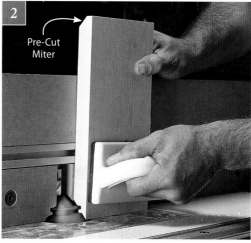

Pre-Cut Miter

Rout the mating piece of a lock miter joint by standing it upright. Pre-cut the ends of all your pieces on a tablesaw to make the job easier.

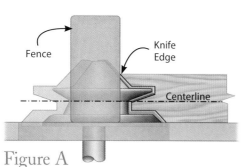

Fence

Knife Edge

Centerline

Figure A

To make a lock miter joint, align the center of the bit with the center of your material. Then, position the fence to produce a knife edge.

Gambler's Micro-Adjust

Precise fence adjustments are a sure bet when I clamp this shop-made device on my router table. I simply drilled and tapped a hole for a ¼"-20 machine screw through the center of a ¾-in. by 1½-in. by 3-in. piece of hardwood. I covered the tip that contacts the fence with a cap nut. My "hi-tech" adjustment mechanism consists of two square nuts squeezed tight together. I've blackened them with a permanent marker and painted on white dots to clearly identify each of the 4 sides. I also added a third square nut, so I can lock the device for repetitive cuts.

With the ¼"-20 screw I used, one full turn of the nuts corresponds to a travel of .05-in. If you prefer working with fractions, switch to a ⅜"-16 screw. Then, one full turn moves the tip ¹⁄₁₆-in. A half turn moves it ¹⁄₃₂-in. and a quarter turn moves it ¹⁄₆₄-in. You can even make one-eighth turn adjustments. Simply position the nuts on edge, as in the photo.

Square Nuts

Make Shallow Climb Cuts

Reversing the normal direction of the router feed is called climb-cutting. Climb-cutting can involve either moving clockwise with a handheld router or pushing wood from left to right on a router table. Climb-cutting almost always eliminates tear-out, but it also makes the router more difficult to control. That's because the stock is fed in the same direction as the bit is spinning, so the bit wants to grab the wood and pull. This makes climb-cutting potentially dangerous. It's not recommended for most routing. If you follow a few rules, though, climb-cutting is a great way to get yourself over those pesky areas where tear-out is almost a sure thing.

Play it safe:
- Always make very shallow, light passes, especially when using a big bit.
- Secure the wood and/or router very firmly.
- Make sure the bit is sharp. A dull bit grabs and pulls, but a sharp bit cuts with less effort.
- On a router table, use featherboards whenever possible to hold the board and keep it from running away.
- When using a handheld router, firmly clamp down the stock. If the workpiece is narrow, add support so the router won't tip.
- Never climb-cut small or narrow pieces on the router table. It's better to cut the profile on a large piece and trim it to the size you want later.

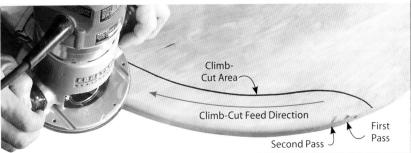

Climb-Cut Area

Climb-Cut Feed Direction

First Pass

Second Pass

ROUTER

Joint with Your Router

I learned this trick about jointing extra-long boards from a
woodworker who only had a short-bed jointer. Jointing with
a router isn't new, but most methods require an absolutely
accurate straightedge to guide the router.

Actually, a perfect straightedge isn't necessary. All you need
is a pretty good straightedge that's longer than the boards. A
little bow in it doesn't matter. The trick is to rout both boards
at the same time, so the edges mirror each other (see photo,
below left). Bowed or not, they'll always fit tightly.

To set up, mill three blocks $^{11}/_{16}$ in. thick. Use them
as spacers to position and clamp the boards to a pair
of sawhorses. Chuck a ¾-in. bit in your router. Clamp the guide
board so the bit takes an equal amount off both boards, about
$^{1}/_{32}$ in. Ride the router tightly against the guideboard,
removing the spacers as needed.

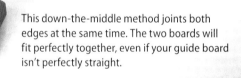

Guide Board

Spacer

This down-the-middle method joints both
edges at the same time. The two boards will
fit perfectly together, even if your guide board
isn't perfectly straight.

Plug-Trimming Router Base

I recently used wood dowels to plug some screw holes. Trimming
them by hand was tough, so I made this handy offset router base.
I used a scrap of MDF and made the offset on my router table.
Then I drilled and countersunk screw holes that match the ones in
my original router base. I attached the new base with long screws
and adjusted the router bit so it cuts just shy of the full thickness
of the new base. It trims the plugs almost perfectly flush, leaving
me just a little scraping or sanding.

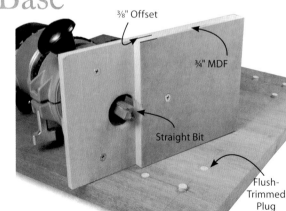

⅜" Offset

¾" MDF

Straight Bit

Flush-Trimmed Plug

Minimize Router Burns

End grain burns easily on maple and cherry, and those burns are hard to remove. After sanding my fingers to the bone following one particularly unfortunate routing pass, I came up with an easy solution that removes those unsightly burns without requiring that I adjust the bit's height or fuss with an edge guide.

Before routing, I put three layers of masking tape on the bottom of the board's edge, where the bit's bearing rides. Then I make two passes. The first pass produces the rough profile, when burning is most likely to occur. After making the initial pass, I remove the tape and rout again. This very fine second pass removes all but the worst burns. If this method still leaves scorches, your feed rate is too slow or you need a new router bit.

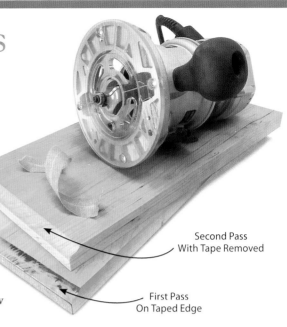

Second Pass With Tape Removed

First Pass On Taped Edge

Overhead Router Table

I've built an overhead router table to simplify a few milling operations, such as making V-grooves, flutes and mortises. On an overhead table, the workpiece faces up. This makes it a lot easier to see the layout marks that indicate where to start and stop a groove or flute.

After some trial and error, I came up with a design that uses a plunge router. It works great, and cost almost nothing. Besides the router, there are essentially three parts: an extended baseplate, a fence and a table. The baseplate is made from ½" MDF with ¾" x 1½" stiffening ribs along the edges. The plate has a 2½" dia. bit hole, large enough for seeing when you get close to your layout lines. I clamp the baseplate to my benchtop drill press table, which is flat, sturdy and adjustable.

The table is made from ¾" melamine. It has two legs with feet for clamping to a bench, and a stiffening rib between the legs to prevent sagging. The table's fence is a 1" x 1" piece of hardwood, fastened to the table at one end with a ¼–20 x 2" bolt and a wing nut. The other end of the fence pivots for adjustment and is secured with a clamp. It's important to note that you push the stock from left to right.

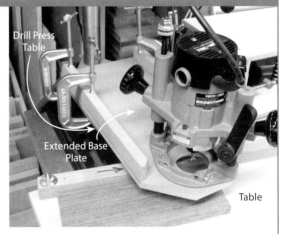

Drill Press Table

Extended Base Plate

Table

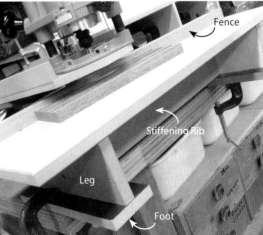

Fence

Stiffening Rib

Leg

Foot

Pull-Out Router Table

Tired of pulling out that heavy router table every time you need it? Save space and your back by mounting your router table under a workbench with sturdy swing-up appliance hardware. Set-up and knock-down are a snap. You need 16 inches plus the height of your router's housing under the table for clearance. Plan your installation so the router table and your workbench meet flush for adequate infeed and outfeed support.

Rigid Routing Sled

A routing sled is a great help when coping the ends of rails and stiles. But I had a problem when I built my first sled. The pressure from the toggle clamp caused the ¼-in.-thick sled base to deflect, which messed up the alignment of the rail-and-stile joints. I solved the problem by adding a board to the front of the sled, plus two top boards that bridge over my workpiece. This setup keeps the ¼-in. base from bending when the toggle clamp is clamped down.

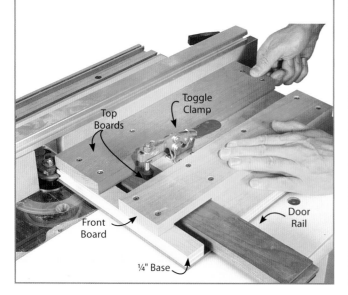

Rounded Corners in a Jiffy

Getting rounded corners that match is a cinch with this template. Legs fastened to both sides automatically center the template on the workpiece. Once the template is in position, only spring clamps are needed to hold it in place.

When you install the template on top of the workpiece, rout the profile with a top-bearing pattern bit. If you install the template on the bottom, rout with a regular flush-trim bit.

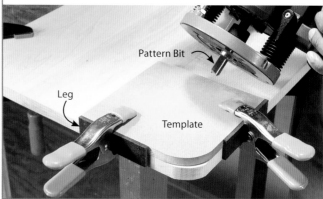

Quick Circles on the Router Table

One afternoon my wife called out to my shop with an urgent request. She needed me to make a round cake plate from ¼" plywood for a charity auction. I assured her it would be no problem. I was in the middle of a project and didn't want to spend all afternoon on this. Then it hit me: I could use my router table.

I ripped a ¾"-wide strip of ⅜" hardwood to fit the miter slot and drilled a pilot hole near one end for a box nail, which I inserted from the bottom. Then I clamped the hardwood strip into my router table's miter slot so the distance from the nail to the bit equaled the circle's radius.

I drilled a center hole in the soon-to-be cake plate, and positioned it on the nail. I held the edge of the plywood up while switching on the router, then lowered it onto the bit very carefully. After the bit bored through, I rotated the plywood counterclockwise, opposite the bit's rotation, to cut a perfect circle.

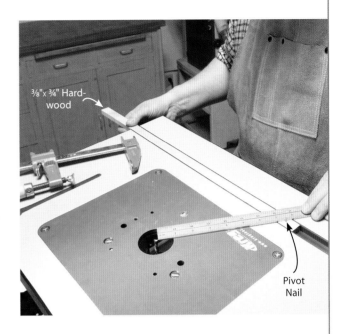

⅜"x ¾" Hard-wood

Pivot Nail

Quick Router Dado Setup

I shorten the time it takes to rout dadoes with a simple jig made from acrylic. A small, 6-in. x 24-in. piece will do. Mark the point where your router base will ride against the straightedge. Then, measure the exact distance from that point to the center of your router bit ("A" in the photo). Mark that distance in from the long edge of your acrylic rectangle. Use a sharp utility knife to score a line exactly parallel to that edge. Then, take a red, fine-point felt-tip pen and run it along the score to create a cursor.

To cut dadoes on your cabinet side, lay out the centerlines of each dado. Then, line up the red line on the acrylic with the dado centerline on the cabinet. Butt your straightedge to the acrylic and clamp it in place. Bingo! You're ready to rout.

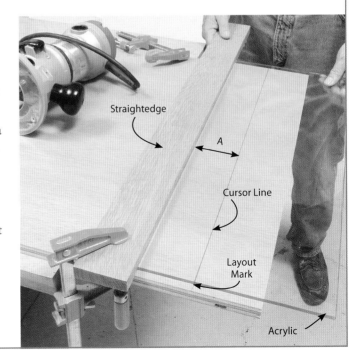

Straightedge

A

Cursor Line

Layout Mark

Acrylic

Router Bit Nest

Watching an expensive router bit roll onto the floor is a heartbreaking experience. In the middle of a project, it can be a disaster. I drilled a few ½" and ¼" holes in the edge of a piece of MDF and fastened it to the back of my router table's fence. In this nest, I keep all the bits I'm using for a particular project at my fingertips without worrying about having them roll off the table.

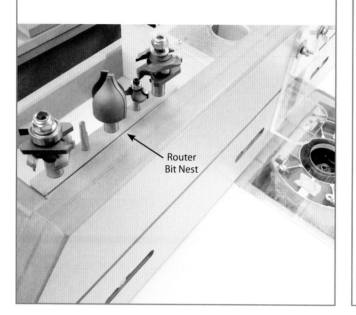

Router
Bit Nest

Rout Narrow Stock with Ease

Since I don't have a router table, routing narrow stock is doubly tough. First, it's hard to hold the stock in position. Second, it's virtually impossible to balance the router as I rout.

My system solves both problems. I use a notched board to hold the narrow stock and an outrigger to stabilize the router. Routing presses the stock securely against the notched board, which is clamped to the bench. The outrigger is simply an offcut of the narrow stock, screwed to the router base. I just replace one of the base's mounting screws with a longer one.

I make sure the surface the outrigger will ride on is smooth and clear of debris and I stop routing about 1 in. away from the notch.

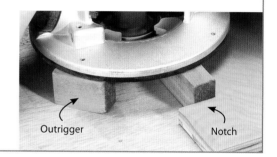

Outrigger

Notch

Router Depth Setter

This jig makes it easy to set the bit for routing flutes or dadoes. I simply drop the appropriate depth gauge into the channel, set my router on top and lower the bit until it touches the gauge. The base is an 8-in. square piece of ¾-in. MDF. Two strips of ¾-in. MDF on top create a channel for the gauges. To make the gauges, subtract the depth of the dado you want to rout from ¾ in. For example, a ¼-in.-deep dado requires a ½-in.-thick gauge.

Router Base Transfer Points

After I lost track of the base plate for the router that goes in my router table, I had to make a new one with accurately marked holes for the mounting screws and a centered hole for the bit. I figured out how to do it while flipping through a machinist's catalog: put a ¼-in. straight bit into the collet and a cone-pointed setscrew into each of the router's threaded mounting holes.

Drill a ¼-in. hole in the base and slide the base over the ¼-in. bit. Give the base a tap and the setscrews mark the drilling locations. Drill and countersink for the mounting screws. Before mounting the base, enlarge the ¼-in. center hole using a holesaw piloted by a ¼-in. bit.

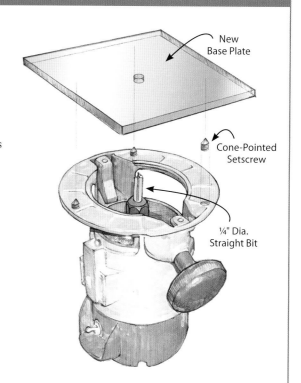

New Base Plate

Cone-Pointed Setscrew

¼" Dia. Straight Bit

Router Rack

I like to keep my fix-based routers handy and ready to go with my favorite bits. Of course the bits prevent me from storing the routers standing up. That's why I built this rack with cutouts for the bits. I made it using ¾-in. MDF. It measures 4 in. tall by 9½ in. deep by 16 in. wide. Each slot measures 2 in. wide by 6 in. deep. I drilled a 2-in. hole at the back of each slot and cut out the rest of the slot on my bandsaw. My router wrenches and extra collets fit nicely under each router.

Router Table Dust Sleeve

To improve the dust collection on my router table, I added a 4" dia., 4" long piece of flexible vacuum hose around my router's body. This helps direct all the dust into the port on the router table's fence. The flexible hose snugs up to the table's plate and can easily be pushed out of the way in order to change bits.

Rusty Router Collets

Returning to my shop after working outside this summer, I noticed a rusty film on my router collets and bits. What's the best way to remove the rust without damaging the collets and bits?

Use a synthetic steel wool or 3M Scotch-Brite pad. To clean a ½-in. collet, wrap the pad around a ¼-in. dowel and spin it inside the collet. Clean the rust off the bit shanks by rubbing the pads around them. Do not use an emery cloth or sandpaper; you don't want to remove any metal that could cause the bit to wobble later. Wipe the collet's inside and the bit's shank with a light, general-purpose grease, then wipe off the excess. A thin film of grease will remain in the surface to slow future rusting.

Clean rusty router collets with a dowel and synthetic steel wool.

Router Table Spring Board

I saw this device in an old woodworking book. I gave it a try and now I use it all the time. With this spring board you get even pressure along the entire fence and better results than either hand feeding or just featherboards. I still use a featherboard on the top to provide some anti-kickback protection.

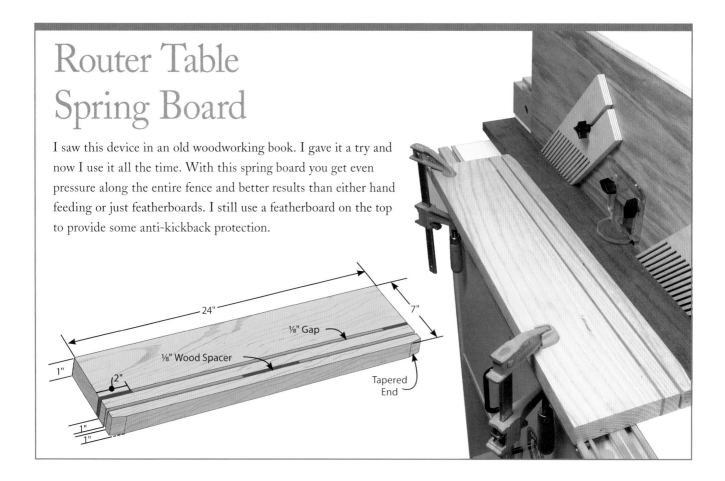

24"

7"

⅛" Gap

⅛" Wood Spacer

1"

2"

Tapered End

1"

1"

Router Table Tenoning Jig

My simple tenoning jig produces flawless tenons in minutes—even haunched tenons. The jig consists of a sled with a glued-on support block and a screwed-on sacrificial backstop. The sled and support block are flush on the work side and square. The backstop protrudes by the thickness of the workpiece, minus 1/16-in.

Before using the jig, install an upcut spiral bit and set its height to the tenon's length. Position the fence and clamp a spacer that's the same thickness as the workpiece against the outfeed end.

To rout the tenon cheeks, clamp the workpiece in the jig, flush against its support block and backstop. Then rout from right to left, while pressing the sled against the outfeed spacer and the workpiece against the infeed fence. I usually make a light scoring pass before routing full-depth: I bear the sled against the spacer, but pull the workpiece away from the fence and guide it freehand through the cut.

To rout the tenon ends, I install the workpiece behind the stop (top photo). To create a haunch, I place an appropriately-thick shim beneath the workpiece before I clamp it to the stop.

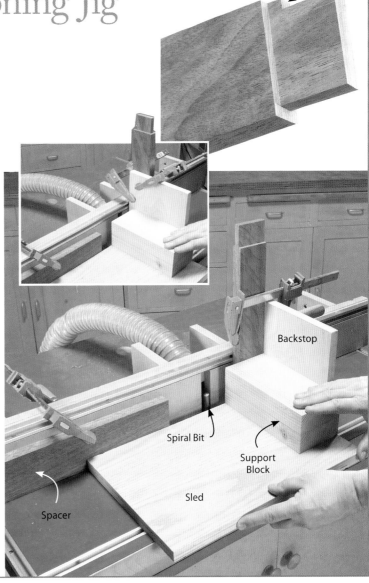

Haunch

Backstop

Spiral Bit

Support Block

Sled

Spacer

Sharpen Your Bits

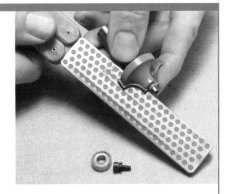

Instead of replacing a dull carbide router bit, re-sharpen it. All you'll need is a good commercial resin cleaner and a couple of diamond paddles. Before sharpening, inspect the edge. If it's rounded over or lightly nicked, take the bit to a pro. Most bits can be professionally sharpened for under $10.

To sharpen the bit yourself, first clean it to remove the pitch and resin build-up. Next, hone the bit with diamond paddles lubricated with water. Use a medium (325 grit) paddle for a somewhat dull bit and a fine (600 grit) paddle for final honing and routine touch-up. Lap the flat face of the bit (not the profile). Four to six passes should do it.

Slot Orients T-Bolt

Aligning the T-bolts on my router table's fence with the T-track slots in the table was a hassle. I could never tell which way the T-bolt heads were facing, because they were hidden beneath the fence. To eliminate the guesswork, I sawed a slot in the visible end of each T-bolt to indicate the head's orientation.

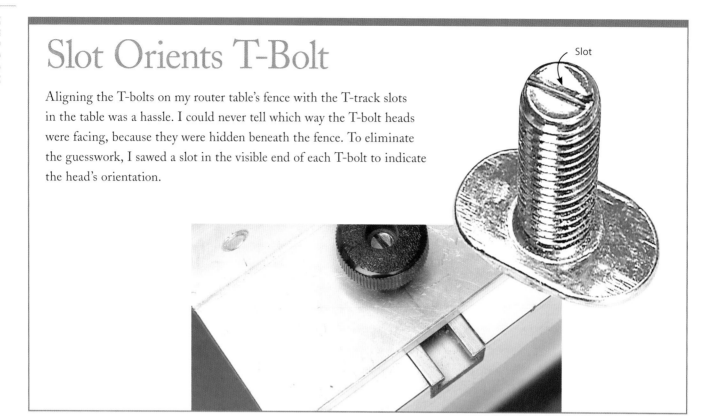

Slot

Safer Small-Parts Routing

When I have to rout a small part on my router table, I reach for a hand screw clamp. It holds the workpiece securely, keeps my hands a safe distance from the router bit and serves as a pair of handles for pushing. It also provides much better control than a pair of push sticks.

XL Router Base

My neighbor needed an edge routed on a large oak table top. Having messed up my fair share of edges by accidentally tilting the router, I was a little nervous, but agreed to take on the job.

While removing my router from the router table, it occurred to me that the table's insert plate would give me the extra support necessary to keep the router from tilting. And it did!

Square Up a Large Tabletop

How do I square up the ends of a tabletop that's too big for my tablesaw?

Use a router with a large-diameter flush-cutting bit (photo, at right), a fence with a square corner and a sacrificial block.

You can guarantee square corners on your tabletop by using a large piece of plywood or particleboard with a factory corner as your fence. Clamp one side flush with the long edge of the tabletop. Make sure the "fence" side extends past the other edge by at least the diameter of the router. Leave as little of the end of the table exposed as possible.

When you rout the end grain, you'll blow out the back edge every time, unless you support it. Clamp a sacrificial block to the fence, making sure it bears firmly against the back edge of the top and is flush with the edge. Use two clamps, so the block won't slip back or to the side. When you rout, simply extend the cut into the sacrificial block. Your fence and block have to be large enough so the clamps won't interfere with the router's path.

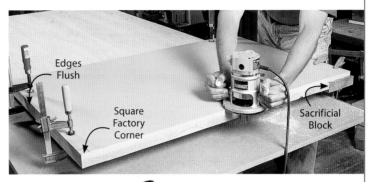

Edges Flush

Square Factory Corner

Sacrificial Block

Bearing

1⅛"

A hefty, large-diameter bit makes a much smoother cut in tough end grain than a ½-in.-dia. bit. A top-mounted bearing makes setup easier. It allows you to clamp the fence on top of the workpiece.

Tablesaw Router Fence

I live in big sky country, but my shop is as cramped as an efficiency apartment in downtown Manhattan! Consequently, I use my tablesaw extension wing as a router table to save floor space. To make use of the tablesaw's fence, I clamp on a shop-made router fence. The combination of these two fences is great. I get the easy adjustment of the saw fence and the router fence is wide enough to accommodate big bits. I also built in a dust port that does a super job of clearing the chips.

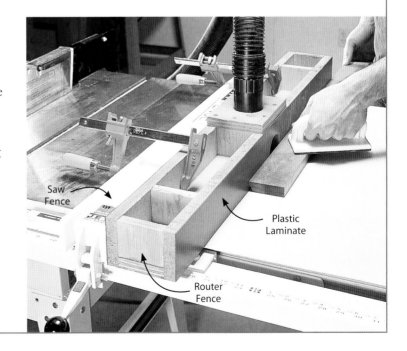

Saw Fence

Plastic Laminate

Router Fence

What's the Deal with Climb-Cutting?

I've often heard that "climb-cutting" with a router gives tear-out-free results. Shouldn't I always rout that way?

Climb-cutting isn't suitable for most routing operations because it's too dangerous. When you make a climb-cut, you move the router in the "wrong" direction, from right to left (on an outside edge), instead of left to right. This backward feed direction is dangerous, because it makes the router very hard to control.

A climb cut allows the spinning bit to kick away from the workpiece. As a result, climb-cuts must be very shallow. The bit's kickback can have surprising force—enough to wrench the router right out of your hands. The only time to consider climb-cutting is when you have to rout directly into the grain. For example, when you rout an arch or a rounded shape, you can't avoid routing into the grain half of the time (photo, at left). In these situations, a climb-cut is likely to produce much less tear-out than a regular cut (photo, below). But before you decide to try climb-cutting, consider sanding to the line as a safer, can't-lose alternative.

Climb-Cut

Routing Into Grain Can Cause Tear-Out Here

Bit Rotation

Normal Routing Direction

Climb-cutting reduces tear-out when you have to rout into the grain. To ensure success, minimize your risk. First, rough-cut as close to the line as you can. Then rout as much as possible using the proper feed direction. When you make a climb-cut, keep a firm grip on the router, make sure it's well-supported and be careful!

Normal Left-To-Right Feed

Grain Change

First Cut Left To Right (Normal)　　　Second Cut Right To Left (Climb-Cut)

Clean Edge

A climb-cut on the right side of the arch eliminated almost all of the tear-out that was caused by a continuous left-to-right feed.

Why do Router Bits Slip?

Today was the third time a router bit slipped in my collet. What's going on?

There are four possible explanations: the retaining nut needs to be tighter; the collet is dirty; the bit shank has been scored; or the collet is worn out and needs replacing. Here's what you should do:

1. Clean the bit shank and outside surfaces of the collet with a Scotch Brite pad and solvent. The least amount of dirt, rust or resin buildup in the collet can cause gripping problems. Blade cleaner (Woodcraft Supply, 800-225-1153, www.woodcraft.com, #142954: $14 for 16 oz.) works best, but you can also use denatured alcohol.

2. Clean the inside of the collet with a brass tubing brush and blade cleaner (Woodhaven, 800-344-6657, #7150; $9 for 3 tubing brushes). Use the brush to clean the vertical relief slots on the collet and the threads of the retaining nut. Apply a dry lubricant (Eagle America, 800-872-2511, #400-0012 Dri Cote, $14) to prevent rust and inhibit resin buildup.

3. Check for scoring on all parts of the collet. If you see any, buy a new collet ($15 to $20) from your router manufacturer's service center.

4. Examine the bit shank and gently remove any burrs with extra-fine emery sandpaper.

Once all the parts are clean, chuck the bit into your router and give it a try. If the bit still loosens up, replace the collet.

Collet

Brass Brush

Workmate Router Base

A Black & Decker Workmate ($70 at home centers and hardware stores) makes an easy-to-store stand for your router table. Screw a pair of blocks that are wider than your router under the router table for the Workmate to grasp. The 8⅜-in. opening of the Workmate is big enough to handle any router and the 31-in. high table is an ideal working height. When you're done routing, the Workmate folds flat and the router table can be hung on the wall.

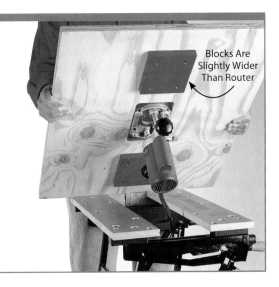

Blocks Are Slightly Wider Than Router

Sanding

Shop-Made Sanding Blocks

Commercial sanding blocks all have some kind of padded bottom. Do my shop-made blocks need to be padded, too?

Yes they do. Padded blocks have two primary benefits: They increase the life of your paper and they make it possible to use pressure-sensitive-adhesive (PSA) paper.

Cork is the easiest way to pad a shop-made sanding block. Cork is flat, firm and stiff enough to sand a plug flush or flatten a finish. The bit of give in a cork bottom provides some shock absorption for the individual grains of abrasive so they are not so easily knocked off the paper. This helps your sandpaper last longer.

It's also much easier to remove PSA paper from a cork bottom than from bare wood. PSA paper can be cut exactly to fit your sanding block, so there's no waste. Regular paper has to be cut oversize so you can hold the paper onto the block with your hand.

To make a padded sanding block, glue a piece of ⅛- or ¼-in.-thick cork (available in hardware stores or home centers) onto the wood. Wood glue works fine as an adhesive; just be sure to keep the glue layer very thin because cork is porous and the glue can easily seep into it.

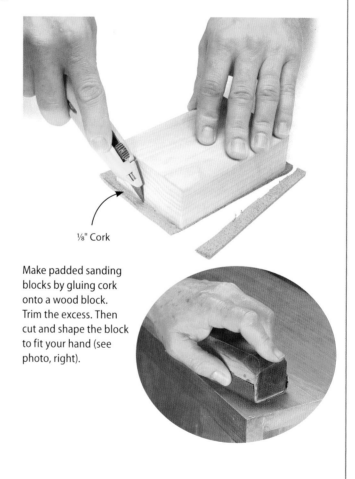

⅛" Cork

Make padded sanding blocks by gluing cork onto a wood block. Trim the excess. Then cut and shape the block to fit your hand (see photo, right).

Contoured Sanding Block

To sand a lot of molding, glue 80-grit sandpaper to several inches of the molding. Rub a block of Styrofoam on the sandpaper until the block conforms to the molding's contour. Glue sandpaper to the block, then sand the molding.

This method works best on large cove moldings; small rounds or hollows can lose their definition if sanded with a large block and coarse paper.

Belt Sanding Block

I do most of my sanding by hand, so I made this convenient wooden sanding block to fit 3-in. x 21-in. sanding belts. The block is split for two-thirds of its length, and the belt is tensioned with a removable dowel. A softer wood, such as poplar or white pine, gives the best results. If the belt stretches and becomes loose, insert a slightly larger dowel.

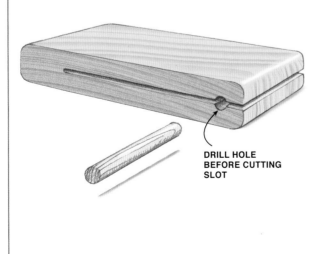

DRILL HOLE BEFORE CUTTING SLOT

Duct-Taped Sanding Block

Sometimes I prefer to sand by hand using a rubber block. This method gives me a better feel for the work than using a random-orbit sander does. Blocks like mine have been around for many years, but I believe I've made an improvement.

I had noticed that most of the work was done by the paper's leading edges. The paper's center didn't seem to have any wear at all. To compensate, I stick a piece of duct tape to the bottom of the sanding block, not quite reaching the ends, before I attach the sandpaper. The tape allows me to apply even pressure across the block's entire surface, but it isn't thick enough to spoil the block's flatness.

Paint-Stick Files

When you next buy paint, ask for a few free stirring sticks. Glue sandpaper to them and soon you'll have a complete set of woodworking "files". They're very handy because you can make the files as coarse or fine as you need.

Pipe Insulation Contour Sander

Sticky-backed sandpaper and foam pipe insulation team up to make perfect custom contour sanders. The flexible pipe insulation can be rolled to conform to almost any size of curve.

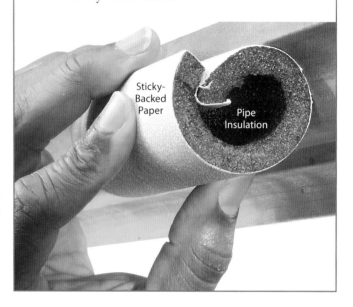

Sticky-Backed Paper

Pipe Insulation

Instant Rasp

I recently built a chest of drawers with sliding-dovetail joinery. During assembly, I found that the fit was just a little too snug. Rather than trying to realign my router jig, I looked around for another solution. I needed something that could slip in along the dovetail. I decided to stick some sandpaper to a scrap of wood with double-faced tape. I beveled the edge of the board, which allowed me to get right in where I needed to be.

Now this instant rasp is almost indispensable in my shop when I'm shaping, sizing or final sanding the edges of parts. I've made myself a whole set, ranging from very coarse to very fine grits.

Sandpaper

Double-Faced Tape

Reinforced Flexible Sandpaper

While refinishing some old chairs, I discovered an easier way to sand the turned legs. I'd been using plain strips of sandpaper, but they tore and wore out so quickly. I reinforced the sandpaper strips with a couple layers of masking tape and they lasted longer and the added stiffness gave them a little extra bite. I save money, too, because this do-it-yourself taped sandpaper costs half as much as cloth-backed abrasives.

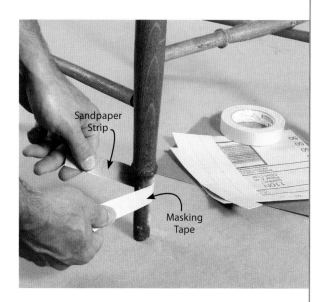

Sandpaper Index

When turning, I like to have all my supplies close at hand, ready for use. I use an index-card box to store and organize cut pieces of sandpaper. It has a lid and dividers, so everything is neat and orderly. When you cut sandpaper into sections, some pieces won't have the grit information on them, so I mark the back of each one using a color coding system.

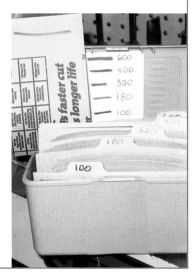

Sandpaper Saver

Sanding between coats of polyurethane is tough on sandpaper. And I make it tougher, because I never wait the recommended 72 hours before recoating. But if the finish isn't bone-dry, the paper is likely to gum up.

When my sandpaper loads up, I clean it using my trusty stripping brush. Its firm nylon bristles remove the gum without wearing out the grit.

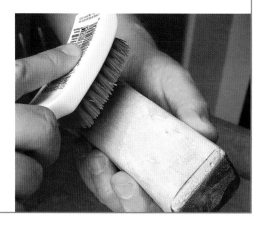

Toggle Clamp Sanding Block

I made this quick-release sanding block from four pieces of ½-in.-thick birch plywood. The top three pieces are glued together. Wrap a quarter sheet of sandpaper around the bottom piece and slip on the top assembly. The toggle clamp (www.rockler.com #20787, $9) locks the top assembly to the bottom.

All four pieces measure 2½-in. wide by 7-in. long. The toggle clamp mounts on the bottom piece. The second piece has a hole just large enough for the toggle clamp's base to fit through. This leaves a lip for the toggle to clamp onto. The third piece has a clearance hole for the entire clamp. The fourth piece is the same as the third, and builds up the block so the clamp sits inside. I glued on pieces of cork to cushion the sanding surface and fortify the toggle clamp's grip.

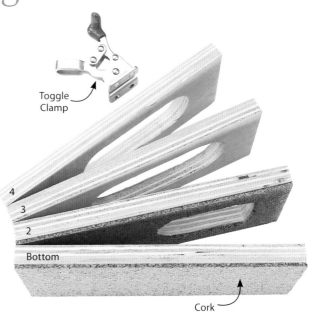

Toggle Clamp

4
3
2
Bottom

Cork

Scrapers Leave Sanders in the Dust

Scrapers have been around for centuries, and for good reason: They do the job fast! A sharp scraper leaves hardwoods with a smooth finish that only needs a little finish sanding. A scraper is faster than an orbital sander and you never have to change grits. The hard part is getting a good cutting edge on a scraper; it takes some practice. But, once you've used a sharp scraper, you'll find yourself reaching for it more often than for your sander.

Scraper Shavings

Shelf Liner Sanding Pad

One roll of shelf liner will provide a lifetime supply of pads for your sanding block–pads which will improve the block's performance. I bought an 18" x 48" roll at a local home center for about $5. At about ³⁄₃₂" thick, I find that shelf liner has just the right combination of firmness and give for finish sanding. I use spray-on contact adhesive to hold the pad in place.

Super Sandpaper

Whenever I was sanding by hand, the sandpaper would roll or slide in my hands, eventually tearing and turning into small, useless scraps. I tried folding it every which way until I finally solved the problem with a little spray adhesive. Now I cut a sheet of sandpaper in half and spray on a light coat of adhesive. Then, I fold the sandpaper to a quarter-sheet size, which is just right for hand-sanding. The glued paper doesn't roll or slide and its double thickness makes it stronger.

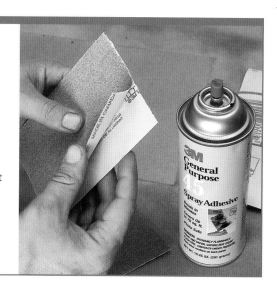

Watch Your P's When Looking for Sandpaper

In my local hardware store, I noticed some sandpaper with the letter P before the grit number. What does that signify?

The P-grade paper assures you of a more consistent scratch pattern because the allowable variation in any given grit size is more tightly controlled. Historically the grit size of paper manufactured in the United States was measured on a scale created by the Coated Abrasives Manufacturing Institute (CAMI). On the CAMI scale, the grit is stated without any additional letters: for example, 120, 180, etc.

In Europe, the allowable variance in grit size is more tightly controlled. Sandpaper made there is graded by the Federation of European Producers of Abrasives (FEPA), which uses the letter P to distinguish its grading system.

The thing to watch for is that the two systems diverge as the grits grow finer (see chart). Not all manufacturers add the P designation to their papers. Here's how the major players label their sandpapers: 3M always uses the P on its FEPA-graded paper. Norton uses FEPA for all but its silicon-carbide paper, but does not display the P. European companies, such as Klingspor and Mirka, only offer FEPA paper and almost always show the P designation.

Little discrepancy occurs between the two grading systems from the coarsest grits up to 180 grit. However, as the grades become finer than 180 grit, the two systems diverge markedly. When using the finer grits, it is important that you know which grading system is used.

Abrasive Grading	
FEPA	CAMI
P24	24
P30	30
P36	36
P40	40
P50	50
P60	60
P80	80
P100	100
P120	120
P150	150
P180	180
P220	220
P240	240
P280	
P320	
P360	320
P400	
P500	360
P600	
P800	400
P1000	500
P1200	600
P1500	800
P2000	1000

Convex Sander Pad

In the process of refinishing an old chair, I found that my random orbit sander's flat surface didn't work for sanding the concave hollow of the seat. My sander uses hook-and-loop paper, so I purchased some adhesive-backed hook-and-loop material at the hardware store. After sticking the material together with the hooks on one side and loops on the other, I cut out a disc shape that was small enough to fit in the center of my sander without blocking the dust collection holes. I then applied the paper over the pad. It worked perfectly to create a slight convex bottom on my sander that conformed to the chair's curve, and held the sandpaper firmly in place.

A Raking Light Finds Hidden Defects

Shine a bright light from different angles across sanded boards to illuminate hard-to-see swirl marks and problem spots while they're still easy to fix. Use the light before each grit change and you'll avoid having to back up several grit levels to remove a deep scratch.

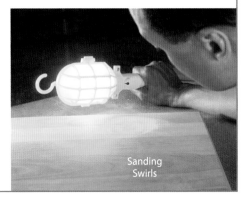

Sanding Swirls

Cool Tip

Changing the sanding sleeves on a spindle sander can be as tough as removing an old rusty bolt. Next time, try this trick: Put the drum in your freezer for 15 minutes. The cold will shrink the rubber drum and the sanding sleeve will almost fall off.

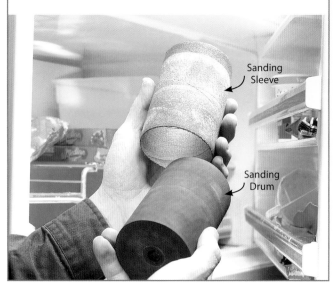

Sanding Sleeve

Sanding Drum

Avoiding Swirl Marks

I just stained a tabletop and found it covered with tiny swirl marks from my random-orbital sander. What did I do wrong?

Swirl marks are inevitable. The trick is to use a technique that minimizes their prominence.

Try this: let the weight of the sander do the work. Guide it, but don't press down. More pressure removes wood faster, but it also leaves more swirls.

Second, use graduated sandpaper grits. Start with 120 to remove mill marks, then move to 150, 180 and 220. Don't skip grit intervals. Swirl marks left by 120-grit paper, for example, won't be easy to remove with 180-grit paper.

Your final and most important step is to hand sand with the same grit you used last on your machine. By the time you get to 220 grit, the swirl marks will be faint, but hand sanding is the only way you will get rid of them entirely.

Set a work light on your bench and shine it at a low angle across the sanded surface. A quick wipe with denatured alcohol will reveal any lingering swirl marks.

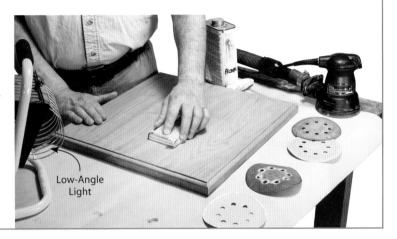

Low-Angle Light

Drum Sander Woes

My drum sander is a great machine, but I throw out way too much sandpaper with burned spots that scorch my wood. What am I doing wrong?

Don't feel bad. We've had a drum sander in the AW shop for four years and had the same problem, until we taped these reminders on our machine:

1. Always start with a coarse grit. Don't try to do it all with a fine grit.
   Rough lumber - 36 grit
   Planed lumber - 80 grit
   Flattening glue-ups - 80 grit
2. Scrape off all dried glue before sanding. Glue lines scorch sandpaper!
3. Sand only the high spots on the first pass.
4. Angle your boards 10 degrees or so. The fibers are cut more cleanly, and glue lines are spread over a wider portion of the belt. Don't feed the wood straight on until the last pass.
5. Rotate the crank one-eighth of a turn at most. Deeper cuts heat up the belt, causing it to wear out faster.
6. Run every board through twice before turning the crank. Make sure the current setting has removed all it can before cutting deeper.

Dampen the Wood for a Clean, Smooth Finish

After your final pass with the power sander, wipe a damp sponge over the wood. As the wood dries, any loose wood fibers will stand up.

Let the wood dry completely. Then lightly sand the whole surface with 220 or higher grit paper to knock off the whiskers. This yields as smooth a wood surface as you can get and is especially important when you use water-based finishes that tend to raise the grain anyway.

Wetting the wood will also reveal any hidden glue smears or sweat drips. Or you can wait until the varnish is on to see them—your choice.

Glue Smear

Dual-Grit Disc Sanding

My disc sander is indispensable for both quick wood removal and final smoothing. I got tired of changing and wasting discs every time I needed a different grit, though, so I made one disc out of two. To make the dual-grit disc, I lay two 12-in. discs together, one coarse and one fine grit. Then I cut a 6-in circle out of the middle of them with a utility knife. This gives me two sets of dual-grit discs and nothing goes to waste. When I mount them to the disc sander, it's just like putting the doughnut hole back in the doughnut.

Coarse Grit Saves Time

If you need to remove a lot of material, using too fine a grit is a waste of time and paper. Use 80- to 100-grit sandpaper to do the hard, time-consuming work. As a rule of thumb, you should spend about 80 percent of your time with these coarser grits. Then the finer grits simply remove scratch marks from the previous grit.

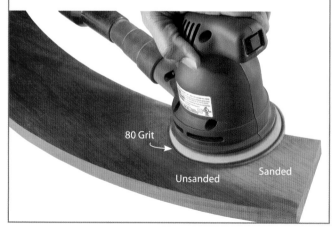

80 Grit

Unsanded   Sanded

Flap Sanders Eat Wood

A flap-sanding disc turns an angle grinder into a great tool for shaping and sculpting wood. You'll be amazed at how quickly these things remove wood. Be sure to take time to practice a bit before you scoop out your first chair seat.

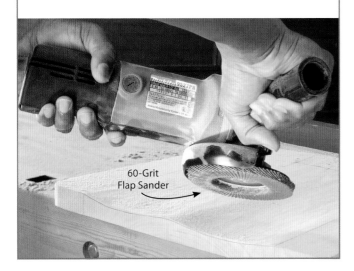

60-Grit
Flap Sander

Hold Wood Steady with a No-Slip Pad

Router pads do a great job of gripping flat pieces of wood during sanding. With a router pad, you don't need to stop and move clamps around or (one of my personal bad habits) try to hang on to a board with your fingertips and work the sander one-handed.

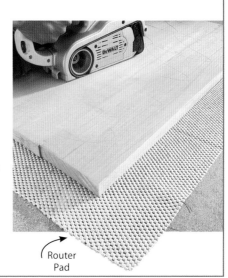

Router
Pad

Dust Collection Improves Sander Performance

Without dust collection, your sander rides on a layer of sawdust, greatly reducing its effectiveness. With a shop vacuum hooked up to your sander, excess sanding dust and grit particles are vacuumed up instantly. This ensures complete contact between the paper and the wood at all times allowing your sander to work at maximum potential. Plus, the lack of dust and grit helps keep you, your shop and your lungs clean.

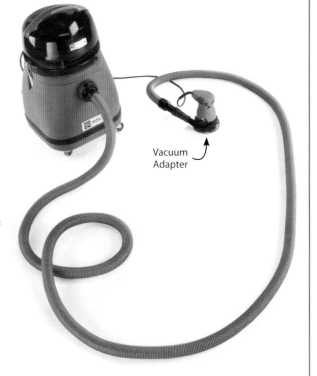

Vacuum
Adapter

Sanding Chalk

I'm making and installing approx. 5000-bd.ft. of hard maple trim. Keeping track of what I've already sanded is difficult, so before sanding, I rub artists non-oil pastel chalks (available at artist supply stores for about $5 for a box of 50) onto the wood and into the grain with a dry staining sponge. Then I simply sand until all the chalk is gone. In addition to showing what has and has not been sanded, the chalk makes blemishes and sanding marks stand out.

Non-oil pastel chalk is a powder that doesn't stick to wood. If any chalk remains in the pores after sanding, I simply dampen the surface with water. This raises the chalk to the surface, so it sands off easily.

I use dark-color chalk on light-colored woods and light-color chalk on dark wood.

Low-Tech Edge Sander

Positioned on a platform adjacent to a table and fence, my belt sander doubles as an edge sander. Front and rear blocks, shaped-to-fit, hold the sander in place on the platform. The platform is fastened to a spring-loaded bar, so I can adjust the depth of cut by turning the wingnuts at each end. Compression springs on the bolts keep the bar under tension. By turning the spring-tensioned setscrews on the back of the platform, I can also adjust the sander's pitch, so it always sands perpendicular edges.

Spring-Tensioned Setscrew

Spring-Loaded Bar

Sanding Guard for Inside Corners

Sanding inside corners used to leave nasty buzz marks from my sander banging into the adjacent face. I still haven't tamed my sander, but now I get buzz-free results by protecting the adjacent face with a painter's edging guide. It costs less than $2 at a home center and is so thin that I can sand virtually all the way into the corner. Now sander-base-whacking won't leave marks.

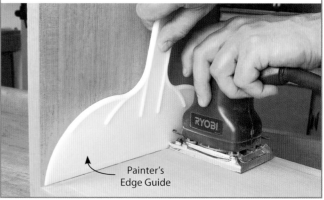

Painter's Edge Guide

Keep Edges Crisp

Lay pieces of scrap wood of equal thickness to bridge the piece you're sanding. This will prevent the sander from tipping and rounding over the crisp edges.

For sanding the narrow edges of doors, clamp the door between two pieces of thick stock to help steady the sander.

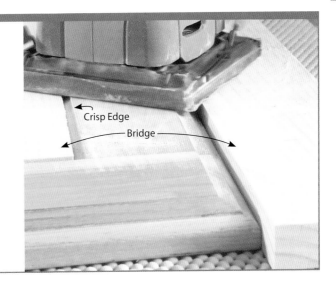

Crisp Edge

Bridge

Longer Life for Hook-and-Loop Pads

I love the hook-and-loop sanding pad on my random-orbital sander, but I had to replace it twice last year. My goal is to get more life out of my pads. Any suggestions?

Manufacturers tell us that heat and pressure are the main culprits for wear on hook-and-loop pads. A worn pad that has damaged hooks has trouble holding the paper when the sander is turned on.

It turns out that prolonging the life of your pad boils down to good sanding habits. Allow the paper and the sander, rather than your arms' strength, to do the work. Bearing down on the sander generates more heat and puts excessive pressure on the pad. Keep the sander flat on the work so pressure is distributed evenly across the whole pad. Don't be tempted to tip the sander on edge to concentrate the pressure. Remember that the outer edge of the pad spins at a much higher speed than the center and thus generates more heat. This explains why bare spots from missing hooks appear at the outer edge of a worn pad first (see photo, right).

Also, remember to change the sandpaper frequently. Dull paper is an open invitation to adding pressure. One last thing: Make sure you always leave sandpaper on the pad. It protects the hooks and keeps you from accidentally running the sander without paper.

Broken Hooks

Pencil Lines Tell You When To Stop

There's nothing worse than sanding right through a veneer. Pencils lines are a great way to gauge sanding progress. I always draw lines on plywood where it meets a solid hardwood edge. The lines will start to disappear when the hardwood edge is flush with the plywood. That's when you know it's time to stop.

Pencil lines work on glued-up boards, too. The boards aren't even until all the lines are gone.

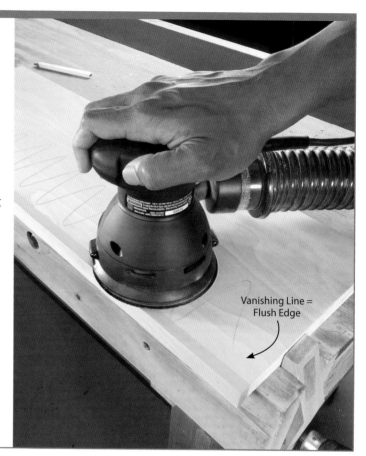

Vanishing Line = Flush Edge

Safer Profile Shaping

Shaping small parts with a template on a router table always spooks me, so I use a sanding disc instead. Now my fingers aren't close to a whizzing router bit and I don't have to worry about tear-out on the end grain.

I make my template a bit undersized to allow for the thickness of the aluminum guide and its distance from the sanding disc. Then I attach my template to my bandsawn wood parts with double-faced tape.

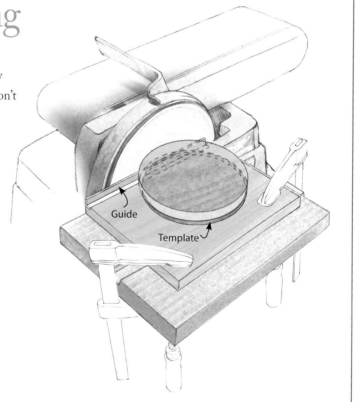

Guide

Template

Template Sanding

A guide bushing on a drum sander transforms it into a template sander. It allows you to create numerous curved parts with sanded edges and is especially useful for softwoods or figured woods that splinter or chip when cut with a router. You don't need to follow a pencil line and the drum sander doesn't leave the annoying ripples that are so common when you're freehand drum-sanding. You can buy drum sanding attachments for a drill press that have built-in guide bushings, which we show in the photo, or you can make your own. To make one, cut a circular disk out of plywood the same diameter as your drum and secure it with screws to a piece of plywood. Attach the plywood to your drill press table so the disc is directly under the sanding drum.

GUIDE BUSHING

Skip Grits

Really, it's OK. We checked with several major sandpaper manufacturers and each one said the same thing: Whatever grit you start with, you can skip every other grit as you progress from coarse to fine. Using each grit in sequence is almost always overkill, not to mention extremely tedious. If you start at 100, skip to 150, then 220. Or from 80, go to 120 and then 180.

Soft Pads Increase Random-Orbit Sanders' Flexibility

A soft replacement pad does a better job than the standard firm pad that comes with your random-orbit sander when it comes to sanding contoured areas. The thick, flexible pad conforms to a soft curve. A stiff pad tends to dig in and ruin the work.

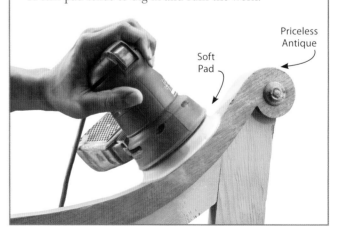

Soft Pad

Priceless Antique

Sharpening

Accurate Paring Requires A Flat Back

Is the back of your chisel really flat? For accurate paring, it has to be as flat as flat can be, for at least 2" to 3". Even though your chisel may look like it's OK, it probably needs to be lapped to make it truly flat.

Lapping consists of two stages: flattening and polishing. First, you flatten the back by rubbing it hard on sandpaper that's adhered to a flat surface. I've used a ¼" thick piece of glass, the cast iron wing of a tablesaw, or the bed of a jointer, but my favorite lapping surface is an inexpensive granite surface plate.

Start with 220 grit paper. Take a few strokes and examine the back. If it's really bad, begin lapping in earnest with 80 grit paper. On most chisels, I start with 120 grit. If the back is pretty good, stick with the 220 grit.

On your first grit, keep sanding until the scratches go all the way from corner to corner and 2" to 3" up the length of the back. This completes the flattening stage.

In the next stage, polish the back with finer and finer grits. A complete sequence is 80, 120, 180, 220, and 320 grit paper. (You can go even further, and save wear on your stones, by using 15 micron and 5 micron 3M PSA-backed Microfinishing paper.)

When you switch to a finer grit, lap in a different direction, so the scratches make a different pattern. Keep lapping on each grit until the scratches made by the previous grit disappear.

Once you've finished with 320 grit, continue lapping on your stones—assuming they're flat.

For abrasives, I prefer 3M's PSA Gold, which is available in discs or rolls at auto supply stores. It cuts faster than any other paper commonly available and doesn't require a sprayed-on adhesive.

3 Ways to Test for Sharpness

If you can see light on the edge, it's not sharp. A sharp edge is too fine to reflect light.

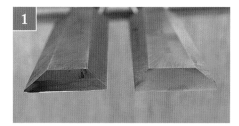

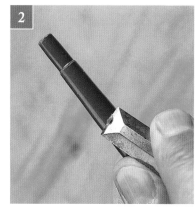

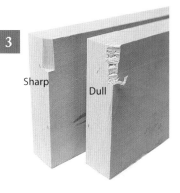

A sharp blade slices softwood end grain cleanly (left). A dull blade tears the end grain (right).

A sharp edge catches easily on the side of a plastic pen barrel. A dull edge slides right off.

4 Blade Profiles

Here's a quick guide on how to sharpen the blades of four major types of bench planes.

Scrub plane. This tool is used to hog off lots of wood, fast. Its blade has a large camber, which is created on a grinder. (No honing is necessary.) The amount of camber depends on the wood's hardness and whether it's green or dry. A 1⁄16" curve will take off shavings up to 1⁄16" thick, just right for kiln-dried hardwoods.

Fore plane. This plane is used to level a large surface. (A fore plane is a 5, 5½, or 6 in the Stanley series.) Its blade has a smaller camber, made on a grinder. This camber is honed.

Smooth plane. A smoother finishes off a surface. Its blade has a very slight camber or none at all. The blade's corners are rounded to prevent them from digging into the surface and leaving a series of steps. This rounding is best done on a grinder. The camber is created by honing only, not on the grinder.

Jointer plane. A jointer is often used to flatten surfaces that will be glued together. Its blade has no camber—it's dead straight across. Block planes are sharpened with a straight profile, too.

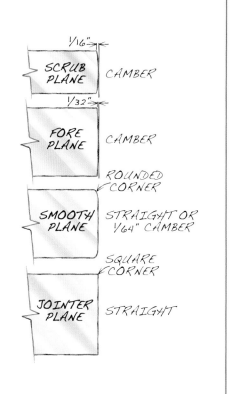

A Bargain Honing Jig, and How To Improve It

When I first learned how to sharpen, I bought a very simple and inexpensive honing jig made in England by Eclipse. Today, the same jig is widely available under many different brand names and often costs less than $15. It works quite well—I've used mine for years—but I've made a few small refinements to it. The jig's body is aluminum, so it's very easy to modify using a file or disc sander.

The jig has two positions for clamping tools: an upper ledge for plane irons and a lower pair of V-shaped grooves for chisels. To set the honing angle, you measure the distance from the tip of the blade to the body of the jig. Here's what you can do to make this good jig even better:

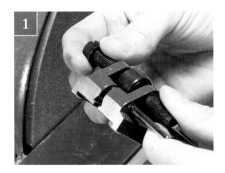

- **Flatten its face**. For accurate and repeatable projection measurements, the two front faces of the jig must be square and even with each other. The easiest way to flatten the faces is by placing the jig on a disc sander's worktable and gently pushing it into the disc (Photo 1).

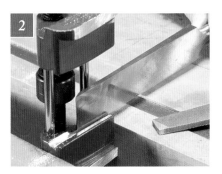

- **Widen the chisel slots**. Many chisels don't fit very well in the V-shaped grooves because their sides are too thick. Clamp the jig in a vise and use the edge of a 6" or 8" mill bastard file to widen the grooves to fit your tools (Photo 2).

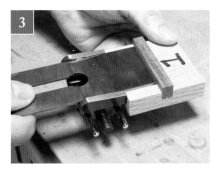

- **Make a projection jig**. You don't need a ruler to measure a tool's projection—use a stepped wooden jig instead (Photo 3). It's more convenient, more accurate, and easily repeatable. I use a single 30mm (about 1³⁄₁₆") projection for most chisels and plane irons. This creates a 30° bevel on a chisel and a 35° bevel on a plane iron.

- **Add a microbevel setting**. I added a second side to the projection jig that is 2mm (about ¹⁄₁₆") shorter than the first side, which increases the bevel angle by about 1°. To sharpen an edge, I use the normal 30mm projection on medium and fine stones (side #1), then reset the projection to 28mm (side #2) and hone on a superfine stone.

- **Form a back-bevel ramp**. Adding a back bevel to a plane iron makes the iron easier to sharpen. To make a back bevel using this jig, you just turn the jig over and rest its top on your stone (Photo 4). Unaltered, the jig produces a back bevel that's quite steep, so I used a disc sander to grind down the top of the jig, sloping from front to back.

Chisel Sharpening Jig

If you've had trouble grinding a straight edge on a chisel or plane iron, try using your disc sander. All you need is a guide that slides in your sander's miter gauge slot and an 80 or 100-grit disc. To make the guide, start with a ¾" x 5" x 8" base. Cut a groove for a runner in its bottom that puts the base's edge about ¹⁄₃₂" away from the sanding disc. Cut the front edge of the base at 25°. This is the standard grinding angle for a general-purpose chisel. Later, use a stone to hone a 30° bevel on the chisel. If you want to use the chisel direct from the disc sander, which is OK for rough work, cut the base's front edge at 30°.

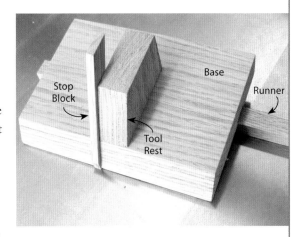

Add a runner to the base, then make the tool rest. It's just a block of hardwood with a stop block glued on one side. The stop block keeps the edge of your tool square to the sanding disc. Cut the front face of the tool rest at the same angle that you cut the base. Glue and screw the tool rest to the base, lining up the angled portions, and you're ready to go.

Before you begin, here's an important cautionary note: To prevent sparks from starting a fire, disconnect your disc sander from your vac or dust collector. Also, clean up any piles of sawdust inside or under the sander; an ember may smolder there and start a fire later on.

To use the jig, position it a little left of center of the sanding disc—if your disc rotates counterclockwise. (The disc's rotation should push down on the chisel, not up.) Place the chisel against the stop block, then slide the chisel down the tool rest until it makes contact with the disc. Slide the jig back and forth.

Blade-Flattening Block

Flattening the back of a spokeshave's blade on sandpaper is a pain. The blade is so small that it's hard to get a grip on it. A 1½" thick MDF block sized to fit my hand makes the job easy. I stick the blade to the block with double-faced tape.

One problem: If the blade gets too hot from friction, it won't stick to the tape anymore. The solution is easy. When the blade starts to get warm, just set the block—blade side down—on a cast-iron surface, such as a tablesaw's top, for about 30 seconds. Cast iron absorbs and dissipates the blade's heat quite rapidly.

Drill Press Sharpening System

Here's a fast, inexpensive way to keep your edge tools razor sharp. First, cut out a few 5" x ¾" MDF discs. Drill a ¼" hole in the center of each disc. Next, glue different grits of sandpaper to each side of the discs, ranging from 50 to 2000 grit. While 50 grit makes quick work of re-grinding a bevel, 2000 grit brings the tool to a mirror finish.

Next, make an arbor using a ¼" x 3" bolt, a fender washer and a ¼" coupler nut. You'll need a jig to hold your tools at the proper angle—I built a ramp that creates a 30° bevel.

Set your drill press to its slowest speed to prevent your tool from overheating, but keep a cup of water handy to quench the tool in case it gets too hot.

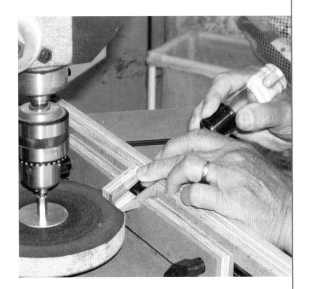

Custom Gouge Strop

Getting a mirror finish on the contoured profiles of carving gouges can be a real hassle. The curved surfaces don't lend themselves to polishing on a flat stone or strop. Making a custom strop is easy. Use the chisel to cut its own contour in a piece of poplar or basswood. Rub chromium oxide polishing compound in the contour and you have a custom-made strop.

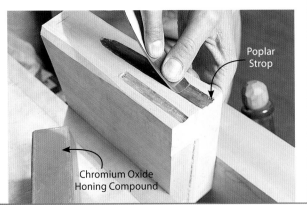

Poplar Strop

Chromium Oxide Honing Compound

Dress for Success

Ever lose your temper? I mean your chisel's temper. Don't get burned by a clogged, uneven grinding wheel. Dressing your grinder wheels periodically to keep them clean and flat helps prevent the excess heat that leads to bluing and loss of temper(s). Single-point diamond wheel dressers do a great job but they're difficult to use freehand. Try a flat-tip diamond dresser instead. It has 36-grit diamond stone particles imbedded in a ½-in. wide by ¾-in.-long face. Simply place it on your grinder's tool rest and make contact with the wheel.

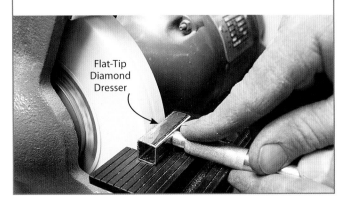

Flat-Tip Diamond Dresser

Back Bevel Avoids Lapping

Conventional wisdom holds that you must lap the back of a plane iron in order to get a keen edge. Well, it ain't necessarily so. There is an alternative: skip the lapping and substitute a back bevel.

The process is quite simple. When it's time to remove the wire edge formed by honing the bevel, place a thin object, such as a piece of plastic or a 6" stainless steel rule, along one side of your finest stone. Rest the blade on this shim when you remove the wire edge. The shim elevates the blade just enough to form a back bevel of only a few degrees.

There are a few provisos, though:

- The back of your blade still has to be relatively flat, so that there are no gaps under the chip breaker.
- A few strokes on the finest stone should do the job. There's no point in making this a large bevel, as long as it goes across the full width of the blade. Once you form a back bevel, you'll have to continue following this method each time you hone.
- In order to maintain a constant angle, always place your shim and the blade on the same places on the stone.
- A back bevel raises the effective cutting angle of your plane. This helps reduce tearout, but it also makes the plane a little harder to push.

Credit for popularizing this technique properly goes to David Charlesworth, a well-known English cabinetmaker.

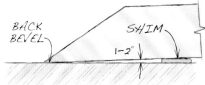

Blunt a Nicked Edge

If your chisel gets a serious nick or ding, you'll have to grind away a lot of metal to renew the edge. The best strategy for doing this is to adjust your grinder's tool rest to 90° and blunt your tool like a screwdriver. Once you've ground past the damage, reset the tool rest at the appropriate grinding angle and have at it.

Consider this as an insurance policy. You're much less likely to overheat and draw the temper out of a blunt edge than an acute edge.

Overheating an edge is all too easy to do when you're removing a lot of material. It's not pretty. The steel turns blue—a definite sign of trouble. The blued portion is softened, and will no longer hold an edge. You have to continue grinding past the blued area to get to good steel again.

Blunting the edge is just a different way to shape a new bevel. You'll have to take off all that metal anyway, so you may as well do it without risking any further damage—a nick is bad enough!

Dress Those Wheels

If your grinder shakes and vibrates, chances are that the wheels aren't round. Sure, they're more or less round, but they have to be perfectly round for your machine to run smoothly. For truing a wheel, you need a wheel dresser.

If your wheels are full of metal particles and have a glazed surface, you've got another problem. All that metal makes the wheel cut slower and build up heat faster—a surefire recipe for drawing the temper from a tool. To renew a wheel's surface, you need a wheel dresser.

You get the picture. A wheel dresser is a must-have accessory for any grinder. It removes material from the face of a grinding wheel the same way that a turning gouge shapes a spindle. As it cuts into the wheel, a dresser removes the high spots, making the wheel truly round. At the same time, it renews the surface by exposing fresh abrasive.

Before you dress your wheels, it's a good idea to mark them all around with a pencil so you know when all the high spots are gone. To mark a wheel, rotate it by hand and hold a pencil against it.

There's more than one type of wheel dresser, but my favorite is a T-shaped tool with a diamond face. To use it, adjust the tool rest to 90°, turn on the grinder, and gently hold the dresser against the wheel. It's that easy. You'll be amazed at the difference it makes.

Belt Sander/Grinder

Getting one tool to do the work of two is a great space saver. I've discovered that my belt sander and a 120-grit belt make an excellent substitute for a grinder. I use a Black & Decker Workmate to hold my sander, but any set-up that holds the sander firmly to a benchtop will work. Grinding produces a shower of sparks, so be sure to remove the dust bag to avoid any fire hazard. The tool rest is made from two pieces of scrap wood. Cut the bottom piece to clamp to the benchtop. The top piece is bevel-cut at whatever angle the particular tool requires. The tops are interchangeable, so I keep a 25-degree and a 30-degree handy. It's easy to make specialized tops with V-grooves for holding carving or turning gouges.

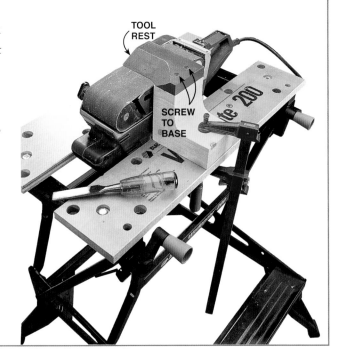

TOOL REST

SCREW TO BASE

Easy Knife Sharpening

Don't keep your sharpening skills confined to your shop tools. Why not tackle that dull set of kitchen knives you've been crushing tomatoes with? Here's a great tip: Go to any office supply store and buy one of those loose-leaf folders with a plastic spline (about 40 cents). Cut and trim the spline to fit over the back of the knife. The spline raises the back of the knife just enough to put a consistent bevel on the cutting edge. Now your knives will glide right through those tomatoes!

Fine Edge On Your Scraper

The edge left after filing a scraper is a little rough for fine work. Use a piece of wood to align the scraper when moving it against the stone and you'll retain the square edge you achieved with your file jig.

An extra-fine (1,200) diamond stone is a good choice for this because the scraper won't wear a groove in the stone.

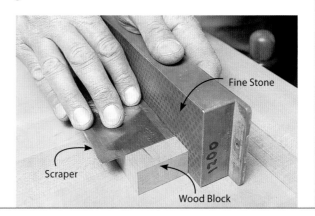

Flatten Blade Backs Fast

It would be great if chisels and planes came from the factory ready to use, but they don't. A perfectly flat, mirror-like finish on the back is essential for a truly sharp edge. Flattening always requires a large dose of elbow grease and patience. The fastest method is to use an extra-coarse diamond stone. It won't dish out the way oilstones and waterstones do and it can easily be clamped in a vise.

Once you have a flat surface, move on to finer stones until your chisels and planes shine like mirrors.

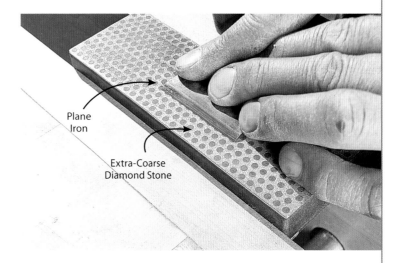

Rust and Mold on Waterstones

My set of Norton waterstones has recently developed two problems. First, a brownish stain appears when I sharpen my chisels and plane irons. Could this be rust? My second problem is mold, probably the result of storing my stones in damp conditions. Can you recommend a way to get rid of the rust and mold?

You're right about the first problem. The brown stain is from the oxidation of small steel particles. This doesn't affect the functioning of the stone and is only an aesthetic concern.

To prevent mold from growing, put a few drops of chlorine bleach in the water that you soak your stones in. To clean up moldy stones, you can lap them on a piece of ¼-in. plate glass with either 180-grit silicon carbide sandpaper, or 90-grit carbide particles (available from auto parts stores). Despite any remaining stains, the stones should function as well as ever. From time to time, your waterstones will need further lapping. This keeps the stone flat and clears it of any clogging particles.

180-GRIT CARBIDE SANDPAPER

Keeping Waterstones Dead Flat

Waterstones are great for sharpening bench tools, but their soft binder makes them prone to dishing out and grooving. Fortunately, flattening them is no big deal. An 11 in. by 12-in. piece of ¼-in. plate glass and a sheet of 180-grit wet/dry sandpaper provide a cheap, perfectly flat abrasive surface for flattening all your waterstones. The glass will cost you about six bucks (be sure to have the edges sanded) and the wet/dry sandpaper about 70 cents a sheet. Both are available at hardware stores. Use water to hold the paper on the glass and to flush away the slurry.

Wet/Dry Sandpaper

Plate Glass

No More Waterstone Mess

There's no getting around it—waterstones are messy. Here's a simple tip for keeping that mess contained: Pick up a heavy-gauge, 13 in. by 19-in. cookie sheet (about $7) at the grocery store, hardware store—wherever. It's large enough to easily hold three stones. Use a ¾-in. board pushed against the stones and clamp down the board and the cookie sheet on your bench. When you're done, just wipe the cookie sheet dry and hang it on the wall.

Hole For Hanging

Cookie Sheet

Hone Scrapers with Diamonds

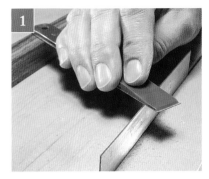

A lot of folks use a stone to put the final edge on a scraper before turning its hook, but I prefer to use a diamond paddle. It cuts faster than most stones and obviously won't develop a rut, which is always a danger when you continually run the edge of a scraper on a stone.

I use an extra-fine diamond paddle, which is roughly equivalent to a soft Arkansas oilstone or a 1000 grit waterstone. While the diamond can't make a scraper's edge quite as sharp as a very fine stone, the edge is good enough for all but the most demanding work. I lubricate the paddle with some 3-In-One oil to float away the metal debris, so it won't clog the paddle.

To hone the scraper's edge, I position the scraper in a vise so that it's level with a small stick. Resting the paddle on the stick ensures that the scraper's edge will be exactly 90° (Photo 1). I also use the paddle to remove the wire edge formed by honing (Photo 2).

Instant Wheel-Dresser Support

I use my grinder almost exclusively for beveling my chisels, so I like to keep the tool rest set to produce the 25-degree bevel I prefer. Having to reset the angle after using my diamond wheel dresser to clean and flatten the wheel bothered me until I made this wedge-shaped support.

Like many of my friends, I've upgraded my grinder by installing a top-quality tool rest. The wedge-shaped support I made fits snugly in the tool rest and instantly positions my diamond dresser correctly, perpendicular to the wheel's face.

After drawing the support's profile on the end of a 12-in.-long, 1¼-in. x 1¾-in. blank, I headed to my tablesaw. First, I cut a rabbet on the back of the blank to create the tongue. Rather than going for a precise fit, I cut the tongue a bit narrow and planned to install adjustment screws later.

Next, I cut the bevel. Its angle depends on your preferred bevel angle, the size of your grinding wheel and the location of your tool rest relative to the wheel.

After checking to make sure the bevel's angle was correct, I cut the support from the blank and installed the adjustment screws. Now, switching from grinding to dressing is effortless.

Adjustment Screw

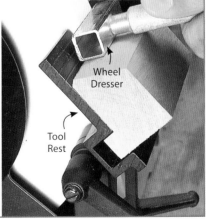

Wheel Dresser

Tool Rest

Plane Blade Lapping Jig

Lapping the back of a plane blade can be a lot of work. My fingers have often complained very loudly, so I've tried many ways to hold the blade comfortably. I've used a magnet, made a holder from a chunk of wood with a shallow dado in it, and worn gardener's gloves–the kind that have rubber bumps all over them. Each method worked OK, but I finally decided that the sharpening world needs another jig.

This one really does the trick. It allows you to put a lot of pressure right on top of the blade, without tipping it, and that extra pressure makes lapping go much faster. The blade is fastened directly to the jig; the knob is elevated on a stack of nylon washers to give you a roomier grip. The knob is threaded and fastened to the jig with a ⁵⁄₁₆" flat head machine bolt.

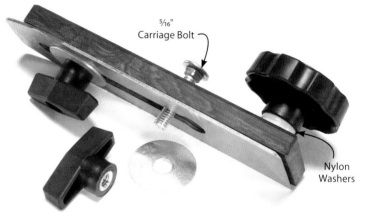

⁵⁄₁₆"
Carriage Bolt

Nylon
Washers

Restoring a Blued Chisel

The first thing I did with my new grinder was to blue the edge of a chisel. Is there anything I can do to save it?

Most woodworkers have faced this problem at some point. The only practical solution is to remove the discolored metal and regrind a new bevel.

Set the tool rest at 90 degrees to the face of the stone and gently grind away the blued edge. Think of it as turning your chisel into a screwdriver (see photo at right). The advantage to flat grinding the end is that it leaves a thick edge to dissipate the heat generated when regrinding the bevel. Be sure to keep the edge square to the side of the chisel.

Regrinding the bevel will take time because a great deal of metal must be removed. Maintain a light touch, and be patient. Once the new bevel has been formed your chisel should be as good as new—just a little shorter.

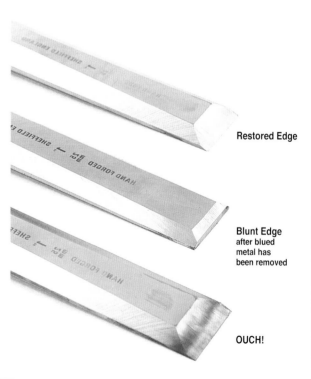

Restored Edge

Blunt Edge
after blued
metal has
been removed

OUCH!

Planer Blade Sharpening Jig

I re-sharpen disposable planer blades a few times, using a shop-made jig, before tossing the blades away. I use a set of three diamond hones to sharpen the blade at an angle 5° higher than the factory bevel to minimize the amount of metal I have to remove.

The jig is a single block that's 1½" thick, 2½" wide and about 15" long. My blades have a 45° bevel, so I cut a 50° bevel on one side of the block. I also cut a rabbet on the top of the block for the blade to nest in. The blade barely protrudes over the block's bevel when it's nested in the rabbet. I drilled some holes in the top of the block so I can secure the blade with screws when honing.

The lower end of the stone rests on the jig when I hone. This maintains the same angle with each stroke. Typically, I make five passes each with coarse, fine and extra-fine diamond hones. I count the number of strokes used on each edge so the knives end up the same width. After honing the bevels, I turn the blade over and remove the wire edges with the extra-fine hone.

Rabbet

Protractor Angle Gauge

When I was in high school, my math teacher showed us an easy way to indicate angles. She simply fastened two see-through plastic protractors on top of one another. I've used this simple devise to draw and check angles in my workshop ever since.

Start with a pair of identical protractors from an office supply store (about $1 each). Carefully drill out the center holes to exactly fit a 6-32 x ⅜-in. flat-head machine screw. Next, drill a countersink for the screw head in the bottom protractor, so the protractor sits flat for drawing angles. Install the screw and nut, making sure the protractors are precisely aligned. During use, the top protractor's zero line indicates the angle on the bottom protractor's scale. The angle matches the opening, because the bottom edges of the protractors are parallel to the zero lines.

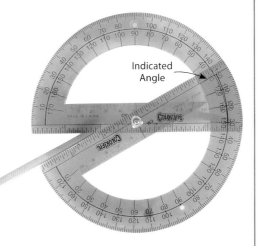

Indicated Angle

Sanding Belt Lapping Jig

You can chew up a lot of sandpaper flattening a plane iron, a large chisel or the bottom of a plane. It makes sense to use paper that lasts a long time–like a sanding belt. But, if you cut a belt to lay open, it won't sit flat, because its backing is too stiff.

To overcome this problem, I devised a jig that stretches a belt very tight. I only use it with coarse grits—60, 80, and 100—for tools that need a lot of flattening. The jig is double-sided, of course, so you'll use the whole belt. It won't slip when you're flattening, because the abrasive on the bottom grips your workbench.

I made this jig for the 6x48 belts that go on my combination disc/belt sander, but it could be any size. The body consists of three ¾"

MDF pieces laminated together. After gluing, flatten the faces by rubbing the blank on sheets of sandpaper taped to the top of a tablesaw. Round the ends by making 45° cuts on both ends of the blank, then soften the sharp corners with a file. Cut off the short end and make opposing wedges to pull the belt tight.

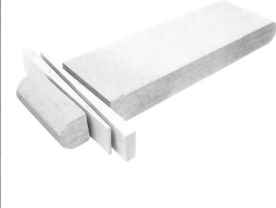

Plastic Shim

Shaky Grinder

My grinder shakes like crazy. Does this mean that the motor shaft is bent or the bearings are shot?

Your problem most likely lies with the wheels, not the motor. They're probably out of round and unbalanced, common conditions of new or old wheels.

Trueing your wheels perfectly round is a simple matter of routine maintenance. After trueing, your grinder should run with little vibration. But if you want your grinder to run even better, and produce a smoother, more even finish on your tools, you can take the extra step of balancing your wheels. This requires purchasing a balancing kit.

Before you true your wheels, try one simple trick to reduce vibration. Unplug the grinder and remove both wheel covers. Loosen the nut on one wheel and rotate the wheel ¼ turn, without turning the shaft (Photo 1). Tighten the nut, replace the wheel covers, plug in the machine and turn it on. If it vibrates about the same amount, try rotating the wheel another ¼ turn, and so on. Grinding wheels may be denser, and thus heavier, on one side. This procedure offsets the imbalance of one wheel with the other, but it doesn't always work.

You'll need a pencil and a dresser to true your wheels. Many types of dressers are available, but a T-style diamond dresser is the easiest to use.

A common problem with trueing is not removing enough material to make the wheel perfectly round, so it's smart to mark your wheels first (Photo 2). Set your tool rest 90 degrees to the wheel, turn on the grinder and true with the dresser (Photo 3). Wheels wear down unevenly, so it's a good idea to repeat this procedure now and then.

Balance your wheels, if you wish, after trueing them (Photo 4). Using a balancing kit is much more effective than rotating the wheels to offset differences in wheel density.

To reduce vibration, try rotating one wheel ¼ turn or more on the shaft. You may find that the wheel runs smoother in one position than another.

Trueing your wheel to make it perfectly round is the best way to reduce vibration. Mark the wheel's entire circumference, rotating the wheel by hand.

Dress the wheel to remove its high spots. Stop the wheel on occasion and check to see whether any pencil marks remain. Keep dressing until they're all gone.

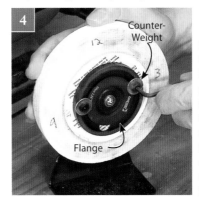

Balance the wheels with a special kit to make your grinder run even smoother. Two new wheel flanges are included. Each flange has moveable counterweights to offset differences in a wheel's density.

Counter-Weight

Flange

Sharpening a No. 80 Scraper Blade

I bought a No. 80 scraper to help me smooth big flat surfaces, but I can't get the hang of sharpening it and raising the burr. What should I be doing?

One of our editors, Tom Caspar, is a long-time user of this scraper, and recommends the simple jig shown here for both sharpening the blade and raising the burr. Make the jig from a thick piece of hardwood, with a wide bevel cut at 45 degrees on one side. Cut a wide bandsaw or handsaw kerf to hold the blade right where the bevel meets the flat surface. Then draw a guide line on the block at a 20-degree angle.

To sharpen the blade, place it in the jig, and clamp the jig in a vise, which secures the blade tightly. Use a mill bastard file to sharpen the blade, holding it against the beveled surface and moving it sideways across the block. When the blade is smooth and straight, remove the wire edge with a slipstone. Then burnish the edge, keeping the burnisher parallel to the guideline.

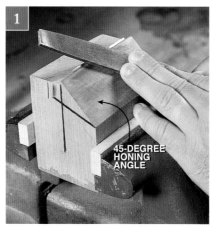

45-DEGREE HONING ANGLE

Guide the file with this simple jig. The scraper's edge must be dead straight and form a wire edge along its entire length.

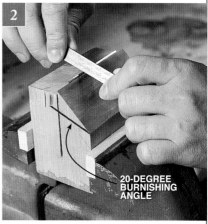

20-DEGREE BURNISHING ANGLE

Turn over a hook on the blade with the corner of a triangular burnisher. Hold the burnisher at the angle scribed on the jig.

Angles to Remember

To keep things simple, burn these three numbers in your memory banks: 25°, 30° and 35°. These are the three most commonly used angles when grinding and honing chisels and plane blades. If you prefer to grind and hone your tools with a single bevel, just remember one number for each type of tool.

If you prefer a double bevel, make the grinding angle 5° less than the honing angle. A general purpose chisel, for example, is ground at 25° and honed at 30°.

The most widely used honing angle for a bench plane's blade is 30°. I prefer 35°, because a steeper edge lasts longer.

CHISELS ———————

PARING   GENERAL PURPOSE   MORTISING

——————— PLANE BLADES

BLOCK PLANE   BENCH PLANES

Sharpening Bits

Can I sharpen my own carbide router bits?

The short answer is no. It takes the specialized equipment of a professional sharpening service to properly sharpen carbide bits, especially if they have any nicks in the edge. However, it is possible to hone the edge of a bit that's just starting to get dull.

You'll need a 1,200-grit diamond stone or fine diamond paddle to cut the hard carbide. Lay the bit so the cutter's face lies flat on the stone or paddle. Take a half dozen strokes or so on each cutter face. Count your strokes. Lubricate the stone or paddle with water or a lightweight oil, such as 3-In-One. It's important to take an equal amount off each cutter. Check for sharpness by visually inspecting the edge. You should see no spots where light reflects back off the cutting edge.

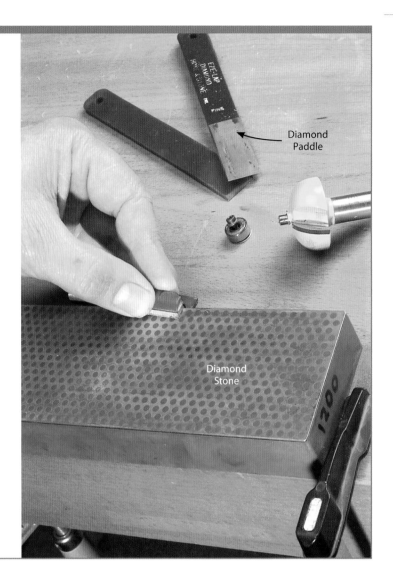

Diamond Paddle

Diamond Stone

Surefire Scraper Filing

You've probably heard other woodworkers talk about what a great tool the scraper is, but maybe you've never had much luck with one yourself. Using them is easy; getting a good edge on them is the tough part. The hardest step in sharpening a scraper is the first one—filing the edge square and flat. Start off right with this easy-to-make file holder:

Cut a kerf equal to the thickness of an 8-in. mill file in a 1¼-in. thick by 4-in. wide by 6-in.-long piece of wood. The kerf should be a little deeper than half the width of the file. This allows you to set the file at different depths to avoid dulling it in one spot. Clamp the scraper in a wood-jaw vise. Push the scraper firmly against the holder while filing for a perfectly square edge.

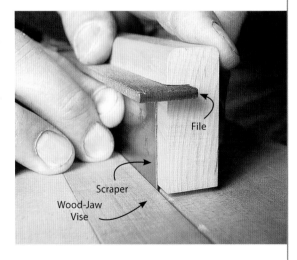

File

Scraper

Wood-Jaw Vise

Sharpening Curved Scrapers

I'm struggling to get a good cutting edge on my concave card scraper. Any tips?

Here's the inside scoop on those inside curves. It's a lot easier to get good results if you concentrate on creating a hook on one side only.

Here's how it works: Start by creating a slight bevel on the edge (Photo 1). Then remove the wire edge (Photo 2). Finally, use your burnisher to roll the cutting hook (Photo 3).

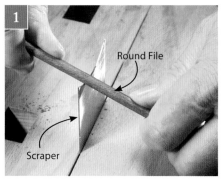

File a slight bevel on the curve. With the scraper held in a vise, push a chainsaw file at a slight angle until you feel a continuous wire edge on the high side of the bevel.

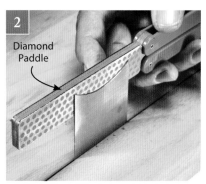

Remove the wire edge with a super-fine diamond paddle. Because you have created a beveled edge, the wire edge will only form on the high side of the bevel.

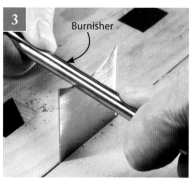

Use a burnisher to roll the edge and create the cutting hook. Hold the burnisher almost flat and use firm pressure to form the cutting hook. A drop or two of light machine oil helps.

Sharp Edge Protection

To protect the sharp edges of my scrapers and fine handsaws, I use the spine from a plastic page protector. They're available at office supply stores. Two bucks will get you a pack of six. They are easily cut to length with a utility knife.

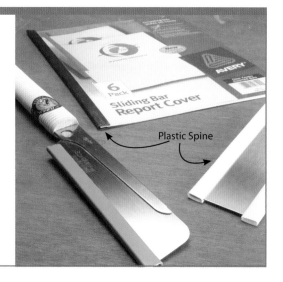

The Hollow-Ground Bevel: What's the Big Deal?

The name "hollow-ground bevel" has been widely misused. I'd like to set the record straight as to what a hollow-ground bevel is, what it's good for, and when to avoid it. It's simply a concave bevel—the natural result of using a grinding wheel. The wheel is convex, of course, so it always creates a bevel that's concave.

A tool with a hollow-ground bevel is easier to sharpen by hand, without the use of a jig. The biggest problem with honing by hand is holding the tool at the correct angle with every stroke. A hollow-ground bevel helps you find and maintain that angle, so there's no wasted effort.

With a hollow grind, you simply rock the tool up and down until it locks in place, resting on the bevel's heel and toe. Two points of support make the difference—it would be much harder to feel the correct angle if the bevel were flat, rather than concave. That's why we have arches in our feet-they make balancing easier.

I often sharpen chisels by hand, without a jig, simply because it's so easy. Ditto for plow plane and rabbeting plane irons that are awkward or impossible to hold in a jig. I do use a jig for honing standard-thickness bench plane irons, though. Even with a hollow grind, their bevels are too narrow for me to maintain that correct angle with every pass on the stone.

So when is a hollow-ground bevel not appropriate? Japanese tools and Western mortising chisels should not be hollow ground. Ideally, Japanese tools should be ground with a flat bevel, to maximize support of the tip. The steel of Japanese tools can be brittle; without adequate support, a tip could fracture. Mortising chisels should be flat ground, too, or made slightly convex, for the same reason. To withstand heavy blows, their tips need to be as strong as possible.

Vacuum Lapping Dust

The best way to keep your sandpaper clean when lapping is to vacuum it. Sandpaper is much less efficient when it clogs up with swarf (a machinist's term for metal debris). Removing the swarf every few strokes makes a tedious chore go faster. Cleaning the sandpaper with a stiff brush or an eraser works so-so, but a vacuum removes everything, almost instantly, with no mess.

Toss or Sharpen?

My large Forstner bit seems awfully dull. Can I sharpen it?

You certainly can. You'll be amazed at how much faster and cleaner a Forstner bit cuts when it's really sharp. In fact, some new bits aren't sharp enough. They'll perform much better if you sharpen them right out of the package.

You'll need two tools for sharpening: a flat diamond hone for the chippers and a convex diamond hone for the rim. Oilstone or ceramic hones will work OK, but you'll probably get better results with diamond hones because they work faster. It's important to retain the bit's original geometry. The more honing strokes you take, the greater the chance that you'll round

over a bevel and create an extra-steep angle. The type of hone that cuts the fastest is thus the best choice, and you can't beat diamond for speed.

Flat diamond hones come in a variety of sizes. I prefer a narrow, tapered style, because it's the easiest one to balance on the bit's chipper (Photo 1). If your bit is particularly dull, use a coarse flat hone.

During each honing step, secure the bit in a wooden-jawed vise, so you don't mar the shaft. Hone the chipper's short bevel first, then move to the long bevel (Photo 2). If the long bevel's surface is quite rough with machining marks, create a smooth micro-bevel by leaning the

hone one or two degrees above the flat surface. Sharpen the rim with a round hone (Photo 3). Some round hones have a small diameter, but a large diameter works better on big bits. The best all-purpose round hone is conical, tapering from large to small diameters.

Begin sharpening by honing the chippers' short bevels. Continue until you feel a wire edge or burr develop on the bevel's tip.

Next, hone the chipper's long bevel. Lay the hone flat on the bevel or raise it slightly to create a microbevel. Stop honing when the wire edge is gone.

Hone the rim's bevel with a convex hone. Follow the original angle, rubbing back and forth around the circle. Don't hone the rim's wall.

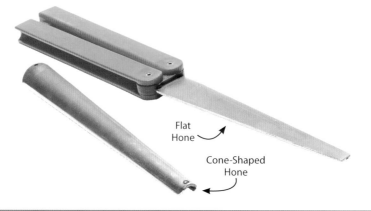

Flat Hone

Cone-Shaped Hone

Sharpening Hollow Chisels

My mortiser's hollow chisels have become quite dull. How can I restore their sharp edges before my right arm gets to be twice the size of my left?

Mortising with a dull hollow chisel can be a strain on you and your equipment. But, there is hope for those aching arm muscles.

Clico Tooling Ltd. of Sheffield, England, makes a hardened-steel sharpener for hollow chisels (Photo 1). The sharpener, which is actually a machinist's reamer, comes with interchangeable guide bushings for each chisel size; ¼, ⁵⁄₁₆, ⅜, and ½-in. Simply attach the right-size bushing to the sharpener and chuck it in a brace. Clamp the bit in a vice, insert the bushing and turn the sharpener using light downward pressure (Photo 2). The reamer shaves the metal so it doesn't take many turns to complete the job. Take off just enough metal to create a tiny burr on the outside edges of the chisel. Lightly hone the outside of the bit to remove the burr. The Clico is a foolproof system and will do a great job of sharpening your hollow chisels. The only drawback is price; around $90. Then again new chisels are around $40 a pop so it almost pays for itself in two sharpenings.

A low-cost alternative is Dremel's conical grinding stone ($3). Chuck the stone in a

CLICO SHARPENER

GUIDE BUSHINGS

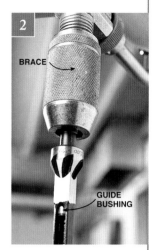

BRACE

GUIDE BUSHING

CONICAL STONE

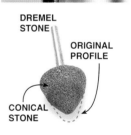

DREMEL STONE

ORIGINAL PROFILE

CONICAL STONE

variable-speed drill to sharpen a chisel (Photo 3). Compared to the Clico, the stone is slow and requires a steady hand, making it harder to get a good edge on all four sides. We also had to flatten the tip of the stone to make it fit our ⅜-in Delta chisel, but this is easy to do. Simply take it to the grinder with the stone chucked in the drill. Turn the drill and the grinder on and hold the spinning stone against the face of the wheel. (Spinning the stone ensures even removal of material.) Rock the drill back and forth a bit as you grind to maintain the conical shape.

Treat Sharpening Stone Water

Waterstones have always been my preferred method to produce a razor-sharp edge. I store them in a plastic tub filled with water, so they're always ready to go. In warm weather, the tub and stones can become rather slimy. To prevent this, I add a capful of bleach when I replenish the water.

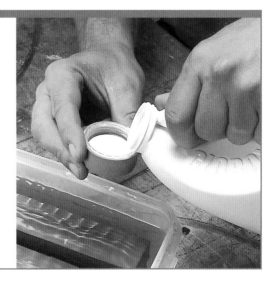

The Right Grinding Wheel for Your Shop

I've been told that the gray wheels that came with my grinder will burn my woodworking tools and that white wheels are better. True?

The stock wheels that come with most grinders are hard, coarse and designed for the metalworking trade. They're way too hard for grinding the hardened steel in chisels and plane irons. It sounds strange, but the harder the steel, the softer the bond in the wheel should be. Here's why: Hard steel quickly dulls the abrasive particles in a wheel. With a soft bond, the dull abrasive sloughs off quickly, leaving fresh, sharp abrasive to do the work. A hard bond, on the other hand, holds tight to the abrasive particles, even after they're dull. The dull or "glazed" wheel rubs as much as it cuts, creating the friction and heat that toast your tools.

The best all-around grinding wheel for woodworking tools is an 80-grit aluminum oxide wheel with a relatively soft bond designated by the letter H, J or K on the wheel label (Photo 1). An H bond is the softest and will provide the coolest grinding. Turners tend to prefer a J grade wheel; its harder bond resists grooving by gouges and parting tools.

Smart buyers read labels. Look for a series of numbers and letters that usually comes after the wheel size (Photo 1). It's best to be color-blind when you are buying a new wheel (Photo 2). Instead, trust the label to give you the precise information you need.

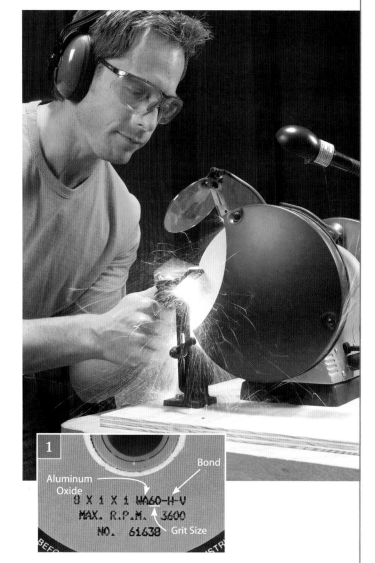

Look for three things on a grinding wheel label. First, the letter A, which stands for aluminum oxide, the abrasive you'll want. Next is the grit size; a 60- or 80-grit wheel is best. Finally, a letter right after the grit size represents the hardness of the bond. Letters from H to K are considered soft bonds, with H being the softest.

Don't let color be your guide. Aluminum oxide is made from bauxite, a naturally white mineral that can be given any color in manufacturing. The only way to really know what you're getting is to read the label.

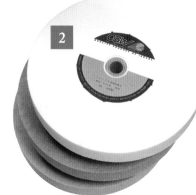

Waterstone Mat

When I switched from oilstones to waterstones back in the Paleozoic era, I thought that I could say goodbye to making a big mess while sharpening. Well, not exactly. Waterstones are messy, too, when you keep their surfaces flooded with water—as you should.

I've been looking for the best method of containing the mess for years, and modern technology has finally delivered: a rubber garden paver. It's about 16" square, ¾" thick, and made from recycled tires. Water beads up on it, and best of all, the surface is a bit rough and sticky, so stones stay put. You don't need a holder or clamps or anything–just your stones and the mat.

Similar material is used for floor underlayment for gyms, so you may be able to scrounge a mat for free, but these pavers are now available at home centers. I'll bet they'll last forever.

What's the Deal with Microbevels?

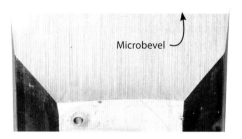

Microbevel

A microbevel sounds like a pretty sophisticated concept, but the idea is really quite simple. A microbevel is just a very short bevel that's honed at a slightly steeper angle than the rest of a tool's bevel. You create it in the last stage of the honing process, using your finest stone.

Why bother? Well, a microbevel has two significant benefits. First, it gives you an extremely sharp edge with a minimum amount of effort. When you're honing on your finest stone, each stroke doesn't remove a whole lot of steel. There's no point in making the whole bevel as smooth and shiny as possible, so it makes sense to concentrate your efforts right at the business end, where it counts. And that's what happens when you raise the honing angle a degree or two.

A microbevel also makes your edge last a bit longer. Think of your blade as a wedge. A thin wedge is going to dull quicker than a thick wedge, right? A 35° edge, for example, will stay sharp longer than a 25° edge. So any increase in a bevel's angle helps an edge stay sharp, even if it's only a degree or two.

What's What With Bevels

So we're all on the same page, here's a visual guide to 5 types of bevels that are used on chisels and plane blades.

Single bevel

A blade with a single bevel is ground and honed at the same angle.

Double bevel

A blade with a double bevel is ground at a lower angle and honed at a higher angle. The difference between the ground bevel and the honed bevel is usually 5°.

Hollow ground bevel

A hollow ground bevel is made on a grinding wheel, which creates a concave shape.

Microbevel

A microbevel is a very short bevel that is one or two degrees steeper than the honing bevel. The blade may have a single bevel or a double bevel.

Back bevel

A back bevel is an optional type of microbevel for a plane blade.

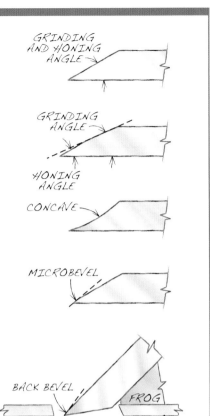

Why Are New Chisels So Dull?

Whenever I buy a blade, like a tablesaw blade or a router bit, it's always sharp. How come when I buy chisels they're duller than a math lecture on the last day of school?

Although it seems reasonable to expect new chisels to come sharp, there are three good reasons why they don't.

First, sharpening is expensive. Some chisels do come presharpened, but they cost about $5 more per chisel. Would you be willing to pay for the first sharp edge when you'll resharpen your chisel dozens of times?

Second, the roughly ground edge on a new chisel is actually a useful secondary bevel. At 25 degrees, it's a lower angle than the chisel is meant to cut at. Your job is to hone the chisel to the primary angle: 30 degrees. The manufacturer has saved you some time by giving you a lower angle so now you have only to hone the tip of the chisel.

Third, a sharp edge is fragile. Chances are it wouldn't survive shipping and handling. With a dull edge, you know what you've got.

Thanks to Zach Etheridge of Highland Hardware for help with this answer.

Factory-Ground Bevel

Which Sharpening Stones?

I'm just starting out in woodworking and need advice on sharpening stones.

We put your question to Peter Korn at the Center for Furniture Craftsmanship and here is his response:

There are four types of sharpening stones used for woodworking tools: waterstones, oilstones, diamond stones and ceramic stones. Each has markedly different working characteristics. Of the four, waterstones and oilstones give the best overall performance. Ceramic stones are the slowest cutting and the finest diamond stone is too coarse to create a satisfactory cutting edge.

The two components of a sharpening stone are an abrasive and a binder. Abrasives vary in sharpness and durability, binders differ in hardness.

Waterstones are the clear choice for most sharpening applications. They give superior results with the greatest economy of effort. Waterstones are characterized by a soft binder, which allows worn abrasive particles to break free, exposing sharp ones underneath. The good news is the stone stays sharp; the bad news is the stone tends to wear unevenly and needs to be flattened regularly. In our shop at the Center for Furniture Craftsmanship we use diamond stones to keep our waterstones flat. A 1000 grit and a 6000 grit make a complete set and cost $50.

Oilstones are the next best choice for woodshop sharpening. They have a hard binder, which makes them slower cutting than waterstones, because the abrasive particles tend to dull and clog with use. However, the hard binder is an advantage for sharpening applications where a waterstone might be gouged or grooved, such as narrow carving tools and odd-shaped blades, such as inshaves. In terms of coarseness, a soft Arkansas and a fine India stone are roughly equivalent to an 800-grit waterstone while a hard Arkansas is closest to a 1000-grit waterstone. (Expect to pay $55 to $64 for a soft and a hard Arkansas.)

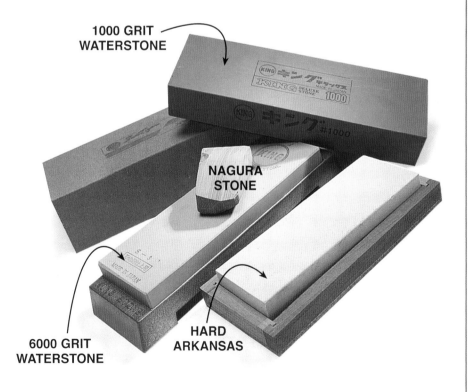

1000 GRIT WATERSTONE

NAGURA STONE

6000 GRIT WATERSTONE

HARD ARKANSAS

Storing Tools & Supplies

Instant Drawers

Large plastic boxes, the kind that restaurants use for bussing dishes, are perfect for shop drawers. They're strong, durable and lightweight, plus they have built-in handles. They're perfect for storing and transporting workshop essentials, from screws to power tools. They come ready-made and they're super-easy to install. I'll never build another storage drawer!

Bus boxes are designed to hang from their rims, so screwed-on cleats make perfect drawer supports. I like to graduate the distance between cleats, so the bottom boxes have more headroom. This wider spacing makes it easier to see what's inside the lower boxes. For large items, I reduce the number of boxes in the stack, so each box has ample headroom.

Ceiling Drawers

To eke out every cubic inch of storage in a basement shop, try these boxes that hang between your ceiling joists. When a drawer is down, you have easy access to its contents. A lag screw or bolt works well for a pivot and a pair of pivoting cleats holds each drawer in place. They're perfect for tools and supplies you don't need to get at all the time.

Cheap, Easy Storage

I found a quick, cheap and easy way to store lots of little stuff like biscuits, screws, wood plugs and the like. Drill a hole in the cap of a plastic soda bottle and insert an eyebolt. Secure the eyebolt with two nuts, one above and one inside the cap. Finally, cut a round hole in the shoulder of the bottle.

One cool thing about this storage system is if I knock one of these bottles off my workbench, all the stuff inside doesn't spill out. It gets trapped in the neck of the bottle rather then spilling out the opening.

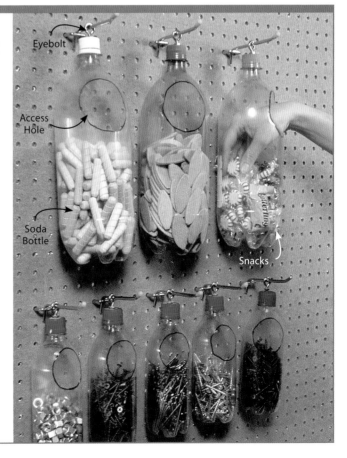

Deep Drawer Organizer

I built a deep drawer for my workbench so I would have lots of storage, but it created another problem. The tools I wanted were always at the bottom of the heap. I solved my frustration by adding an upper and lower tray. The upper tray slides forward or backward on top of the lower tray, making the lower tools fully accessible. Both trays are removable, so I can carry them closer to a project, if I need to.

I made my trays out of ⅜-in.-thick pine and assembled them with glue and brad nails.

Upper Tray

Lower Tray

Get the Clutter Off Your Bench

I found a new place to store dispensers right under my nose. Any lightweight stuff that comes in a box can be fastened to the bottom of a cupboard and still leave plenty of room over the counter below. A little double-faced tape or hot-melt glue makes a strong but temporary bond.

Double-Faced Tape

Hardware Storage Cabinet

Plastic bins are excellent for storing hardware and other small items. After purchasing all the types and sizes of bins I needed, including some complete cabinets, I made this shelf unit to neatly house them in one place.

Quick ID Parts Bin

Like most people, I keep lots of different screws, bolts, nails, washers, and other small parts in bins. Instead of paper labels, I hot glue a sample of the actual part on the outside of the bin. It's much easier to locate what I need by eye than by name. If I ever run out of parts, I can always remove the one on the bin's front!

Shop Apron Magnets

Small tools are easier to reach since I added two rare-earth magnets to my apron. I epoxied the ½" dia. magnets to two 1" square pieces of leather, punched ½" holes in the apron, and then epoxied the leather squares to the apron's back side.

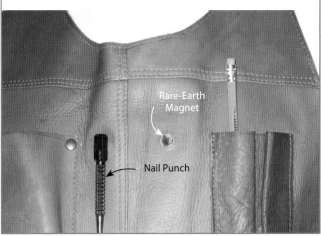

Rare-Earth Magnet

Nail Punch

Easy Sliding Drawers

Wood cleats make good drawer runners for shop storage cabinets because they don't gum up like ball-bearing slides and they're cheap. The downside is that wood runners wear down and are likely to stick. The fix is simple: Glue a strip of plastic laminate to the top of the cleats. The drawers will slide like they're on ice.

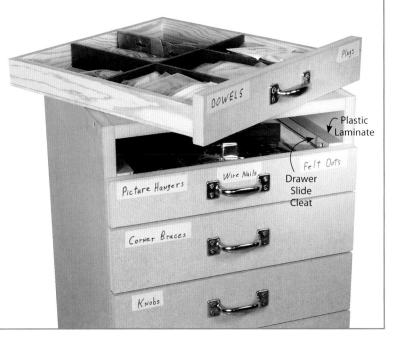

Plugs

DOWELS

Plastic Laminate

Felt Dots

Wire Nails

Drawer Slide Cleat

Picture Hangers

Corner Braces

Knobs

Jumbo Tape Dispenser

I have five or six different kinds of tape in my shop, and last weekend I got fed up with rooting through a drawer to find the one I wanted. To solve the problem, I built this tape dispenser that holds a variety of tape widths and types.

I made my dispenser from scraps of ¾-in. birch lumber but plywood will work. Almost all regular-size rolls of tape have a 3-in. center hole, so the same size filler block will work for most rolls.

I made my filler blocks 2³⁄₁₆-in. square and rounded the corners until I got a tight fit inside the roll. The axle was simply a ¾-in. dowel. The axle fits into a slot in the dividers. I cut the slots on my router table using a ¾-in.-dia. straight bit. They are ¼-in. deep and 1½-in. long.

A hacksaw blade on the front panel serves as the tape-cutting edge. If you need a roll closer to your project, just lift it out and take it with you.

Hacksaw Blade

Filler Block

Wall-Hung Storage Bins

I recently bought a big stack of plastic storage bins at a flea market. I got a great deal on them, but they didn't come with any hanger strips. I came up with my own hanger by using a piece of colonial-style base molding attached with the good side toward the wall. The bins hang perfectly from the thin top edge. Boy, now my hardware is going to finally be organized!

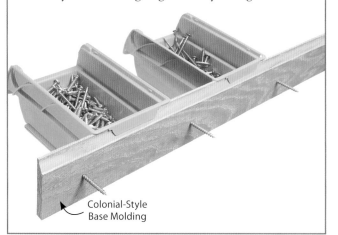

Colonial-Style Base Molding

Quick-and-Easy Storage Boxes

I finally found a use for all that scrap plywood I've been hanging onto. I made a bunch of small storage boxes with it and a small shelf to put them on. They're quick to build. Just glue and nail the ends to the bottom and then glue and nail on the sides. That's it! They're so handy I think I'll go and build some more right now.

Storage Hang-Up

I'm a neat freak and I jump at any idea that keeps stuff off my bench. I built a glue bottle perch for my pegboard just for that reason. It's just a couple of boards with a cutoff section of PVC pipe screwed to the back and a pair of holes for the peg hangers. The PVC ring keeps the bottle secure on its perch. The glue bottle loves it's new home above the fray on my bench. I've expanded the idea to include my biscuit container and I'm making one for my coffee cup next.

Spray Can Storage

I'm a great fan of aerosol finishes, especially now that many of them have adjustable tips that make much less splatter. But my shop got so cluttered with half-used cans that I had trouble finding the color I wanted, so I built this simple storage rack for all the cans. Now I can instantly find just the color I'm looking for. The shelves need to be 5-in. deep, but the angle isn't critical. Anything between 45 to 75 degrees will work. Mine is 70 degrees.

Tackle Box Storage

This is my all-time favorite way to store screws, small hardware and router bits. Fishing tackle boxes come in a variety of sizes and shapes but I picked this one because the inner utility boxes have lids to keep stuff from spilling and the adjustable dividers allow me to use the trays for both short and long items. This tackle box, including the three big lower utility boxes, cost $25. The five small upper utility boxes are sold separately for $2 each. I have over 70 different items stored in my tackle box!

Driver-Bit Storage

Upper Utility Boxes

Lower Utility Boxes

Drill Press Storage

I packed plenty of storage under my drill press by recycling an old kitchen cabinet. To make it fit around the column of the drill press, I moved the cabinet's back panel in about 8 in. and shortened up the drawer a few inches. I added a new plastic-laminate top and mounted pull-out dividers inside, using full-extension drawer slides. A set of casters makes the whole thing easy to move when I have to sweep. The removable drill bit indexes make storing and handling different bits a breeze.

Angled Hanging Strip

Full-Extension Drawer Slide

Pullout Divider

Benchtop Lazy Susan

I finally got fed up with rummaging through a drawer of small screwdrivers, nail sets and dental picks to find the one tool I needed. I built a revolving tool stand to make them more accessible.

The stand is composed of three layers, glued together, and mounted on a lazy Susan ring (www.leevalley.com, #12K01.3, $3.10). The bottom layer is 2" thick and 8" square; the middle layer is 1" thick and 6" square; the top layer is 1" thick and 4" square. I drilled lots of holes for my tools in the 1" rim on each layer and on top.

Hanging Bit Box

I use my tablesaw extension wing for a router table. It's a great space saver, but I got tired of running back and forth to my bench to get router bits and wrenches. Then the lightbulb went on! A simple plywood box with pullout trays for bits and wrenches fits perfectly under the router table. I hung the box from the table extension with screws and used carpet tape to stick the extruded polystyrene insulation board to the ¼-in. hardboard tray. I added a door to keep out dust and shavings.

Sliding Door

1½" Polystyrene Insulation Board

Benchtop Tool System

My shop is in a two-car garage, which (outrageously enough) I must share with two cars. That's why I use benchtop tools. Unfortunately, they're somewhat hard to store.

My solution is a two-part benchtop tool system that's as versatile as it is compact. The first part is a simple storage rack to keep all my tools off the floor. The second part is a Black & Decker Work-Mate that I bought at a home center. It serves as a sturdy workstation for each tool.

My benchtop tools are bolted to four plywood bases that slide into the rack. Nothing special so far. But the plywood bases have a center 2x2 frame that's slightly smaller than the maximum opening on my Work-Mate. Once I set the tool in place, a single turn of the clamping handles holds the tool securely. The resulting workstation is remarkably solid, doesn't "walk" across the floor, and can be quickly stowed away when I need the space for something else.

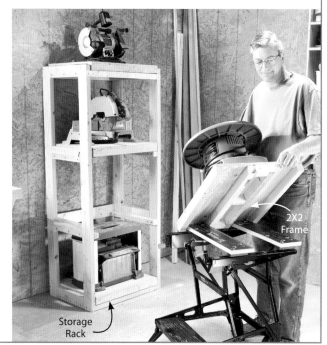

2X2 Frame

Storage Rack

Cordless Drill Stand

Even though most cordless drills are designed to stand on their own, they still fall over easily. Mine took one too many dives off the workbench. This drove me to build this stand to give my drill a secure home. It also provides a handy place to keep my most commonly used driver bits.

To make the stand, I glued and screwed together boards that are 1 in. thick by 6 in. wide. I positioned the holster board (B) at a comfortable grabbing angle of 60 degrees. The holster slot measures 2 in. wide by 3½ in. deep. The angles on the brace (A) are 15 degrees at the top and 45 degrees at the bottom. You may need to adjust the angles and dimensions to match your particular drill.

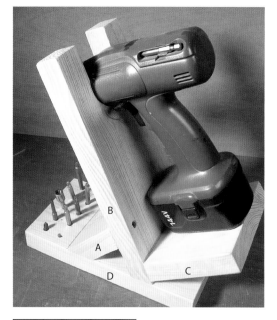

	Part	L
A	Brace	3¾"
B	Holster	12"
C	Support	5"
D	Base	10"

Clandestine Tool Chest

I transformed this dresser for my daughter, who didn't like the way her husband's metal tool chest looked in their apartment. For these newlyweds, shop space wasn't in their budget and he needed a place to park his tools.

My daughter had always liked this old relic, which occupied a corner of our attic for years. I simply knocked apart the two middle drawers and attached the fronts to a piece of plywood. I removed the divider that originally separated the two drawers and installed new plywood shelves, using the drawer runners as supports.

I mounted the new door with a continuous hinge and installed a spring catch to hold it closed. My daughter loves the stylish addition to their décor and my son-in-law is happy to have his tools handy.

Hideaway Tool Stand

My bench grinder is out of the way but instantly accessible, thanks to this sturdy flip-up table. It works great and it's simple to make. You'll only need a scrap of ¾-in. plywood that's ½-in. narrower than the overhang, four 3-in. butt hinges, a strap hinge and a length of 1x4.

Build It

1. Mount three butt hinges to the underside of the plywood table, with the barrels centered on the edge.
2. Fasten the table to the benchtop.
3. Install the remaining butt hinge on the far side of the foot. Make sure it's aligned with the outer hinge on the table.
4. Make the hinged brace from two 1x4s of equal length. The brace's overall length is the distance between the barrels of the two centered hinges with the table fully open.
5. Attach one 1x4 to the foot hinge and the other to the top hinge. Rejoin the two halves by attaching the strap hinge.
6. Fasten the 10-in.-long brace lock to the upper 1x4.
7. Install pivoting support blocks to hold the table in the folded-under position.
8. Open the table and install the benchtop tool of your choice.

Strap Hinge

Butt Hinge

Brace Lock

Hinged Brace

Perf-Board Shelving

I use a perf-board over my bench to keep tools organized and within easy reach. These shelves take the concept one step further and remove the clutter that tends to build up on a workbench. Use 2x4s and ¼-in. L hooks to make the shelves. Chamfer the top back edge so the shelf can be tipped in and tighten the L hooks for a snug fit against the perf-board. These shelves are surprisingly strong and can be sized to fit your specific needs.

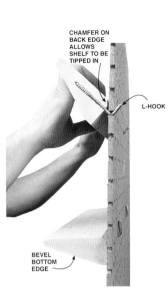

CHAMFER ON BACK EDGE ALLOWS SHELF TO BE TIPPED IN

L-HOOK

BEVEL BOTTOM EDGE

SCREW A SUPPORT BRACKET ONTO DEEP SHELVES

Hook Your Cordless Drills

I've been using an old metal-working vise in my shop for years. Occasionally I really do need a metal-working vise, but most often I use it to hold drawer sides up high when cutting dovetails. Unfortunately the metal jaws can be a hazard to edge tools and they can mar the surface of the wood. I solved these problems by adding a pair of soft jaws to the vise. The jaws are just two pieces of pine with a couple holes for recessed rare earth magnets. The soft jaws literally snap in place to provide a non-marring clamp surface for my stock plus a non-threatening surface for my edge tools.

Simple Storage for Layout Tools

I used to keep my layout tools in a toolbox, but they always banged around against each other. I needed a better way to store them, so I came up with this simple rack. All it took was a chunk of 2x6 and some angle cuts spaced about 1½ in. apart. Now my layout tools are protected from damage and readily available. Plus, it turned out to be a good way to store my scrapers too.

Tablesaw Blade Rack

I'm always trying to eke out more space in my shop, and I found some hidden under my tablesaw behind the bevel crank. There's just enough space back there to hang a blade rack. I made the rack with an angled bottom shelf so the blades stay in their slots when I'm rolling the saw around.

Angled Bottom Shelf

See-Through Chisel Holder

Here's a chisel rack that protects those sharp edges and allows me to see the right chisel for the job at hand.

The rack is easy to customize for any size chisels. Glue a 1-in.-wide strip of ½-in.-thick wood across a plywood backer board. Next, arrange your chisels across the 1-in. strip in whatever order you prefer. Add spacer blocks to fit the width of each chisel blade. A third ½-in. strip creates the chisel holes. A piece of acrylic screwed to the last strip protects the chisel edges and your hands.

Mobile Tool Cabinet

I bought my current house because of the big detached garage, which is perfect for my woodshop. However, when I started remodeling the house I got really tired of lugging boxes of tools from the garage to the house every weekend. To make things easier on my back, I made this mobile tool cabinet. It holds a variety of essential tools, which are easy to swap out for different tools when your needs change. I built this cabinet using 1x10 pine boards which are lightweight yet rugged. I fastened the cabinet sides to the top, bottom and shelves with biscuits, screws and glue. Then I glued and screwed the boards for the back. I added the pegboard inside to hang a variety of tools.

I surface-mounted the leaf hinges to the outside of the cabinet. This approach allows the doors to stop in an "open book" position. This makes accessing the tools on the doors much more convenient than if the doors swung all the way around to the sides of the cabinet.

I also added a small block of wood underneath the front edge of the cabinet so it tips backward slightly which helps keep the doors open when in use. To keep the doors closed I used a sliding bolt, but a screw eye and hook is equally simple and effective.

I attached the cabinet to a dolly with four conduit straps. All the materials, including the dolly, were purchased at a home center for about $40.

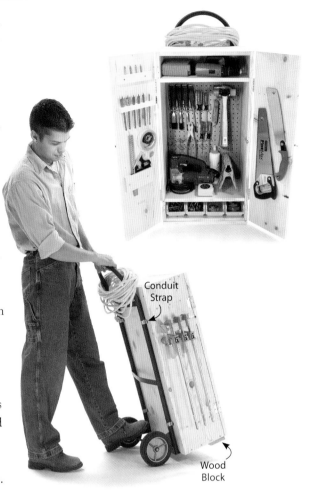

Conduit Strap

Wood Block

Cutting List		
Overall Dimensions: 18½" W x 36" T x 9¼" D		
Part	**Qty.**	**Length**
Doors, Sides and Back Panels	6	36"
Top, Bottom and Shelves	4	17"

Scraper Wallet

I love to use card scrapers for removing chatter marks, tear-out and any other smoothing that requires a delicate touch. Trouble is, they get dinged up in my toolbox.

When my wife bought herself a new leather wallet, I immediately snatched her old one. The leather compartments are perfect for storing and protecting my scrapers.

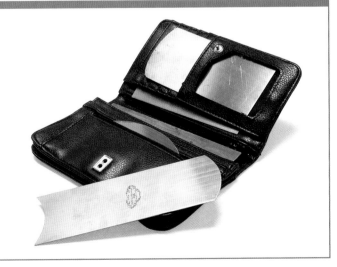

Storing Wood

Sheet Goods ATV

My shop is in a walkout basement with a steep grassy slope from the driveway. The skateboard-like devices made for moving stock work well on hard surfaces, but not on grass. My solution is an 8-ft.-long two-wheeled cart.

To build the cart, start with a 2½" wide strip of ¼" plywood, 8 ft. long. Glue and screw two ¾" square wood rails flush with each edge, leaving a 1" space between them. Fasten a stop block between the rails at one end. It doesn't matter if the rails go all the way to the other end.

Attach 7" lawn mower wheels with 3" lag screws and washers to the ends of an 18"-long 2x4. Screw and glue the 2x4 axle assembly to the plywood about 5 ft. from the stop block. To use the cart, load the sheet on edge between the rails with one end against the stop block. Lift the top corner of the sheet on the stop block end and roll it wherever you need it.

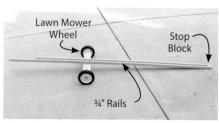

Lawn Mower Wheel

Stop Block

¾" Rails

Free Storage

I'd been using my typical cantilevered lumber rack for years when I realized I was wasting precious storage space. By screwing ¼-in. hardboard to the top and bottom of each support I created free storage space between the supports. I can fill the spaces with drawers or use them for general storage. Plus, I can store short stock without stacking it on long stock. Now there isn't a single inch of wasted space in my lumber rack.

Hideaway Bin for Short Stock

I've been using an old metal-working vise in my shop for years. Occasionally I really do need a metal-working vise, but most often I use it to hold drawer sides up high when cutting dovetails. Unfortunately the metal jaws can be a hazard to edge tools and they can mar the surface of the wood. I solved these problems by adding a pair of soft jaws to the vise. The jaws are just two pieces of pine with a couple holes for recessed rare earth magnets. The soft jaws literally snap in place to provide a non-marring clamp surface for my stock plus a non-threatening surface for my edge tools.

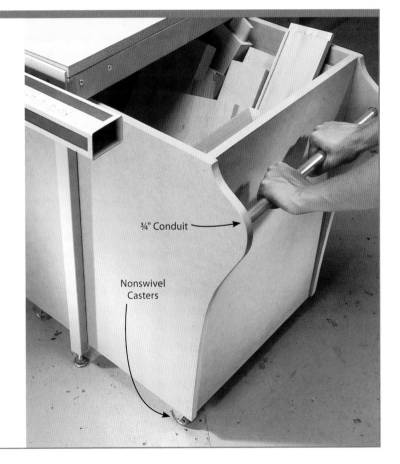

PVC Lumber Storage

In need of some quick lumber storage, I rummaged around my shop for a solution. I discovered a length of PVC pipe left over from a plumbing job and cut it into three 12" long pieces. I also found some ½" rope and cut it into three 5' long pieces. I tied knots on the ends of each piece, slipped them through the pipes, and used heavy-duty wire staples to attach the ropes to the ceiling joists. The knots keep the ropes from slipping through the staples. Once my racks were hung, I gave them the "pull-up test." They held my 250 lbs. with ease!

Rolling Scrap Bin

Who says you can't put a square peg in a round hole? My scrap bin is made from round cardboard tubes made for concrete forms. These tubes are available at home centers; they're durable, come in various diameters, and are easy to cut. I use their different diameters and lengths as a filing system for my scraps. My bin is on wheels so that I can move it from tool to tool.

To make the bin, I cut the tubes to length, glued and screwed a ¾" plywood disc inside the bottom of each tube, and screwed the tubes to a plywood base equipped with 3" casters. After the tubes were mounted, I glued them together where they touch for extra strength. Obviously, painting is optional.

High and Dry Ply

After ruining four $90 sheets of plywood by storing them on a damp floor, I came up with a simple fix: PVC feet.

Cut several 12" sections of 2" dia. PVC pipe in half, lengthwise. Apply traction tape to the convex side, so the plywood doesn't slide. Place the feet on your shop floor, and your sheet goods on the feet. It doesn't matter if the PVC gets wet—it'll last forever.

Plastic Stickers Don't Stain

I use plastic conduit to make stickers for stacking and drying my wood. These stickers provide consistent spacing and excellent air circulation with minimal contact. I've never had problems with insects, mold or staining, which can occur around wooden stickers, especially when the wood is green and the air is damp.

For strength, I use 1¼-in.-i.d. Schedule-80 rigid PVC electrical conduit. Available from home centers and electrical supply stores, it costs about $12 for a 10-ft. length. Schedule-40 rigid PVC conduit is much less expensive but thinner-walled, so it doesn't support as much weight. I only use it for small stacks. Both Schedule-40 and Schedule-80 rigid PVC conduit are suitable for indoor and outdoor use.

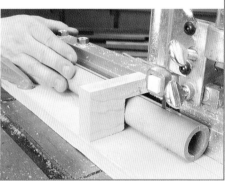

After cutting the conduit to sticker lengths, I cut them in half on my bandsaw, using a simple jig to hold the sticker in position (see photo, above). To keep the conduit from rotating during the cut, I follow a straight line drawn on its surface. To draw the line, I simply lay a flat board next to the conduit and use the board as a straightedge.

Plywood Carrier

You don't have to be built like an orangutan to carry plywood! This simple carrier extends your reach and turns an awkward job into an easy one. It's quick to build out of ¾-in. plywood, a scrap of 2x2, some glue and a few screws.

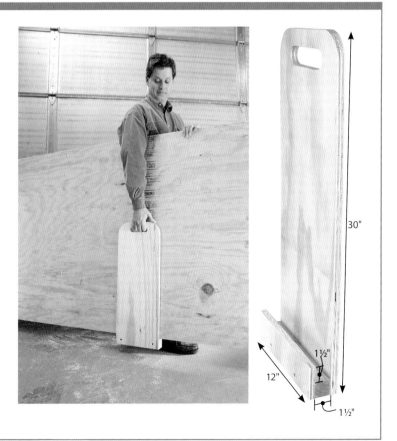

30"

12"

1½"

1½"

Sheet-Stock Dolly

Moving sheets of plywood around in my cramped shop was a real hassle until I made this little sheet-stock dolly. The weight of the plywood makes the base sag, which in turn makes the vertical supports pinch the plywood, securing it to the dolly. A little self-stick felt on the inside of the supports protects the veneer. Buy inexpensive casters, two swivel and two fixed, to attach to the bottom. Once the sheet stock is in place, you can roll it to where you need it. You can even let go of it because the dolly offers plenty of support and it won't tip over. Try this and your back will thank you!

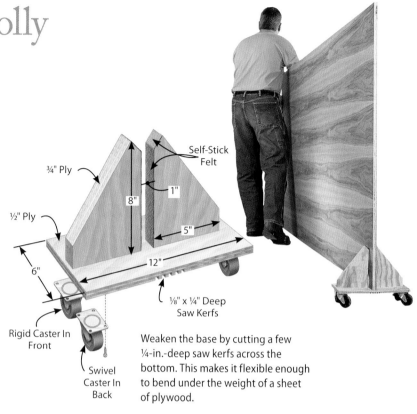

¾" Ply

Self-Stick Felt

1"

8"

5"

½" Ply

12"

6"

⅛" x ¼" Deep Saw Kerfs

Rigid Caster In Front

Swivel Caster In Back

Weaken the base by cutting a few ¼-in.-deep saw kerfs across the bottom. This makes it flexible enough to bend under the weight of a sheet of plywood.

Sneaky Sheet-Stock Storage

I built my lumber rack about 9 in. out from the wall. This allows me to store sheet goods behind the rack without losing any more wall space. The concrete floor in my garage shop gets damp so I protect the edges of my sheet stock by laying a strip of plywood on the floor. The only downside is I have to move my car and the compressor to get anything larger than 4 ft. out. But hey, that's life in a small shop!

Plywood Tipper

Hoisting heavy sheets of plywood and MDF onto my tablesaw is not my idea of workshop fun. That's why I devised this pivoting rack—and began storing my sheet stock vertically.

The rack's frame fits around the two base uprights and pivots on bolts. A cleat at the bottom keeps the sheet from sliding off.

After installing a sheet on the rack, I simply tip it down toward the saw. A horizontal stop with adjustable feet holds the rack at tablesaw height. The feet are oriented upside down, so they thread into the top of the stop.

Pivot Bolt

Cleat

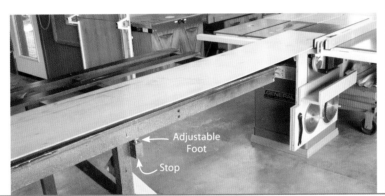

Adjustable Foot

Stop

Rollers Ease Plywood Storage

Before I installed these rollers, sliding plywood in and out of my storage rack used to wear me out. It also damaged the edges of the sheets. Now plywood sheets glide in and out.

I cut the 2½-in.-dia. rollers from ¾-in. hard maple on my drill press using a fly cutter. You could also cut them on a bandsaw with a circle-cutting jig. I drilled out the centers to $^{17}/_{32}$ in., so they would spin on the ½-in. hex-head bolts I use as spindles.

My rack consists of four evenly spaced blocks attached to uprights and a 4-in.-wide x 6-ft.-long solid-wood backboard. The backboard is screwed to the wall; the uprights fasten to a board mounted on the ceiling.

Before assembling the rack, I laid out and drilled holes in the uprights and backboard for the hex-head bolts. I counterbored the backboard's holes for the ½-in. nuts that the 7-in.-long bolts screw into. After screwing the blocks to the backboard and installing the nuts, I screwed the assembly to the wall. Then I screwed each upright to the block on the floor and the board on the ceiling. Installing the rollers and their ½-in. washer spacers was the last step. I slid them onto the bolts before screwing the bolts into the backboard's housed nuts.

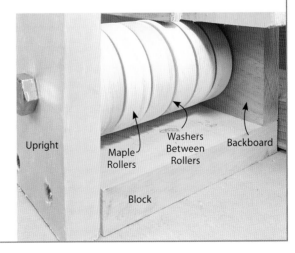

Upright

Maple Rollers

Washers Between Rollers

Backboard

Block

Swing-Out Plywood Storage

Pipe Flange

⅝" Plywood

Pipe Strap

2x10

1" x 48" Pipe

1" x 4½" Pipe

Elbow

Caster

Caster

I was looking for a way to keep my small inventory of plywood organized and easy to access. The garage at my town house is small, but I did have a narrow space along one of the sidewalls next to the overhead door. After some head scratching I designed this swing-out storage unit. It fits the space perfectly and allows me to access any piece of plywood that I want because it works like a file folder.

I bought all the materials for it at my home center for around 75 bucks. The hinge is made out of 1-in. pipe parts and fastened to the end of the storage container with 1¼-in. pipe straps. The pipe is connected to the wall with pipe flanges. The unit rolls on four 3-in. non-swiveling casters.

Utilize Your Corner Space

If you use a lot of sheet stock like I do, you know what a problem storage can be. A growing colony of sheet goods, offcuts and scrap forced me to get organized and build this lumber rack. The rack makes perfect use of wasted corner space without taking up a lot of floor and wall space. The center slot can handle full sheets of plywood and the two outside slots work for partial sheets and scrap. I added shelves in one corner for general storage and left the other open for stacking lumber vertically.

Hollow-core doors make perfect dividers because they're flat, smooth and cheaper than plywood. I used two 36-in. and two 24-in. doors for my rack. If you're lucky, you can find used or damaged doors really cheap. Even with new doors, the entire rack can be built for less than $80.

1x2 Support

Hollow-Core Doors

1x4 Cleat

1⅜" Hollow-Core Doors

35"

1x4 Cleat

51-1/2"

43-1/4"

36"

24"

10-1/2"

10-1/2"

12"

38-1/2"

1x4 Cleat Run Long For Shelves

1x2 Supports

Store Lumber Vertically

When you're alone, it's a real chore to unearth boards from the bottom of a horizontal stack. Boards stored upright against brackets are easy to see and sort. Just flip through the boards and tip out the ones you want. You don't have to lift anything.

Tablesaw

Tablesaw Tapering Jig

I recently built a pair of garden benches that required several identical parts that were tapered on both sides. To make the job easier, I built this jig that worked for both angles. The two screws make setting the angles quick and precise. On the first cut, the edge of the board rests against the first screw head with the end of the board resting on the second screw. For the second cut, I just flip over the board and move it to the second screw (as shown in the photo), and rest the end of the board against the wood stop block. The toggle clamp holds the board in place during sawing. Once the screws are set you can cut perfect angles all day long.

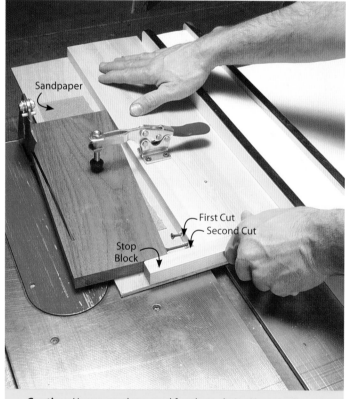

Sandpaper

First Cut
Second Cut

Stop
Block

Caution: Upper guard removed for photo clarity. Use yours!

Aluminum Angle Sled Runners

If you've had a problem with the wood runners on your tablesaw sled shrinking or swelling, make new runners from ⅛ in. x ¾-in. aluminum angle. These runners will fit most miter slots and will not shrink or swell like wood.

Here's how I built mine: First I fit the angle to the miter gauge slot in my tablesaw. You may need to file the angle a little to get a good fit. The angle should glide smoothly in the miter gauge slot without binding, with minimum side to side play.

Next I cut a saw kerf in the bottom of the sled base. The kerf makes runner alignment automatic. Turn the sled over and fasten the first angle to the base with a ¼-in.-thick spacer. You may have to adjust the thickness of this spacer. You want the angle to ride above the T-slot in the miter gauge. If your miter gauge slot does not have a T-slot, use a thicker wood spacer. Just leave a little clearance between the bottom of the miter slot and the bottom of the angle.

Now I set the sled on the tablesaw with the first runner in a miter slot. I pulled the sled back a bit and put another piece of angle in the second miter slot, carefully marking the location for the saw kerf. I cut the kerf and attached the second runner. I've used my sled for years with perfect alignment and smooth action year round.

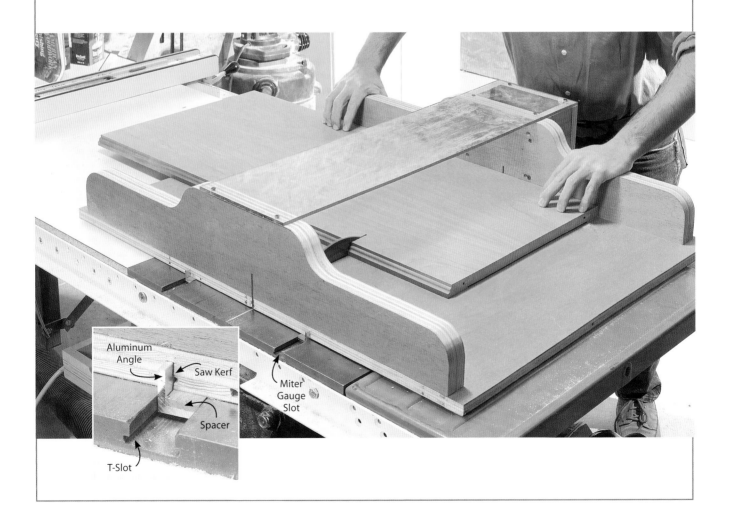

Aluminum Angle

Saw Kerf

Spacer

Miter Gauge Slot

T-Slot

Compact Crosscut Sled

I don't get perfectly square cuts with my saw's miter gauge. Is there another way?

Make a small crosscut sled. It's a reliable substitute for your miter gauge because it's dedicated to one operation: making perfect 90-degree cuts. Unlike your miter gauge, a sled tracks in both miter slots, so it won't wiggle when you cut. A compact sled is ideal for cutting stiles, rails and legs to length, and is easier to store than a large sled.

Make the sled about 12 in. deep and 24 in. wide. Use ½ in. Baltic birch for the base and thick pieces of maple, 2½ in. wide, for the fences. Make a dust shield from ¼ in. clear acrylic.

To build the sled, rip two 12-in.-long runners that fit tight in the saw's miter slots (Photo 1). Not too tight, though—they must be loose enough to slide. Hardboard works well because it won't shrink or swell with changes in humidity. Cut the base and glue it to the runners (Photo 2). When the glue is dry, remove the spacers.

Glue and screw the rear fence to the base. Attach the front fence with a single screw, located at the fence's right end. Screw a block to the base, from below, at the base's left end (Photo 3). Place shims between the block and the fence, clamp the fence to the block and make a test cut. Add or subtract shims until the sled cuts exactly 90 degrees, then screw the fence to the base and remove the block. Add the shield to deflect sawdust.

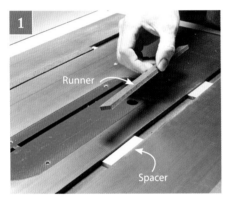

Make runners for the sled from ¼-in. hardboard. Raise the runners above the saw's top by placing them on ¼-in. thick spacers.

Glue the sled's base to the runners. Align the base with the saw's fence, then place weights on it.

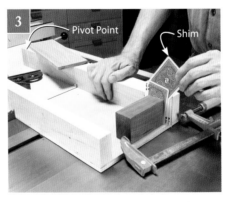

Pivot the front fence on a single screw. Clamp the fence's other end to a temporary block that's screwed to the base, then add shims to adjust the fence until it is square to the blade.

Crosscut Sled Cam Clamp

I use a sled for crosscutting ¾-in. melamine and plywood panels up to 24 inches wide. These panels can be hard to hold in position while making a cut, so I installed a cam lever that securely locks the panel to the bed. The radius of the cam increases from 1⅛-in to 1⅜-in. Now I can keep both hands on the sled and concentrate on making smooth cuts.

Crosscut Sled Upgrade

Adding a hold-down to my shop-made crosscut sled makes the sled easier and safer to use. My parts don't slip and my fingers are far from the blade because I don't have to hold the workpiece. The hold-down swivels so I can place it on either side of the blade.

To build the hold-down, you'll need three hardwood blocks (the arm, the foot and a support block), two ¼-20 threaded inserts, two ¼-20 jig knobs (one with a through hole and one with a 1" stud), a ¼-20 flathead machine screw, two ¼" washers, and three ¼-20 nuts. Make the arm ¾" x 2" x 8". The foot is 2" x 2" x 2½" and the support block is 2" x 2" x 6". Glue the support block to the sled's fence, flush to the top.

Rout a ¼" x 4" slot in the arm and install a threaded insert in one end of the arm. Install another threaded insert in the fence's top, in line with the blade slot. Drill a ¼" hole through the foot, countersink the bottom end of the hole and insert a ¼-20 machine screw through the hole. Slip a washer onto the screw, then thread two nuts onto the screw all the way down to the foot. Tighten the nuts against each other, leaving the foot free to swivel.

Thread the machine screw through the arm's insert. Install a jam nut about ½" down from the end of the screw. Thread a through-hole jig knob onto the screw, then tighten the jam nut against the knob.

To use the hold-down, slide the arm over the piece to be cut. Tighten the arm, then tighten the foot.

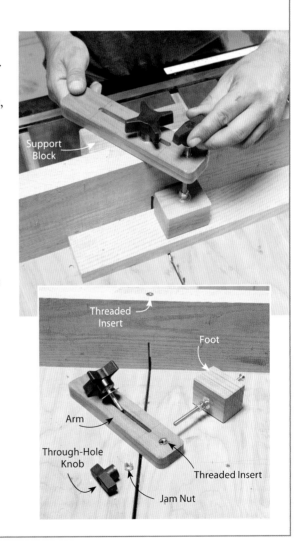

Cutting Sled for Inlay Strips

This sled allows me to cut the ⅛-in.-wide strips of veneer that I often use for inlays. I can cut strips all day without having to measure or reposition the saw's fence. The sled consists of a 13-in. by 24-in. piece of ½-in. MDF with a hardwood runner attached to the bottom. Battens and a fence are glued to the top. The fence is parallel to a saw kerf that runs the length of the sled.

After attaching the runner and the ½-in.-thick battens, I made a cut with the blade height set at ⅝-in., to create the kerf without sawing through the battens. Then I attached the fence ⅛-in. from the kerf.

To use the sled, I set the blade at ⅝-in. and install the sled's runner in the miter slot. I position a piece of veneer flush against the fence, secure it with a ¾-in. MDF cover and make the cut.

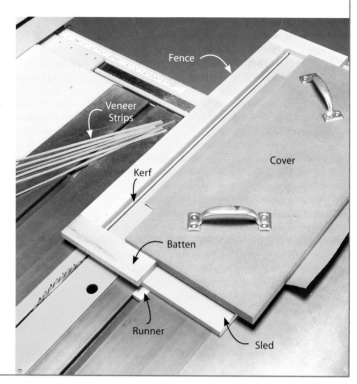

Long Tenoning Sled

Here's a tablesaw-tenoning jig that combines the light weight of a miter gauge with the support of a wide tablesaw sled. I made this sled for use on the right side of my blade so my saw's right-side table supports the sled. I also added an auxiliary wood fence to my rip fence to act as a stop guide and to protect the fence from being cut by the dado blade. The toggle clamp holds the work flat when cutting the faces of my workpiece. When I cut the sides of the tenon, I just hold the part up against the sled's rear fence.

Caution: Guard must be removed for this operation. Use caution!

Long-Reach Stop for Crosscut Sled

I built the "Ultimate Crosscut Sled" featured in AW #75 (October 1999, page 38). It works great, and recently I've added an adjustable stop, which makes it even better. I thought other AW readers would be interested in my upgrade.

My 50-in.-capacity stop consists of scrap wood, a 48-in. length of T-track (I used Mini Track from www.prairieriverwoodworking.com), ¼-20 hex-head bolts and a couple of plastic knobs. I spent less than $25. My stop makes repetitive crosscutting of long stock—shelves for a bookcase, for instance—a breeze. Any hardwood will do for the rail and stop; I used a ⅞-in. x 2-in. x 60-in. piece of hickory. You can increase the crosscut capacity by using a longer rail.

I cut a stopped dado in the back of the rail to house the T-track, which I installed with screws. I attached the stop to the end of the rail with a glued half-lap joint. I counterbored a pair of holes in the sled's fence and installed the bolts and knobs.

T-track makes the stop easy to install and adjust. When the stop isn't necessary, tightening the knobs draws the bolts into the counterbored holes, so they don't protrude.

T-Track

Knob

Counterbored Hole

Saddle Stop Block

Here's a no-frills, adjustable block for making stopped cuts. Cut three pieces of ¾" plywood sized to fit your tablesaw's rip fence. Install a T-nut in one of the side pieces before assembly. Thread a short piece of threaded rod into the T-nut, and then secure a wing nut on the end of the rod with a jam nut. A plastic knob with a stud would work, too.

To use the stop block, position it behind the blade at the desired setting and twist the wing nut. That locks the block in place.

Plywood Crosscut Guide

I use this jig, which I made from leftover materials, to cut plywood into manageable sizes. Melamine provides a slick surface for the saw to ride on and shelf standards guide the saw base in a straight line.

The stops at the end of the guide keep me from sawing too far. Two boards (A) help square the guide on the sheet of plywood, but I still double-check the guide's position by sighting through the 1-in. holes to make sure the saw blade lines up with my pencil line. Two more boards (B) hook over the top of the plywood and provide a simple way to secure the guide to the sheet of plywood.

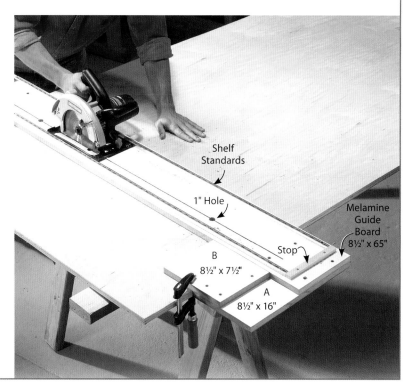

Shelf Standards

1" Hole

B
8½" x 7½"

Stop

Melamine Guide Board
8½" x 65"

A
8½" x 16"

Raised-Panel Tablesaw Jig

Rather than buy a set of raised-panel router bits, I use this tall fence on my tablesaw. It's simply a plywood box that slides on the rip fence. I use two bar clamps to hold my ¾-in.-thick panel to the fence. The stop at the back of the jig also keeps the panel from shifting. To saw the bevel, I set the saw blade at 15 degrees and raise it 1½ in. high. I use a scrap board to test the setting and adjust the rip fence so the beveled edge of the panel ends up slightly less than ¼ in. thick. This permits the panel's beveled edge to fit snugly into the slot in the rails and stiles of my project. I also adjust the blade height so it creates a ⅛-in.-wide shoulder on the inner edge of the bevel.

Tall Fence
12" x 20"

Back Panel
8" x 20"

Stop Block
2" x 12"

Tablesaw Finger Saver

Trimming small parts on a tablesaw using a miter gauge can be a little nerve wracking. In order to do this job safely, I use a handscrew-jig instead of a miter gauge.

To make the jig, I cut a piece of plywood. Next, I gripped a try square in the handscrew and clamped it square to one edge of the plywood. Then I fastened the front jaw of the handscrew to the plywood. The opposite edge of the plywood rides against the saw's fence.

I mounted a piece of clear acrylic on top to prevent cutoffs from flying up. I also use a zero-clearance throat plate to keep small cutoffs from getting stuck.

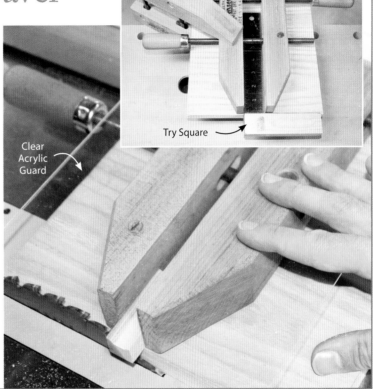

Try Square

Clear Acrylic Guard

8-ft. Straightedge for $4

Whenever I have to cut down a sheet of plywood I reach for one of my trusty metal stud straightedges. Metal studs are available in different thicknesses for different applications. A 20-gauge non-load-bearing drywall stud (about 35¢/ft.) won't deflect significantly when it's clamped to an 8-ft.-long sheet of plywood.

I bought 3⅝ in. x 9-ft. metal studs at my local drywall supplier (look in the Yellow Pages under drywall). Home centers usually stock lighter 25-gauge studs, but they can special-order the heavier gauge for you (25-gauge studs deflect about ⅛ in. over 8 ft).

I trimmed one stud down to 8-ft. 6 in. for ripping and cut the other stud to use for crosscutting.

Metal Stud

Tablesaw Template Trick

A simple addition to my tablesaw fence allows me to cut dozens of identical odd-angled shapes in a hurry. It works just like a flush-cutting router bit. The auxiliary fence's ledge is exactly lined up with the blade's outer edge. I use double-face tape to attach a template to a slightly oversize workpiece, then push the template along the ledge. The result is a perfectly clean cut—with no router bit tear-out—that precisely follows any template. It's perfectly safe on sides down to 4 in. long.

I used ¾-in. solid wood to build the fence, but plywood would do as well. The ledge is screwed and glued to the horizontal piece, 1 in. above its base. This gives enough clearance for the blade to be set higher than the ¾-in.-thick workpiece. On the bandsaw, I rough-cut each workpiece ⅛ in. larger than the template on all sides. Presawing eliminates large offcuts, so there's no chance of kickback. All I get are sawdust and perfect copies of my pattern.

This jig is perfect for making dozens of identical odd-angled parts.

Ledge

Template

Flush Cut

Position the saw's fence so the ledge is exactly in line with the blade's teeth. Every cut will be flush with the template.

Auxiliary Fence Scale

I have difficulty making accurate measurements when I install my auxiliary fence, because the plywood is a weird thickness. My solution is to create a new scale based on the plywood. Zero the sacrificial face next to the blade and slide a thin ruler under the plastic curser (the ruler must rest under the curser without touching). Once the curser line is aligned with the ruler's zero mark, tape the ruler in place. Make sure the ruler is accurately scaled—inexpensive rulers may be inaccurate.

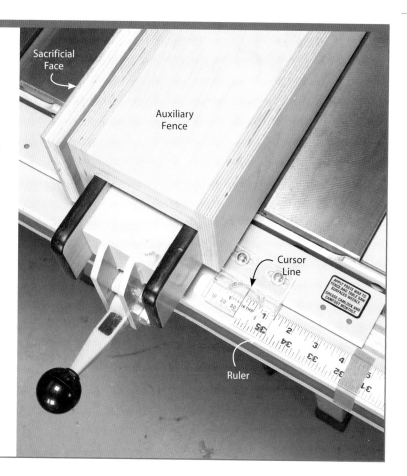

Best Plastic for Shop-Made Guards

I want to make a transparent guard for my tablesaw crosscut sled. My hardware store carries acrylic and polycarbonate plastic. Which should I buy?

Polycarbonate plastic is your best choice for shop-made guards. Polycarbonate is more shatter-resistant than acrylic. In fact, it's the stuff most safety glasses are made from. Because it's softer and more flexible than acrylic plastic, polycarbonate is also easier to cut and drill. We recommend using a bandsaw to cut it. Tablesaw blades generate enough heat to melt the plastic and gum up the blade. Be sure to use a hold-down when drilling, because the plastic has a tendency to climb up the bit.

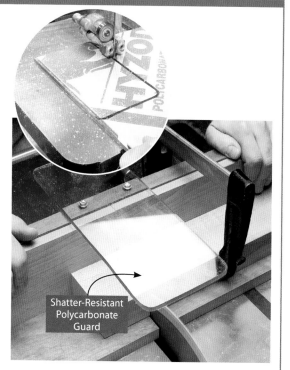

Acrylic has uses in a shop as well. It's a very stiff plastic better suited for things that hold weight, like a router table insert.

Adjustable Push Shoe

A push stick is a familiar device to prevent kickback while ripping a board, but I prefer to use a "push shoe." It's shaped like a shoe with a handle, and has a heel, just like a boot. The heel pushes the work through the saw. I'm more comfortable using a push shoe because the entire sole of the shoe is in contact with the board, unlike a push stick.

I've modified my push shoe's heel to accommodate boards of different thicknesses. Rather than cut a simple notch to form the heel, I added a ⅜" dowel to do the pushing. The dowel fits quite snug through a hole near the shoe's back end. I just adjust the dowel's protrusion to match the stock's thickness.

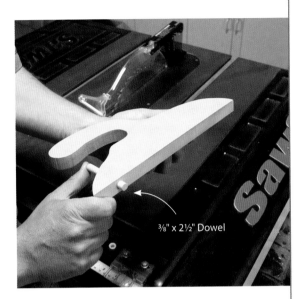

⅜" x 2½" Dowel

Circular-Saw Depth Gauge

Setting the depth-of-cut on my circular saw was awkward at best before I made this handy gauge. It's just a thick block of wood with ¼" wide slots cut at precise, incremental depths. I made the slots on the tablesaw.

To set the depth-of-cut, I place the circular saw on the appropriate slot on the gauge, loosen the saw's depth stop, drop the blade until it bottoms out, and then re-lock the depth stop. The gauge also works upside down for setting the height of a tablesaw blade.

Cheesy Dado Shims

While looking around the shop to find a shim for my dado set, I saw the plastic lid from a cottage cheese container in the trash. Hmm, I thought, that could be it.

I trimmed away the edge and measured the thickness. At .022 (about ³⁄₁₂₈), it complemented my thinner paper shims perfectly. To cut the arbor hole, I just folded the top in half. I've kept several of these cheesy shims handy ever since.

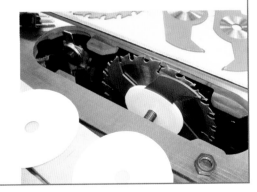

Bit-Bridging Featherboard

This wraparound featherboard produces chatter-free moldings, because it provides continuous pressure ahead of and behind the cutter. Cut a 2-in. arc in the end of the blank before you cut the feathers.

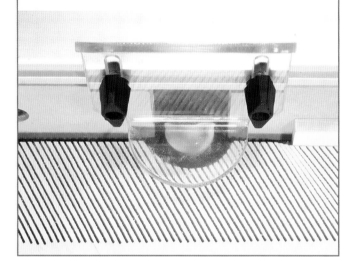

Changing of the Guard

After years of use, I could hardly see through my tablesaw's guard. While at a car show, I heard that polish for renewing aluminum wheels also worked to clear up old headlight lenses—so I tried it on my saw's guard. After two applications, it was as good as new! Since then, I've cleaned all my guards and my face shield as well.

Arbor-Washer Upgrade

Chances are, your tablesaw's arbor washer is made of stamped metal. Unlike the machined-metal washer that's permanently mounted to your saw's arbor, the stamped metal may not be perfectly flat. This can lead to unnecessary vibration in your saw blade. Here's an easy fix. Tape some 120-grit sandpaper on a flat surface. Your cast-iron saw table should work fine. Sand the washer until all the high spots are removed (see inset). Now your washer will make complete contact with the saw blade. Few tablesaw enhancements are as easy and cheap as this!

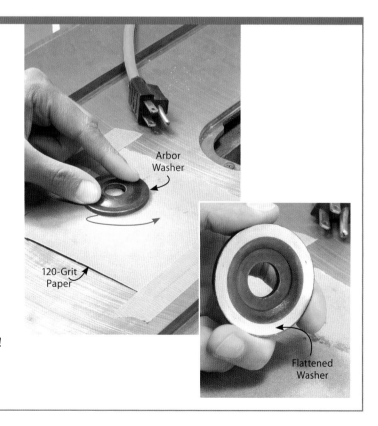

Arbor Washer

120-Grit Paper

Flattened Washer

Clamp-Free Rip Fence

After years of fumbling with clamps, I decided there must be a better way to attach featherboards to my tablesaw's rip fence. Two T-tracks screwed to the fence allow me to mount a piece of plywood with a side-mounted track for attaching featherboards. Now I can set and adjust my featherboards with ease.

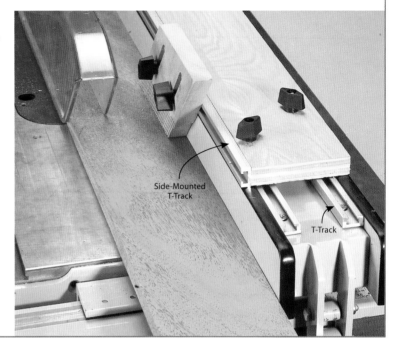

Dado Scale for Left-Tilt Saws

Installing a dado set on my left-tilt saw makes the scale on the rip fence un-usable. Here's why: The cutters stack from left to right, toward the fence, so each cutter I add knocks the scale off by the width of the cutter.

Fortunately, recalibrating the scale is easy. After installing my dado set and checking it to see that it cuts the width I want, I unplug the saw and lock the fence in place next to the blade. Then I place a piece of tape on the scale's zero mark. The edge of the tape is the new cursor line. Now I can use the scale for dado cuts without altering its regular setting.

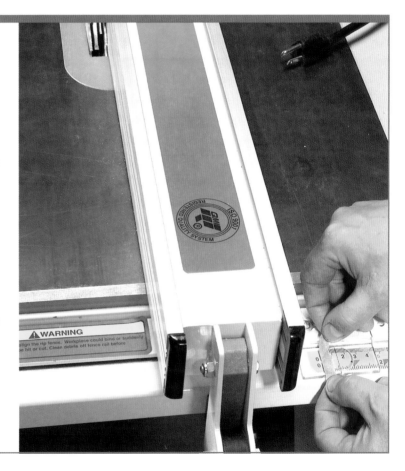

Double-Duty Push Stick

To change the blade on my tablesaw, I used to wedge the front end of my push stick between the saw table and the blade teeth, so I could loosen or re-tighten the arbor nut. It worked, but the teeth always mangled the end of the push stick.

Then I realized that by cutting a saw kerf into the bottom edge of the push stick, I could capture the blade securely during blade changes.

Adding the kerf is easy because I saw it while the bottom edge of the blank is still flat. First I trace the push stick profile on the blank, including the notch and heel at the bottom. Then I lower the blade below the saw table and set the rip fence to center the kerf in the blank. After making sure the kerf won't extend into the heel, I clamp the blank to the fence, turn on the saw and raise the blade about 1¼ in.

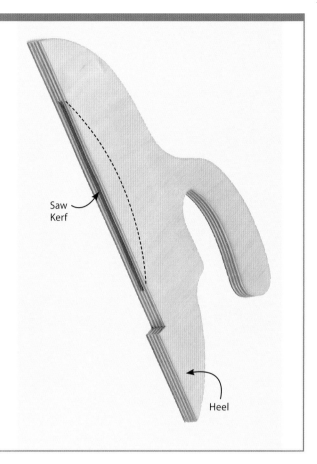

Saw Kerf

Heel

Easy-to-See 90-Degree Blade Check

Most tablesaw cuts require the blade to be set perfectly at 90 degrees to the table. As a check, I used to crank the blade all the way up and set a square between the table and the protruding portion of the blade. I had a hard time discerning the tiny gap that might appear over the 3 in. of exposed blade.

Happily, I discovered a way to use the full diameter of the blade so what would be a tiny gap across 3 in. of blade, becomes a much larger gap across the full 10-in. dia. With the throat plate removed, I set a combination square down through the table so it bears against the entire surface of the blade. Even if the blade is off by only a fraction of a degree, it's easy to see.

Gap

Contact With Blade

Do Blade Stiffeners and Stabilizers Really Help?

I'm trying to get a super-smooth cut on my contractor's saw. I've seen blade "stabilizers" for sale. Do they work?

Two devices can help both standard and thin-kerf blades make smoother cuts: a blade stiffener (at right) or a pair of blade stabilizers (below). Their names are often interchanged but they're actually very different accessories.

Stiffeners cost about $15, while stabilizers cost about $20 per pair.

Before you buy either one, make sure your saw is properly set up. The blade and fence must be parallel to the miter slot. Upgrade your pulleys and belt. Use a high-quality blade and make sure it's clean and sharp. (Stiffeners and stabilizers improve average-quality blades more than high-quality ones.)

If your cut still isn't smooth enough, buy a stiffener or stabilizer. By virtue of their larger diameters and added mass, both reduce the amount of vibration the motor, pulleys and arbor pass on to the blade.

A stiffener is a precision-ground, flat disc. It's far easier to add than stabilizers. It goes right on top of the blade, behind the arbor washer. You may lose ¼-in. depth of cut.

Stabilizers replace or supplement the arbor washers on either side of the blade. Most outer arbor washers are simply stamped steel, and may not run true, but stabilizers are machined flat. If your inner arbor washer is also stamped steel, slide it off and replace it with one of the stabilizers. If you can't remove it, place one stabilizer on top of it.

The big downside to thick stabilizers is that the inner piece pushes the blade farther out on the arbor. You must adapt your saw to fit the new position of the blade. The spot in your saw's throat plate may not line up with the blade. If it doesn't, substitute a zero-clearance insert. Shift the splitter on your blade guard so it lines up with the blade. In addition, realign the cursor and scale on your fence.

4" Blade Stiffener

Pair of 3½" Blade Stabilizers

Blade stabilizers are used in pairs, one on either side of the blade. In effect, they're oversized, precision arbor washers.

Featherboards Made Easy

The safest way to make featherboards is on the bandsaw using a simple sled with a miter slot runner. Cut a 30-degree angle on one end of the featherboard blank first. Mark a parallel line about 2½ in. from the angled end. Set the blank on the sled and make the first cut from the end to the line. Then, slide the featherboard over to the next mark to make the second cut and continue across the board's width.

A feather length of about 2½ in. with cuts made every ⅛ in. provides the right balance between flexibility (for firm pressure without being too stiff) and strength (so the feathers won't snap off) for most hardwoods or multi-ply birch. Increase the feather spacing to ³⁄₁₆-in. when you are using softer woods, such as pine or basswood, or regular hardwood plywood. You can always fine-tune the length and spacing to suit your own needs.

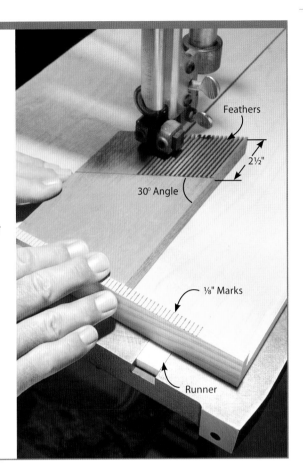

Glue-Line Rip Blade

I use my jointer to clean up sawn edges before glue-up. The results are great except when I try to joint figured wood. Any suggestions?

Jointing highly figured wood often leaves nasty tear-out. It's times like these that a tablesaw and a specialized blade called a glue-line rip blade come in handy. A glue-line rip blade produces a much smoother edge than even the best 40-tooth combination blade can.

Glue-line rip blades are designed and used differently than standard rip blades. General-purpose rip blades are made for fast, rough cuts. Typically, they have 24 flat-ground teeth. A typical glue-line rip blade, on the other hand, has 30 teeth with every other tooth having a "triple-chip grind." The triple-chip tooth hogs out most of the material and the flat tooth cleans up what's left. This produces an ultra-smooth cut that's ready for glue-up. You set up a glue-line rip blade differently than you do a typical blade. You'll get the best results by feeding the stock at a slow, steady rate.

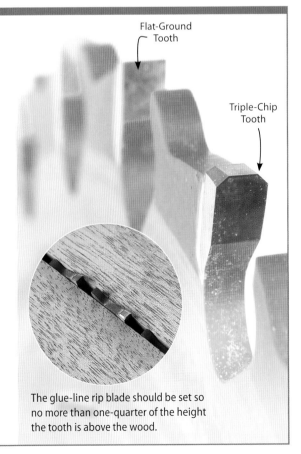

The glue-line rip blade should be set so no more than one-quarter of the height the tooth is above the wood.

Guaranteed Square Edges

Jointing an absolutely square edge on a wide board can be tricky for someone new to the jointer. The least little tip away from the fence and you'll have to start over. This paddle-style featherboard can bridge your jointer's guard while keeping your stock pushed firmly against the fence. The paddle featherboard is easy to make and is just as useful on a tablesaw or router table (Fig. A, below).

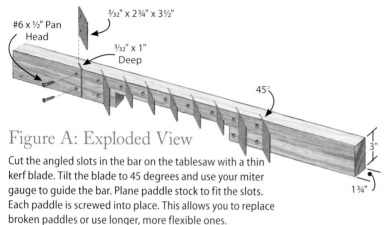

Figure A: Exploded View

#6 x ½" Pan Head

³⁄₃₂" x 2¾" x 3½"

³⁄₃₂" x 1" Deep

45°

3"

1¾"

Cut the angled slots in the bar on the tablesaw with a thin kerf blade. Tilt the blade to 45 degrees and use your miter gauge to guide the bar. Plane paddle stock to fit the slots. Each paddle is screwed into place. This allows you to replace broken paddles or use longer, more flexible ones.

Paddle

How Flat Does "Flat" Have to Be?

My new saw table has a dip of about .005 in. from side to side. Is that a problem or am I being too picky?

Relax. For most projects that little dip shouldn't make any noticeable difference. After all, once you've cut your wood it'll probably bend or twist that much anyway.

Most tablesaw manufacturers consider twice that error, or .010 in., the margin of acceptability. (That's equivalent to two thicknesses of the cover of our magazine.) If you've just bought a new saw that's out of flat by substantially more than this amount, such as .015 to .020 in., give the manufacturer a call.

To check your saw, you'll need a high-quality straightedge and an automotive feeler gauge or our magazine cover. Feeler gauges have an assortment of steel blades with thicknesses precisely graduated in thousandths of an inch. They're available at all auto-supply stores.

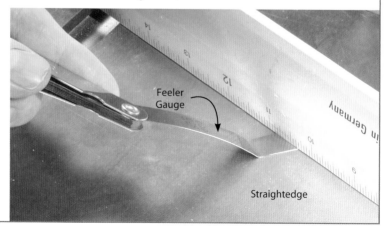

Feeler Gauge

Straightedge

How Tight Does My Blade Have to Be?

I have a heck of a time loosening the arbor nut when I switch blades on my tablesaw. How hard do I really have to crank on that nut when I tighten it?

Don't knock yourself out tightening that arbor nut! It only has to be snug.

Every saw's arbor is threaded so the nut will self-tighten. The arbor on a right-tilt saw is a left-handed thread; on a left-tilt saw it's a right-handed thread, just like a standard screw or bolt.

For either saw, the force of the blade will tighten, not loosen, the nut as the blade is spinning. It's highly unlikely the nut will come loose from inadequate tightening, so there's no reason to crank down on it with a ton of force.

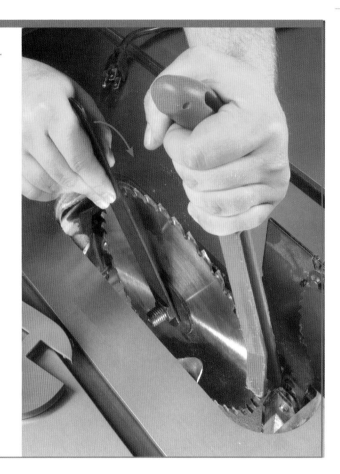

Laminate Flooring for Zero-Clearance Inserts

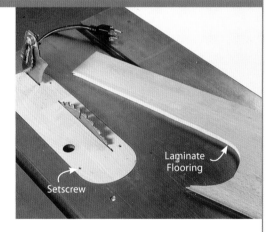

Setscrew

Laminate Flooring

Rather than mess with gluing up plastic laminate, I use a piece of laminate flooring when making zero-clearance inserts. Laminate flooring is great because it's stiff, with a nice slick surface. It's between ¼-in. and ⅜-in. thick, which is just right for inserts. It also saws and routs nicely.

I bought a couple of sample pieces of laminate flooring for $6 per 8-in. by 48-in. piece. You can find it at home centers and flooring stores. Each plank makes four inserts.

To make my inserts I followed the directions in "Zero-Clearance Inserts," AW #95, September 2002, page 50. The only change I made was to use #10-24 by ⅜-in.-long socket-head setscrews for the leveling screws rather than flat-head screws. I prefer setscrews because I don't have to drill a countersink. Some saws require a ½-in. long setscrew because the support flanges that the insert rests on are lower. To determine the screw's size, measure from the top of your saw table down to the support flange. Buy setscrews that are about ¹⁄₁₆-in. to ⅛-in. shorter than this measurement. You can buy socket setscrews at most hardware stores for about 25 cents each.

Left or Right Tilt?

Can you advise me on the pros and cons of right- versus left-tilting tablesaws?

Tablesaw blades tilt for making beveled cuts. Twenty years ago, blades almost always tilted toward the rip fence—a right tilt. Blades that tilt away from the fence, called left-tilt blades, are now almost as popular.

Both tilt directions have advantages, so the choice ultimately depends on personal preference. While weighing the pros and cons, it's good to remember that the vast majority of your cutting will be done with the blade at 90 degrees—not tilted at all.

A left-tilt blade is more user-friendly, because it allows working consistently on the right side of the blade, a practice most woodworkers prefer. It provides a clear view during the cut, because the blade guard angles away from the fence. This orientation also means the guard doesn't interfere with feeding stock that's less than 6 in. wide.

In addition, a left-tilt blade allows cutting mitered pieces face side up. This eliminates any chance for the face to be scratched during the cut. Also, any bottom-side tear-out caused by the blade occurs on the inside edge of the bevel, where it's most likely to be hidden.

A right-tilt blade allows you to use the rip-fence scale no matter what kind of blade is installed. The blade installs against a fixed washer mounted on the arbor. On a right-tilt saw, this washer is on the same side as the fence, so the blade's dimension, whether it's a regular kerf, thin kerf or dado set, doesn't change the distance between the edge of the blade and the fence.

The blade height-adjustment wheel is more convenient on a right-tilt saw, because it's on the left side of the saw. Many woodworkers build storage cabinets on the right side, under the saw's extension table.

Kickback is possible with either orientation. A right-tilt blade can trap the workpiece between the blade and the fence. If the workpiece happens to drift over a left-tilting blade, the teeth can catch and throw it up and back—the most dangerous type of kickback.

The biggest left-tilt inconvenience is having to reset the scale when you change blades. Guard interference is the right-tilt bane. To bevel-rip narrow stock, you have to move the fence to the other side of the blade.

A good way to test your tilt preference is to consider how you would make a beveled crosscut using the miter gauge. If you would make the cut with the blade tilting away from the miter gauge, you'll probably prefer a left-tilt blade.

Left Tilt

Levitated Alignment Guide

By holding a straightedge parallel to the blade, rare-earth magnets make it easy to align your table saw fence.

Using digital calipers, find two ½-in.-dia. rare earth magnets of exactly the same thickness. Crank the blade to maximum height and place the magnets toward the outer edge of the blade, about ¾-in. above the table's surface. Place the straightedge—I use an 18-in. rule from a combination square—on edge against the rare earth magnets. The magnets' thickness positions the straightedge beyond the blade's teeth. Align the fence parallel with the straightedge.

Rare Earth Magnet

Long-Reach Featherboard

A long arm on a featherboard takes the hassle out of clamping it on a tablesaw. Featherboards need to be secured at two points to prevent pivoting. Securing a single featherboard across a tablesaw's large expanse can be difficult, if not impossible. The solution is to biscuit an arm at a 30-degree angle to the featherboard. Position the featherboard just in front of the blade for rip cuts.

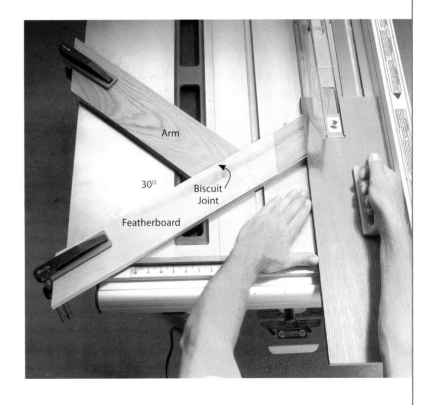

Arm

30°

Biscuit Joint

Featherboard

Memory Stick

Here's a simple way to guarantee that duplicate parts turn out the same size every time, whether its next week or next year.

First, cut a stop block to fit between the guide tube and the support rail, and below the miter slots, if necessary. Next, set the fence against the blade and slide the stop block up to the fence's tee. Secure the stop block in place however you wish. It's best to make it easily removeable, though.

To verify your stop block's zero position, cut a memory stick about 2" wide. Loosen the fence and slide it to the right. Position the memory stick so that it's held between the fence's tee and the stop block, then lock the fence.

Take out the memory stick, and make a test cut. The board you cut should come out the same 2" width as the memory stick. Make and label memory sticks, including the thickness of the blade's kerf, for any parts you want to duplicate.

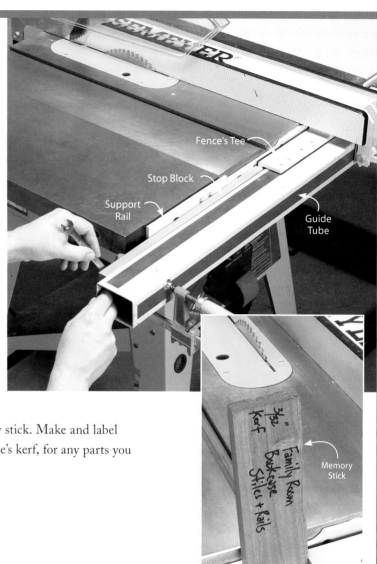

Never-Lost Push Stick

I really got tired of digging around to find my tablesaw's push stick each time I needed it, so I figured out a way to attach it to the fence using a rare-earth magnet. I drilled a ½" counterbore in the push stick's face, 1½" up from the bottom (so the magnet won't be hit by the blade), and super-glued the magnet in the hole. I drilled a similar hole in my fence, on the right side, to hold the magnet's mating washer.

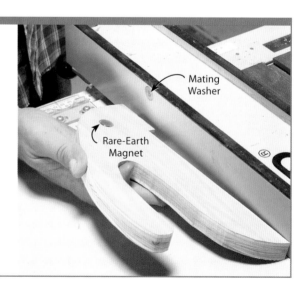

Make Your Own Tablesaw Moldings

I'm restoring an antique that's missing a piece of trim molding. I can't find a router bit profile that even comes close. How can I make a small section of molding to match the original?

You can use your tablesaw to rough out the profile and then finish the shape with sanding blocks or a few basic carving chisels. First, trace the profile of the original on the end of a board. Use an extra wide board to provide legs for the molding to stand on as it's being shaped on the saw. Adjust the blade height so the cut is just shy of the mark. Cutting too deep will ruin the molding, and you know Murphy's law says that'll happen on the last cut.

Position the rip fence to guide the stock through the cut. Readjust the fence and the blade height as you work your way across the entire profile.

When you've rough-cut the molding, turn it on its back and rip to finish width. Refine the shape with sandpaper, a block plane, scrapers or carving chisels.

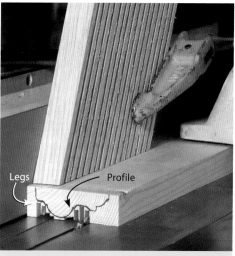

Legs Profile

Caution: The guard is removed for this operation.

Low-Tech Alignment Tool

This simple jig enables you to quickly and accurately align your saw's blade with a miter slot. Perfect alignment helps prevents kickback and burned cuts. You can also use the jig to align your fence with a miter slot.

First, make a 12" long runner that fits snug in the slot. Position a block of wood on the runner ½" away from the blade and glue or fasten the block to the runner. Screw a round-head brass screw into the end of the block facing the blade.

To check your blade, unplug the saw and color one tooth with a marker. Rotate the blade so this tooth sits just above the front of the throat plate. Back out the screw until it just touches the tooth. Rotate the blade so the marked tooth sits at the back of the throat plate and check the distance between the screw and the tooth. If the screw just touches the blade, alignment is correct. If not, you'll need to loosen and adjust the saw's top or trunnions.

Caution: Unplug your saw.

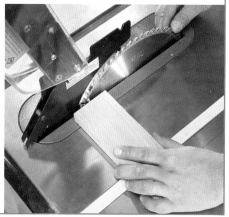

No-Slip Miter Gauge Face

Trimming miters used to drive me crazy, because I couldn't hold the piece I was trimming securely enough against the miter gauge. The piece would always slide away from the blade during the cut. I solved the problem by covering the miter gauge face with 120-grit PSA (pressure sensitive adhesive backed) sandpaper. One 5-in. disc will cover most gauges. I clean the face with denatured alcohol, to assure good adhesion. Then I simply cut the disc to fit the face and press on the pieces.

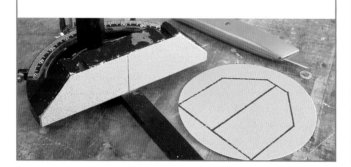

Perfect Pressure Every Time

Positioning a featherboard can be a pain. Too close to the fence or table and the squeeze is so tight you can barely feed the stock. Too loose and you've lost effectiveness. Try taking about ⅛ in. off the first feather. Set that end against the stock you plan to machine and clamp the featherboard parallel to the table's fence. The pressure should automatically be just right.

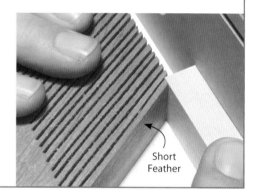

Short Feather

No-Clamp Featherboard

I added a pair of powerful handled magnets to my shop-made featherboard. They fit snugly into two notches and hold the featherboard absolutely rigid. The magnets enable me to place the featherboard anywhere I want on my tablesaw or bandsaw without fumbling with clamps. Each magnet exerts 100 pounds of force—plenty of clamping power. To remove the featherboard, I just grab each magnet by its handle and tip it over.

Magnet

Mobile Saw Base with Bonus Storage

My tools need to be mobile because I share my shop with two cars. This mobile tablesaw base offers portability and abundant storage. The base provides enclosed storage, including a full-extension drawer for small items. I made a hinged outfeed table and added a couple of wood blocks under the outer corners to provide a place for drilling the leg sockets. The legs are 1-in.-metal electrical conduit with leveling feet inserted in one end. When the outfeed table is folded down, I store the legs in a couple of spring clips on the side of the base.

The locking casters keep everything stationary when sawing. I used MDF because it's cheaper than plywood and the extra weight seems to help the case absorb vibrations better. I found all the materials at my local home center for about $100.

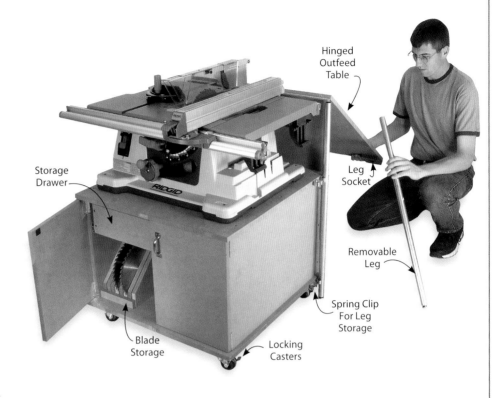

Hinged Outfeed Table

Storage Drawer

Leg Socket

Removable Leg

Spring Clip For Leg Storage

Blade Storage

Locking Casters

Perfectly Parallel Fence

Here's a quick and easy way to align your tablesaw fence with your miter slot. Plane down a board until it fits into your miter slot without play. Now slide the fence up to the board and use a feeler gauge to determine your fence alignment. It's that easy.

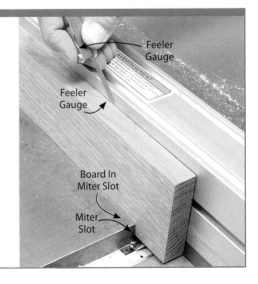

Feeler Gauge

Feeler Gauge

Board In Miter Slot

Miter Slot

Precision Fence Setting

I use a set of shop-made gauge blocks to adjust my fence for cutting rabbets and tenon shoulders. The blocks are precise thicknesses and about 2" wide.

To set the fence, I insert a ½" spiral bit into the collet, upside down, and then tighten the collet by finger only. (A piece of ½" drill rod would work as well.) Why upside down? The bit's shank provides a smooth surface for the square to register against. Right-side up, a router bit is difficult to use because you must precisely rotate its cutting edge to the outermost point of its travel.

Next, I insert a gauge block between the fence and the square. Then I adjust the fence until the square is flat against the gauge block and touching the bit's shank. After turning the bit right-side up, I'm ready to go.

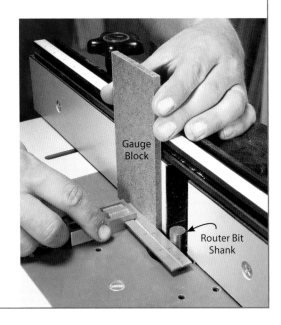

Gauge Block

Router Bit Shank

Playing Cards in the Shop

A deck of playing cards can be very useful around the woodshop. One of my favorite uses is for shimming my dado set. I drill a ⅝-in. hole in the center of several cards and keep them with my dado set so they're ready when I need them.

Playing cards are also handy as disposable glue spreaders and for leveling the feet on my rolling workbench. Waiting for a finish to dry? How about a game of solitaire?!

Quick, Easy Featherboard Fasteners

Clamping a featherboard on a tablesaw can be a hassle. T-track fasteners allow you to quickly and easily position a featherboard just ahead of the blade for rip cuts. To make this style of featherboard, cut deep slots for the T-track fasteners as you cut the feathers on your bandsaw.

T-Slot Hold Down

No Math Octagons

I'm not a numbers guy, so I hate complicated formulas for figuring out dimensions. I'd given up making octagonal wood blanks for my lathe until I discovered this technique. No measuring required! You can also do this on your bandsaw.

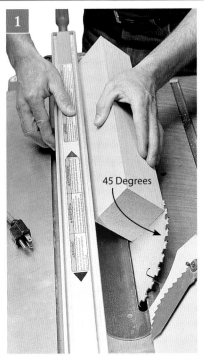

45 Degrees

Tilt your tablesaw blade to 45 degrees. Rest the stock flat against the blade and slide the fence over until it touches the corner of the stock. Then lock the fence into position.

Lower the blade half way. Then lay the stock flat and saw off the corners.

Outfeed Table: Melamine or Laminate?

I'm building an outfeed table for my tablesaw. Should I use melamine or plastic laminate?

Plastic laminate is more durable than melamine, but it will cost you more time and money to install.

Laminate provides more abrasion and impact resistance than melamine. You're less likely to wear through the top layer or dent and scar it. A top with laminate on both sides will sag far less than a melamine top. Thermofused melamine, the kind most commonly found at lumberyards and home centers, has a single layer of paper adhered to the front and back of a particleboard substrate, heat-fused with melamine resins. Laminate is much thicker. On top is a similar layer of paper, but under that is a decor sheet (which carries the color or pattern) and three to five layers of kraft paper fused to the first two layers with tough phenolic resins.

Before choosing laminate, however, consider cost and labor. A 4x8 sheet of thermofused melamine costs about $25. Cut it to the size you need, and you're ready to go. For the sake of comparison, a 4x8 sheet of laminate costs about $55. Add to that the cost of the particleboard or medium-density fiberboard (MDF) substrate ($20 to $25), and the contact cement. You have to apply laminate to a substrate yourself and trim it with a router. You can wear out and replace several melamine outfeed tables for the same cost as one laminate table.

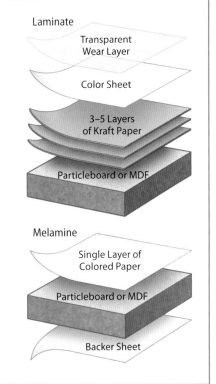

Laminate

Transparent Wear Layer

Color Sheet

3–5 Layers of Kraft Paper

Particleboard or MDF

Melamine

Single Layer of Colored Paper

Particleboard or MDF

Backer Sheet

Quick Featherboard Clamp

Clamping featherboards to my tablesaw was always a hassle until I discovered locking welding clamps. Their C-shaped jaws adjust to fit the webbed castings on the bottom of the extension table. They clamp and release easily, so adjustments and realignments are a snap.

I use locking welding clamps all over my shop. They're much lighter and easier to use than long-reach woodworking clamps. Be sure the ones you buy have swivel pads. I glue on plywood faces, for no-mar clamping.

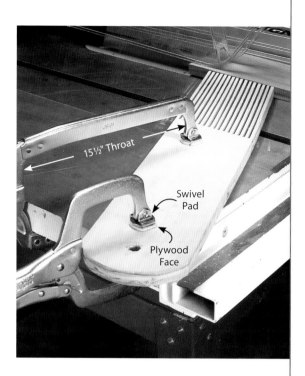

15½" Throat

Swivel Pad

Plywood Face

Ribbed Saw Table Fillers

I like my contractor's saw just fine, except for the ribbed extension tables. The openings can be a real finger pincher when sliding the rip fence across them. After my last bruised fingernail I decided to do something about it. I custom fit some ¼-in.-thick plywood and attached it to the ribs with construction adhesive. You may have more or less space on your tablesaw than I do, but a little shimming or sanding should give you the fit you need.

Rough-Cut Plywood

It's awkward to manhandle plywood in a small shop and sometimes your cuts aren't accurate just because the sheets are so unwieldy. One solution is to rough-cut the pieces with a circular saw and then make final cuts on your tablesaw. Lay the plywood on top of a piece of building foam, use a fine-tooth blade in your saw and set the saw so it cuts just 1/8-in. deeper than the plywood. Then simply kneel on top to cut. It's much easier than sawhorses.

Make sure that you leave a factory edge on each piece that you cut. Although you may have to trim it off later, it's essential as a reference for your first cut on the tablesaw.

BUILDING FOAM

Replaceable Fence Faces

It's hard to improve on the performance of a T-square fence, but I think I've done it. I got frustrated with clamping on an additional subfence every time I wanted to make a rabbet with a dado set (where part of the blade is actually housed in the fence), so I made a new set of fence faces with interchangeable inserts. One insert has a cutout for rabbeting; the other is plain for ripping. When the arc in the rabbeting insert becomes too large, I just install a new insert.

To maintain the usefulness of the fence's scale and cursor, I removed the original ½-in.-thick faces and replaced them. I made the new faces from ½-in. MDF and mitered the ends at 45 degrees. The original faces were glued to the fence; I attached the new faces with self-tapping hex-head screws. The inserts don't need to be screwed because they slide firmly in place.

Rip Fence for Plastic Laminate

I used to work in a cabinet shop that churned out countertops by the truckload. We used this simple jig to keep plastic laminate from lifting during the cut or from slipping under the saw's rip fence, since most fences rest slightly above the saw's table.

The jig is a simple box that fits snugly over the saw's fence and is clamped or screwed in place. A subfence and a piece of plastic laminate glued to the bottom of the box arm corral the piece of laminate that's being cut. To set the fence when using the jig, simply add the ¾-in. thickness of the box arm to the overall width.

Box Arm

Subfence

Laminate

Tablesaw Trap

Even with a zero-clearance throat plate in my tablesaw, thin cut-offs slip through now and then. These pieces can clog a vacuum hose or damage the blades of a dust collector. I made a trap to catch them by attaching a piece of hardware cloth inside my saw, in front of the dust port. The trap also catches a dropped arbor nut or washer.

Safer Ripping

I recently had a thick piece of wood pull apart as it came off the blade of my tablesaw. The spreading wood pushed off the fence and against the spinning blade. Is there a safer way to rip?

Wood often has built-in tension due to drying stresses. Ripping the board releases the tension causing the wood to either pull apart or pinch together. A splitter keeps the wood from pinching the blade but it is ineffective when the wood pulls apart. In Europe, tablesaw fences end just past the blade. That way the wood is free to splay apart. In North America, we're used to a fence extending well past the blade but there's really no need for this additional fence length when rip-cutting.

You can easily make your own Euro-style fence. Use double-faced tape to add a subfence that ends just past the far end of the blade. Make the subfence exactly 1-in. thick and it'll make direct-read measurements easier.

Subfence

Shallow Cut Eliminates Tear-Out

When I crosscut hardwood plywood, I use an old technique to minimize tear-out on the bottom face. I simply make two passes with my general-purpose blade. After setting the rip fence, I cut a shallow groove, no more than ¹⁄₃₂ in. deep. Then I raise the blade and cut all the way through. Cutting plywood this way takes longer, but I'm not in a hurry and the tear-out-free results are worth the extra effort.

First Cut

Short-Fence Featherboard

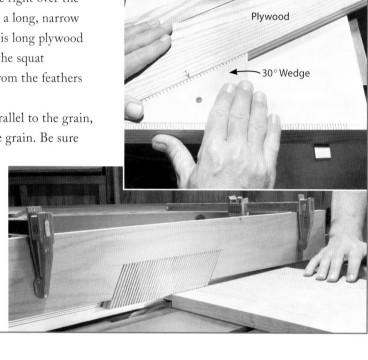

Plywood

← 30° Wedge

Sometimes you want a featherboard to apply pressure right over the blade, as when you're cutting a rabbet. But clamping a long, narrow featherboard onto a short fence can give you fits. This long plywood featherboard is just the ticket. It clamps easily onto the squat tablesaw fence because the clamps are far removed from the feathers and the blade.

Most featherboards are made with the feathers parallel to the grain, but this one requires the feathers to be cut across the grain. Be sure to make it from plywood or your cross-grained featherboard will start to look like my 8-year-old's smile—lots of missing teeth. To cut these feathers, use the same sled as you do for the parallel-grain boards, but add a 30-degree wedge.

Should I Spend More Money on Cast-Iron Wings?

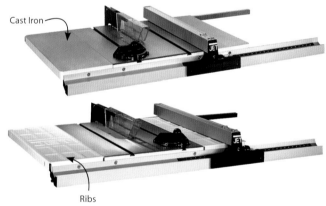

Cast Iron

Ribs

I can save money by buying stamped steel rather than cast-iron extension wings for my new tablesaw. What do cast-iron wings offer that steel wings don't?

Over the long haul, you'll find that cast-iron wings have at least four valuable benefits that are worth the extra money.

First, a cast-iron wing is much more rugged and is more likely to remain flat after years of use. You can inadvertently bend a steel wing by grabbing it when you move your saw or by dropping something heavy on it, such as a full sheet of plywood.

Second, a cast-iron wing adds about 25 lb. to the top of your saw table. That additional mass helps soak up vibration. Two wings are even better.

Third, a cast-iron wing provides a dead-flat surface that's useful even when the saw isn't running. An unplugged tablesaw makes a great assembly table, and a single cast-iron wing adds almost 50 percent more flat surface area to the main table. The ribbed surface on a stamped steel wing is anything but flat.

Fourth, believe it or not, a cast-iron wing is a convenient surface for sharpening tools. Simply attach some sandpaper with low-tack spray adhesive. The wing is flat, rock solid and more accessible than the main table—perfect for lapping the backside of chisels and plane irons.

Silencing a Squeaky Tablesaw

My tablesaw screeches like nails on a chalkboard whenever I adjust the blade. WD-40 made the noise go away for a while, but now it's back. What do I do?

That sound can drive you crazy! It's a clear sign that the gears under your saw are due for lubrication. The original lubricant has either hardened or worn off, so now you're hearing the bare steel of the worm gears scrape the bare cast iron of the tilting trunnion and raising gear. You're unlikely to wear out the gears this way, so it's not a cause for alarm, but the noise will continue to get worse.

The best fix is to lubricate the gears with lithium grease, the same stuff they use at the factory. You can buy a lifetime's supply ($6 for a 1-lb. tub) at an auto supply store. An alternative is powdered graphite, available at a hardware store or a locksmith's shop for about $2 a tube. One advantage: it won't attract dust and chips the way grease does.

Clean the gears with a small brass brush or an old toothbrush and WD-40, which helps soften the grease. Apply a thin layer of new grease to the teeth of the raising gear and the trunnion. Turn the handles a few cranks to transfer the grease to the worm gears and enjoy the sound of silence.

Thanks to Chris Cooper at Powermatic and Roger Amrol at Delta Tools for help with this answer.

Splitter for Narrow Pieces

How can I avoid burn marks when ripping thin strips?

Add a splitter to your zero-clearance throat plate. A splitter keeps the wood from binding on the back of the blade.

For most rip cuts, you should use your blade guard and its built-in splitter to prevent binding, but it's often not practical when ripping pieces less than 1" wide. For these cuts, remove the guard and install a shop-made or commercial zero-clearance throat plate so there's full support under the workpiece.

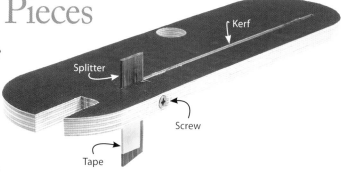

To add the splitter, first extend the length of the throat plate's kerf by raising the blade all the way, under power. Next, make the splitter from a piece of wood that's two paper thicknesses thinner than the kerf, for adequate clearance. Cut the piece ½" wide and 1½" long. Remove the throat plate from the saw and clamp it in a vise. Wrap the splitter with masking tape (so it fits tight in the kerf) and put it in the throat plate, butted up to the back of the kerf and extending about ½" above the throat plate. Drill and countersink a hole for a long No. 8 screw through the side of the throat plate and through the splitter. Remove the splitter and slightly enlarge the hole, so the screw won't split the splitter. Put the splitter back in place and drive in the screw. Cut off the tape above the throat plate. Taper the front of the splitter with a file, and you're all set. Be sure to use a push stick to keep your hands out of harm's way.

Tape-On Miter Gauge Shim

While doing some precision tablesaw work, I discovered my miter gauge was a bit sloppy in the slot. I was in the middle of a project, and I needed a quick fix. After adding a layer of aluminum tape to each side of the bar I was back in action.

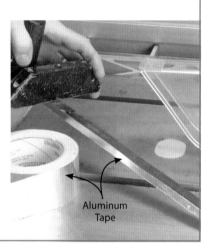

Aluminum Tape

Two-Sided Tablesaw Insert

I needed a ¼" zero-clearance throat plate for cutting dados the other day, but my throat plate only had a ¾" slot in it. I didn't want to interrupt my project to make or buy a new throat plate, so I turned the old one 180° and cut a new slot in it. Why hadn't I thought of that before? Now, whenever I make a new throat plate, I make it two-sided right off the bat.

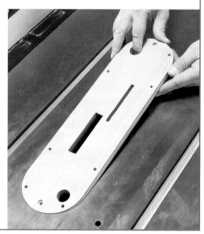

Tall Support for Tall Stock

A tall featherboard can apply pressure against the entire height of the fence. It's especially useful for holding tall, narrow stock—for instance, a door panel—against a fence. Just glue some scraps to create a block that is as tall as your fence is. Then, cut the feathers on your bandsaw sled.

Door Panel

Template Cutting on the Tablesaw

If you have a lot of parts with cuts at odd angles, template cutting on the tablesaw can make fast work of them. Add an extension fence (see photo) to your tablesaw fence and set it so the edge is flush with the outside edge of the blade and slightly higher than the thickness of your workpieces. Make a template of the shape you want and attach it to your blanks with double-sided tape, hot-melt glue or a couple small screws. You can also simply glue coarse sandpaper to the bottom of the template so it grabs the blank well. For added safety, attach a handle to the top of the template. Now run the template against the fence, swiveling it to do all sides, and your piece is cut. Be careful about the cutoff pieces that will accumulate under the extension guide. Poke them through with the saw turned off.

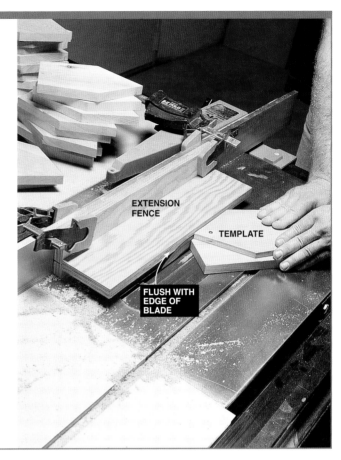

EXTENSION FENCE

TEMPLATE

FLUSH WITH EDGE OF BLADE

Thrifty Square

You can't beat a 12-in. standard drafting triangle for an extremely accurate and inexpensive set-up tool. It's particularly useful for adjusting a tablesaw's miter gauge at both 90 and 45 degrees to the blade.

This precision tool is superior to a combination square or a framing square for setting up a saw. While a combination square has only one long arm, a drafting triangle has two. A metal framing square is unwieldy and can bang against the fragile carbide teeth of your saw blade. This plastic triangle is compact and can't possibly damage your blade. Hang it under the saw or store it with your saw blades.

In addition, kid gloves aren't required when handling this precision tool, even when you're in the thick of cutting on your tablesaw. Unlike a very expensive metal square, this tool can take a beating and is easily replaced. Buy one for about $5 to $10 at any office supply store.

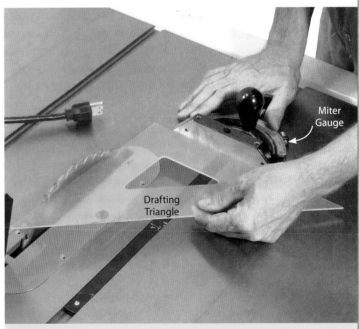

Miter Gauge

Drafting Triangle

Caution: Unplug your saw before placing any measuring tool against its blade.

When Should I Sharpen My Blade?

How can I tell when my carbide tablesaw blade needs to be sharpened?

There are three signs that a blade is getting dull: burning on both sides of the cut, more resistance when ripping a board, and worn teeth.

Burning. If your blade consistently leaves burn marks on only one side of a cut, your fence or splitter is probably out of alignment. If you see burning on both sides of the cut, the blade is getting dull.

Feed resistance. If it takes a lot of pressure to push a board through a rip cut, either the wood or blade is to blame. Boards may spread or close up when cut, binding against the fence or splitter. Try testing the feed resistance with plywood instead. Is it the same as when the blade was new?

Worn teeth. Remove pitch buildup with a blade cleaner and examine the teeth with a magnifying glass. A 10X works best, but any magnifier will do. If any of the corners of the blade have started to wear away, or if you see any rounding over of the tops and sides, the blade should be sharpened. Cleaning the blade can also improve its performance. Pitch build-up won't dull the blade, but it can affect the quality of your cut.

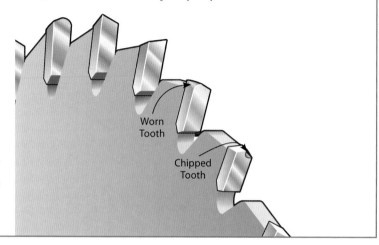

Worn Tooth

Chipped Tooth

Why Coat Sawblades?

Why are some saw blades covered with a slick coating when only the teeth actually touch the wood?

All the parts of a blade come into play when it's cutting. The purpose of a coating, beyond preventing corrosion and rust, is to keep a blade running cool and straight so it makes a smooth cut.

As the teeth cut, a swirl of sawdust moves around the plate and inside the gullets. This dust contains pitch from solid wood or resins from plywood. The dust is constantly rubbing against the blade, producing friction and adding to the heat made by the blade's teeth. The hotter the blade gets, the more this gummy stuff clings to the sides of the teeth, the gullets and plate. When the pitch and resin start to build up, the reduced clearance behind the teeth creates even more friction. It's a vicious cycle. Too much heat causes a blade to slightly distort and wobble, making a noticeably rougher cut. Thin-kerf blades are particularly prone to this problem.

A coating reduces the friction between the sawdust and the plate. Plus, it resists gummy build-up, just like a coated frying pan. Both factors help a blade run true. Coated blades still get some gummy build-up. A coating doesn't eliminate the need to regularly inspect and clean your blade.

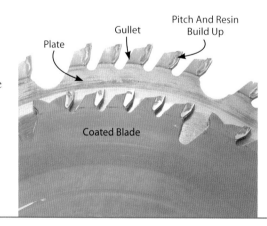

Plate Gullet Pitch And Resin Build Up

Coated Blade

Tool Smarts

Moisture Meters

I've been looking at moisture meters and wondering why I should buy a pin type if a pinless can do the job without poking holes in the wood?

If you buy your wood already surfaced, then a pinless meter will work fine. If you buy your wood rough or if you dry your own wood, a pin-type meter is the way to go.

A pinless meter's greatest asset is its ability to scan over an entire board or even a finished piece of furniture, without leaving a mark. Pinless meters are also unaffected by temperature, which eliminates the conversion charts needed with pin-type meters.

The biggest drawback to pinless meters is the flat, smooth surface required for the sensing pad. This means they can't be used effectively on rough-sawn lumber without first planing a flat area.

Pin-type meters work equally well on rough or surfaced wood. These meters can also be adapted to take accurate readings at depths beyond their normal range. Simply drive uncoated nails to the depth you wish to measure and use alligator clips to connect the pins on the meter to the nail heads (see photo). If you dry your own lumber, these nails can

be left in place allowing you to monitor your wood as it dries.

Still can't make up your mind? Electrophysics (800-244-9908) offers a dual mode pin-type and pinless meter for $330. Good quality moisture meters are also available from Highland Hardware (800-241-6748), Woodcraft Supply (800-225-1153) and Woodworkers' Supply of New Mexico (800-645-9292); prices range from $50 to $250. For further reading on moisture meters call Forest Products Laboratories (608-231-9200) and ask for the report, "Electric Moisture Meters for Wood," by William James.

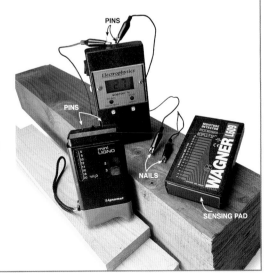

Air Hose Rack

Air tools are great, but the air supply hose is hard to store conveniently. This rack solves this problem, and it's cheap! All you need is some 1¼-in. PVC pipe, a 45-degree elbow, two 1¼-in. conduit straps, and a wooden disc. I made the rack so it stands 48-in. tall but you can make it any height that is convenient for you. A coiled air hose drops onto the upper pipe section and rests on the disc. The conduit straps hold the rack to the wall or a workbench. Connect the lower end of the hose to your air compressor and the upper end to an air-powered tool. Uncoil as much air hose as you need for a job, and when you're finished working, disconnect the hose from your tool and drop the coiled hose back on the pipe. The whole thing pivots toward your work for use, and back for storage. A separate rack holds air tool accessories. Not counting the hose, the whole thing cost about $14 to build.

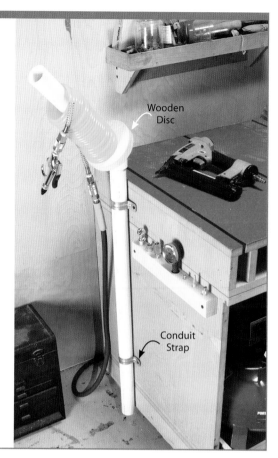

Wooden Disc

Conduit Strap

Ban Toolbox Corrosion

Placed in any enclosed space, these anti-corrosion emitters provide continuous protection for up to two years, even on odd-shaped parts or difficult-to-reach areas. They give off a harmless corrosion-inhibiting vapor that forms an invisible crystal barrier on both ferrous and non-ferrous metals. The 10" by 10" foam sheet protects a total of 8 cu. ft. Or, cut it to fit—1 sq. in. of foam shields 138 cu. in. of volume). The round emitters have self-adhesive backings. The small size is suitable for areas up to 5 cu. ft. and the large size for up to 11 cu. ft.

Auxiliary Compressor Tank

My small air compressor cycled so often during use that the noise almost drove me crazy. As much as I hated to spend the money, it looked like a bigger compressor would be my only option. That's when I discovered air-storage tanks. By connecting a 5-gal. storage tank to my compressor's tank, I more than doubled its air-storage capacity. Now my compressor cycles much less frequently.

Standard plumbing components, available at any hardware store, connect the storage tank to the compressor (see photo, right). The storage tank is still portable because the input ball valve allows airtight disconnecting and reconnecting.

The tank is mounted upside down, so the moisture produced by the compressed air collects in a 4-in.-long trap. Cracking a ball valve mounted at the end of the trap expels the moisture.

My total cost was about $50. Make sure the pounds-per-square-inch (psi) pressure rating of the storage tank you buy is equal to or greater than your compressor's psi rating. An onboard safety switch prevents the compressor from pressurizing higher than its psi rating, so I fully open the compressor's regulator and use the storage tank's regulator to adjust the line pressure. This arrangement pressurizes both tanks to the compressor's limit and provides maximum air storage.

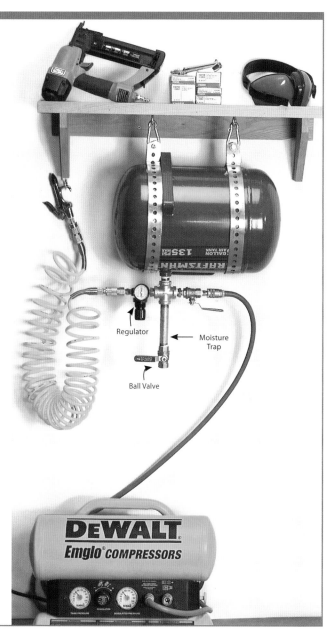

Regulator

Moisture Trap

Ball Valve

Planer Blade Drawknife

My portable planer uses disposable blades. When the first set got dull, I didn't throw them away—I turned the two blades into very useful drawknives. I wrapped duct tape around the ends of the blades and touched up their cutting edges with a diamond paddle. The narrow profiles of these tools are perfect for cutting tight curves.

Electrolysis Cleans Rusty Tools

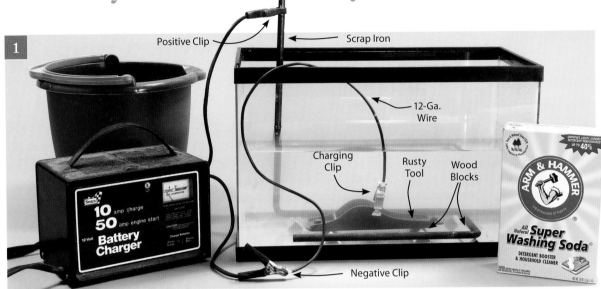

1 Positive Clip · Scrap Iron · 12-Ga. Wire · Charging Clip · Rusty Tool · Wood Blocks · Negative Clip

I've heard there's an easy way to remove rust from small tools using a battery charger. How does it work?

Electrolysis is a gentle, safe way to chemically remove all the rust, leaving the iron untouched. An abrasive can remove rust, too, but it may require removing a large amount of metal, either weakening the piece or destroying its value.

Here's what you need: A small battery charger, a plastic or glass container, washing soda (available in the laundry-detergent aisle at grocery stores), scrap iron, a charging clip and a couple feet of wire.

Here's how it works: Follow the setup in Photo 1. The tool gets a negative charge and the scrap iron gets a positive charge. The rust flees from the negatively charged tool and is attracted to the positively charged scrap iron. The cleaning action occurs only in a line-of-sight manner, so it's best if the scrap iron surrounds the tool. When you've wired the tool and scrap-iron rod, plug in the charger. The lowest

setting is all you need. Bubbles mean it's working (Photo 2). Eventually, a reddish brown crud will appear on the water's surface (Photo 3). When bubbles no longer form on the tool, you're done. Clean the tool with water and a gray 3M finishing pad. Treat your restored tool to a coat of rust-inhibiting wax or spray.

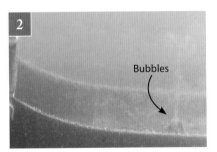

2 Bubbles

Bubbles indicate the process has started. Now all you have to do is wait until the bubbles stop. This plane iron took a day and a half.

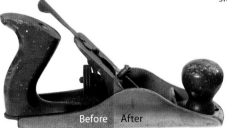

Before   After

Electrolysis is not a complex operation. Mix one tablespoon of washing soda in one gallon of water. Pour this solution over the tool until it is covered. Hook the charger's black negative clip to the tool using a length of 12-gauge wire and a charging clip. This keeps your charger lead out of the soup. The red clip must be hooked to a portion of scrap-iron rod that is out of the water, because it would be eaten away in the water. Wooden blocks suspend the tool so the bottom gets cleaned as well.

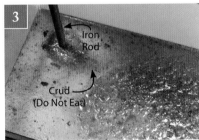

3 Iron Rod · Crud (Do Not Eat)

The orange crud on top is all that rust fleeing from the negatively charged tool to the positively charged iron rod. This is a good thing. It looks terrible, but this nontoxic sludge can be poured down the drain.

Safety Considerations

Electricity and water can be dangerous. Keep the charger away from the water in case of an accidental spill. Unplug the charger prior to placing your hands in the water.

Non-Slip Bench Hook

Planing or scraping parts with angled or mitered ends is tricky. Bench dogs will damage a crisp corner, and clamps get in the way. To hold the work, I use an oversized bench hook with a new twist: a layer of 3M's grip tape, made for slippery sidewalks and steps. The grit doesn't mar the wood—even soft wood—and when I apply downward pressure with a plane or scraper, the part stays put.

Better Winding Sticks

Winding sticks are very useful for gauging twist in a board, but they're difficult to read. My improved version of these time-tested helpers makes the twist stand out.

I start with a pair of straight, flat 2-in.-wide sticks made from ¾-in.-thick light-colored wood. Then I stain both of them dark—the darker, the better.

When the stain is dry, I cut shallow rabbets in both faces at the top of both sticks. This exposes a ribbon of light-colored wood above the stained surface on each face. To cut the rabbets, set the blade's height to ½ in. and the rip fence ⅟₃₂ in. narrower than the stick. Rip all four rabbets from this setting.

Joint the top edge of one board to remove the stain. Then rip this board narrower by the width of the rabbet on the other board. That's all there is to it.

During use, the narrow stick goes in front. Any twist in the board shows as a dark-colored wedge between the top of the rabbet on the near stick and the bottom of the rabbet on the far stick.

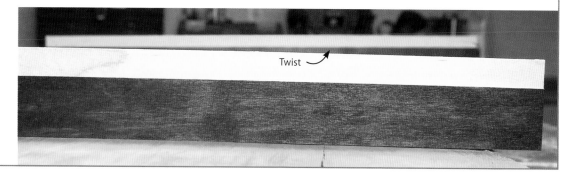

Twist

Pare Thin Dovetails

A while back, you ran a story on making precise half-blind dovetails by paring. The pins were ⅜ in. at the gauge line, narrowing down to ¼ in. I prefer smaller pins, narrowing down to less than ⅛ in., but I can't find a chisel thin enough to pare into this smaller opening. Can you make a recommendation?

Make your own chisel from a standard-thickness plane blade. This is a very cool tool! You'll find many other applications for it.

With this plane-blade chisel, you can pare drawer dovetails that are ¼ in. wide at the gauge line and have a 1-in-8 slope, as shown in the photo.

Sharpen the plane blade straight across to enable it to pare into a corner. Make the handle from ½-in. thick wood. Round the sides and top edge and chamfer the bottom edge. Fasten the sides with 1-in. long ¼-20 machine screws and square nuts. The handle is easily removable for sharpening the blade, which can go back in the plane when needed.

Rust Removal

My shop's roof leaked and I've got a light coating of rust on my tools. How can I restore them?

There are lots of ways to remove rust, but here's one that's inexpensive and uses materials you probably already have. Basically, you sand off the rust using light oil as a lubricant. WD-40 works great. It floats the swarf (the metal particles) so the paper doesn't clog up. Use a fine paper, such as 320-grit. Standard paper is OK; it doesn't have to be the wet/dry type.

The process is a bit messy, though, so you won't want to contaminate a good sanding block. Make a throwaway block from scrap and glue a piece of corrugated cardboard to its bottom (for all sanding, a block with a slight cushion works better than one with a hard bottom). Wipe up the rusty oil residue with paper towels.

Low-Angle Planes Provide Versatility

What advantage does a low-angle bench plane have over a standard bench plane?

Low-angle bench planes allow you to change the blade's effective cutting angle to suit specific tasks. Because the bevel points up on a low-angle plane, the effective cutting angle can be varied based on the iron's bevel angle. The bevel-up configuration also means the plane blade is fully supported right up to the cutting edge. With the bevel down, the cutting edge remains unsupported along the bevel, which can lead to blade chatter (Fig. A, below).

To get the most out of your low-angle bench plane, it's best to have two or three blades on hand with various bevel angles already ground on them (Fig. A). A 25-degree bevel ground on the cutting iron will produce a low cutting angle of 37 degrees that's ideal for shaving end grain (see photo, left). A 35-degree bevel approximates the 45-degree cutting angle on a standard bench plane, which is best-suited for general planing tasks. A 50-degree bevel creates a high cutting angle of 62 degrees for more of a scraping cut that reduces tearout on squirrelly grained wood, such as bird's-eye maple.

Figure A

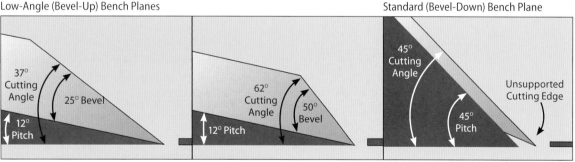

Low-Angle (Bevel-Up) Bench Planes

37° Cutting Angle — 25° Bevel — 12° Pitch

62° Cutting Angle — 50° Bevel — 12° Pitch

Standard (Bevel-Down) Bench Plane

45° Cutting Angle — Unsupported Cutting Edge — 45° Pitch

The cutting angle is simply the sum of the bevel angle and the plane-bed angle or pitch. The pitch of a low-angle bench plane is 12 degrees, but its effective cutting angle can be varied based on the iron's bevel angle. Standard bench planes usually have a pitch of 45 degrees, often referred to as common, or York, pitch. Since the plane is bevel down, the effective cutting angle remains at 45 degrees no matter what angle is ground on the bevel.

Remote Compressor Drain

To save precious floor space, I mounted my air compressor up high. This works great except when the time comes to drain the condensation from the tank. To solve the problem, I replaced the original drain cock with a safety release valve available wherever compressors are sold. Then I attached a cord to the drain valve to put it within easy reach. To drain the tank I get to play train engineer and pull the cord to blow the whistle. When I release the cable, the valve closes automatically. (Don't forget to wear your safety glasses and hearing protection.)

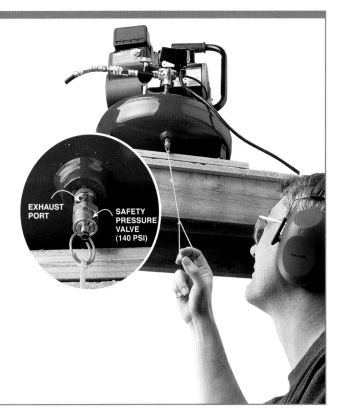

EXHAUST PORT

SAFETY PRESSURE VALVE (140 PSI)

Recycle Old Gloves

Here's a simple way to protect your chisels from getting nicked and rusty while they're rattling around in your toolbox. Just cut the fingers off some old leather work gloves. Poke holes with an awl at the open end and thread a drawstring through them. Slide the chisel's blade into the finger, then close it tight with the drawstring.

To keep the chisel rust-free, drizzle a little 3-in-1 oil into the finger. The oil will soak into the leather. Wipe the chisels with a clean cloth before use so the oil doesn't get on the wood.

Rx for Rusty Tools

How do I prevent my edge tools from rusting?

Rust is the curse of all woodworkers, but you've got three weapons at your disposal. First, lower the amount of water vapor in your shop's air with a dehumidifier. Second, isolate your tools in small drawers containing reusable packets of silica gel. These packets absorb moisture in the air and can be renewed by heating in a microwave oven. Third, coat your tools with oil, wax or volatile corrosion inhibitors (VCIs) emitted by strips you can stick in a drawer. You must renew oil and wax coatings often, but the VCI strips do the work for you for up to two years.

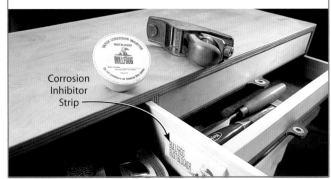

Corrosion Inhibitor Strip

Saber-Saw Cushion

The next time you use your saber saw, forget about hauling out the sawhorses or cantilevering a hard-to-hold workpiece off your bench. Extruded polystyrene insulation board, the rigid pink sheets used in housing construction, makes saber-sawing easy, whether you're cutting a small piece of hardwood or a full sheet of plywood. During the cut, the workpiece is always fully supported, so your saw has constant, stable support. The 2-in.-thick insulation houses saber-saw blades as long as 3½ in. The same piece can be used repeatedly; one 4-ft. x 8-ft. sheet (about $17 at home centers) will probably last you a lifetime.

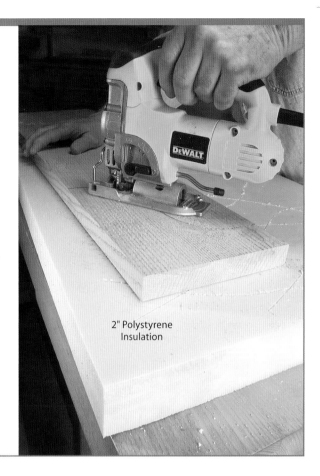

2" Polystyrene Insulation

Shaper Wings

I love my shaper, but always wished it had a bigger top to help balance large parts. Rather than buy a new shaper, I enlarged the top by adding hardwood extensions. The extensions on the sides are 1" thick and 3" wide; the extension on the front is 1" thick and 6" wide.

To fasten the extensions, I drilled and tapped holes in the edges of the table. Then, I glued and screwed 1" by 2" cleats to the edges of the extensions. I used a Forstner bit on the side extensions and a dado set on the front extension to create recesses for tightening the bolts.

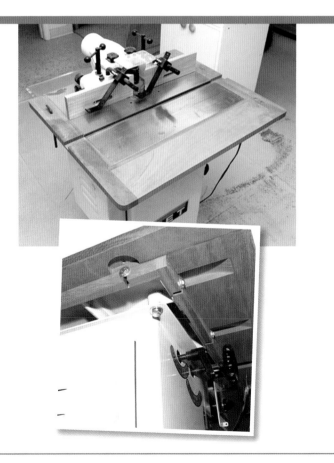

Scratch-Free Flush Cuts

No matter how carefully I cut with my economy-model flush-cutting saw, it always left scratch marks on the wood's surface. To solve the problem, I attached a playing card with double-faced tape. Now I don't have to worry about scratches, because my carded saw doesn't quite cut flush. Attaching the card limits the saw's depth of cut, so I saw the dowel halfway, then finish from the opposite side. Sawn dowels stand a wee bit proud, but they're easy to sand flush.

Shop-Made Straightedge

Every shop should have a long wooden straightedge. It's got a hundred and one uses, but I primarily use mine for checking jointed and sawn edges, and for guiding my router.

This 4-ft. one is pretty fancy, I admit, but there are good reasons for going to the extra trouble. Most of it is pine, so it's lightweight. It's laminated from strips, so it will stay straight for years. I added a hardwood strip to the bottom to prevent dings. The holes are for hanging this beautiful tool on my wall.

Steamer for Small Parts

To steam small pieces of wood, I made a plywood cover for my electric kettle with a 2½" hole drilled in the center. A piece of perforated rubber shelf liner over the hole creates a gasket around the PVC pipe, keeps the parts from falling through, and allows steam to flow into the pipe. Tie a length of string to the end of the parts you're steaming so you don't burn your fingers trying to get them out of the pipe. Also, be careful not to let the water level get too low or you'll ruin the kettle's heating element.

Steam Bending Gear

What do I need to know before building a simple steam-bending rig?

Steam bending doesn't require sophisticated equipment. For a single bending project, you can quickly cobble together an apparatus from ordinary materials.

The box. Build a box that fits your pieces out of any untreated solid wood or exterior plywood. Add a hinged or lift-off lid, but don't make it airtight. Add a simple rack to support your pieces so the steam can circulate. Tilt the box slightly and drill a ½-in. hole 6-in. from the end to drain condensate and relieve pressure.

Schedule 40 PVC pipe is another option, as shown above. A 10-ft. section of 4-in. schedule 40 PVC pipe and two end caps cost about $20. Drill ³⁄₁₆-in. holes every couple of feet to suspend your pieces on 12-gauge electrical wire.

Schedule 40 PVC is safe to use for steaming, but it will soften and droop when hot. Nail two boards in a "V" for support. Don't forget the ½-in. drain hole.

Water container. Use any type of metal container to which you can attach a hose, such as a new gas can or an old tea kettle.

Heat source. Electric hot plates or camp stoves will do, but they are not very efficient. Pros often use a propane gas burner available from camping stores. Caution: propane must be used outdoors.

A convenient alternative is an electric tea kettle kit. It comes with a 6-in. section of 1½-in. pipe to insert into the kettle's spout. The kettle holds enough water for an hour's worth of steaming and will shut off automatically when the water runs out.

Hose. A garden hose will do the job, but an automobile radiator hose (about $10) is a better choice. It's much easier to attach to the steam kettle kit, but you must drill a 1½-in. diameter hole in your box or pipe end cap. Radiator hoses are available in many sizes at all auto parts stores.

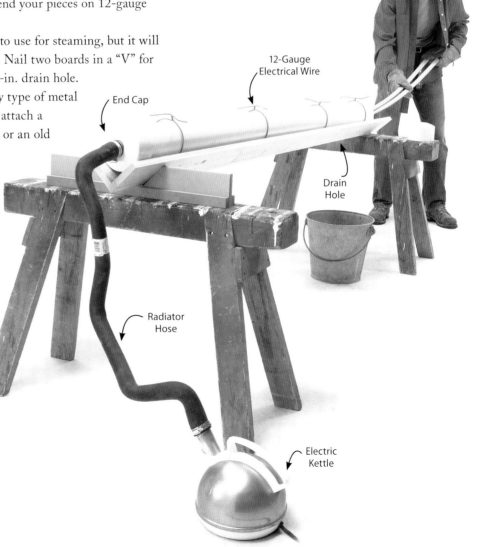

End Cap

12-Gauge Electrical Wire

Drain Hole

Radiator Hose

Electric Kettle

Filosophy

What are different kinds of files used for?

There are four kinds that you'll find handy in your woodshop:

Cabinet Rasp. Use this coarse tool with a heavy pressure to rapidly remove wood, such as shaping a rounded leg. Its teeth are individually formed and separate from one another, leaving behind a rough surface. A Wood rasp is similar to a Cabinet rasp, but has coarser teeth.

Pattern Makers File. Use this specialist's tool with a light pressure to remove wood fast. It leaves a much smoother surface than a Cabinet rasp. Its teeth are also individually formed, but set in wavy rows.

Double-cut Flat File or **Half Round File.** These tools, used with a heavy pressure, remove wood slower than a Cabinet rasp or Pattern Makers file. They leave a relatively smooth surface that requires further

sanding. Both files have two rows of teeth set at an angle to each other. Flat files are rectangular in cross section; Half-round files have one flat side and one curved side.

Single-cut Mill File. Used with a light pressure, this tool produces a very smooth surface. It's generally used on metal rather than wood, such as sharpening a scraper blade. It has a single row of teeth. Mill files are rectangular in cross section.

When buying a Flat, Half Round or Mill file, notice its *cut* and *length*. Both factors affect the coarseness of its teeth, and thus the smoothness of the surface it leaves behind. In order of coarseness, the various cuts you'll find are: Coarse, Bastard, Second Cut, and Smooth. A Flat Bastard file, for example, cuts faster but makes a rougher surface than a Flat Smooth file. Generally you'll find a file's cut marked just above the tang,

next to the maker's name.

Within each type of cut, the longer the file, the coarser are its teeth (see photo, left.) A 10 in. Single Cut Mill Bastard file, for example, has coarser teeth than an 8 in. Single Cut Mill Bastard file. Files range from 4 in. long to 16 in. long, in 2 in. increments. Files that are either 8 or 10 in. long are about the right size for most jobs.

For more information, see the "Nicholson Guide to Files and Filing," a PDF available at www.cooperhandtools.com/brands/nicholson_files/. It's based on File Filosophy, an out-of-print 48-page booklet published in many editions since 1878 by the Nicholson File Co. Old copies are available through used-book stores and on the web.

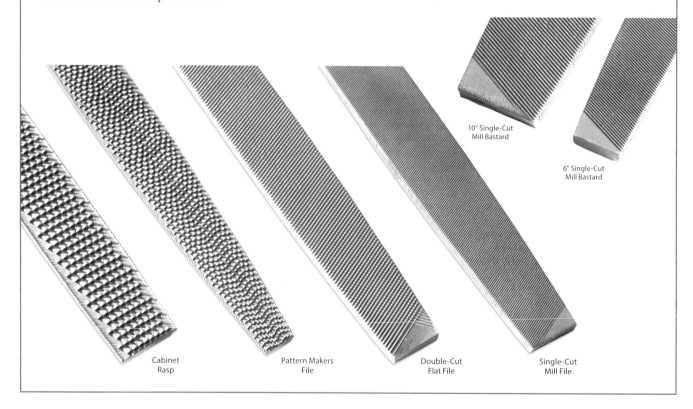

10" Single-Cut
Mill Bastard

6" Single-Cut
Mill Bastard

Cabinet
Rasp

Pattern Makers
File

Double-Cut
Flat File

Single-Cut
Mill File

Spray Gun Cleaning Jug

When I clean my HVLP spray gun, this shop-made container captures the liquid solvent and fumes. When the gun is clean, I simply pour the waste into a storage container for disposal.

Drill a 3-in. hole in the back of a paint thinner jug. Cut a 3-in. circle from an activated carbon filter pad (available at pet shops with aquarium products) and place it in a 3-in. ventilation louver (from the home center). Insert the louver into the hole in the jug,

making sure the fins face down. The activated carbon captures fumes while allowing the pressurized air to escape. Finally, drill a hole in the jug's cap, slightly larger than your gun's air cap but smaller than its sleeve nut. This way the tip of the gun forms a tight seal when pressed against the jug's cap. I used a 1¼-in. Forstner bit.

To clean your gun, simply hold the jug in one hand and press the spray gun's tip into the cap.

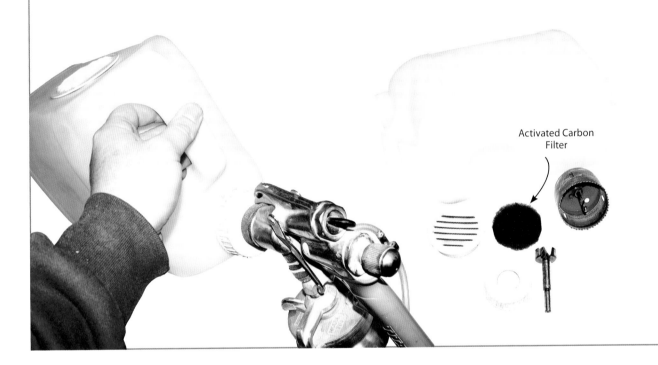

Activated Carbon Filter

Stop Cutting Creep

When you're cutting miters on a miter saw, the spinning blade tends to push or pull the workpiece along the fence. A hold-down clamp will stop the creeping, but molded stock can be hard to clamp. In that case, dampen the back side of the wood. Moistened wood is less slippery and easier to hold in place.

What's a Pattern Rasp?

A friend told me that a tool called a pattern rasp is a must-have for woodworking. What's so special about it?

A pattern rasp cuts aggressively but leaves a smooth surface. A standard wood rasp makes a rougher surface requiring additional filing because its teeth are set in rows. The teeth of a pattern rasp are set in a random pattern.

Pattern rasps cost almost four times as much as standard wood rasps, however. The higher cost is due in part to the complexity of manufacturing random-set teeth. But the real difference is the steel. Pattern rasps have hardened teeth made to handle material harder than wood. You can use a pattern rasp to shape brass, bronze, aluminum, mild steel and even ceramic tile. If you stick to wood, a pattern rasp will far outlast a standard wood rasp.

As their name suggests, pattern rasps were originally designed for pattern makers. These artisans build very precise wood patterns for casting metal machine parts.

Two types of pattern rasps are available, the #49 and the #50, which has finer teeth. The #49 is generally the best choice for woodworkers.

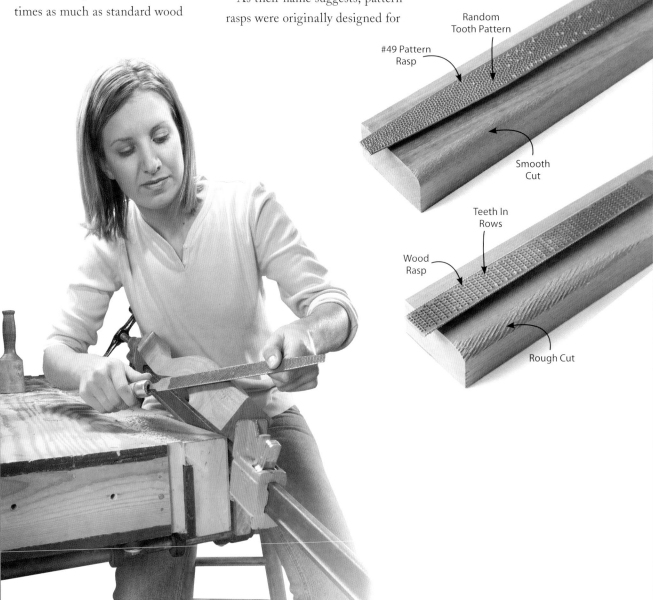

Random Tooth Pattern

#49 Pattern Rasp

Smooth Cut

Teeth In Rows

Wood Rasp

Rough Cut

Cheapest Plumbing Ever

Whenever I need a cup of water or a damp rag, I just turn the spigot on my $3 water jug. That's much cheaper than plumbing my shop!

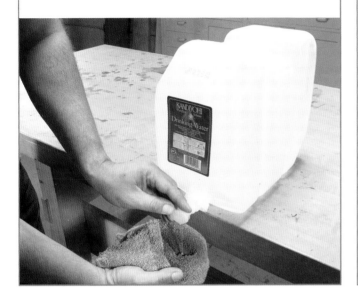

Garden Variety Wrap

Hook and loop tie wrap is nothing new, but you may not be aware that it comes in two different varieties. The two-piece kind sells for about a dollar per foot. One piece has hooks; the other has loops. The one-piece "garden variety" kind, which has hooks on one side and loops on the other side, comes in a ½" wide by 45' roll that only costs about 3 bucks! It really is made for gardeners, but I've found dozens of uses for it around the shop, such as binding cords, securing box lids, and bundling wood scraps or dowels.

Do-It-All Shop Paper

You may think I'm crazy for getting excited about a roll of paper, but if you ask me, this product should be in every shop. If it's brown it's called builder's paper and if it's red it's called rosin paper. You'll find it at home centers for about nine bucks for a roll 144-ft. long by 36-in. wide. I originally bought it to save my tablesaw from glue drips but it has tons of other uses around the shop, for example:

- Making full-scale drawings
- Laying out templates
- Masking off the back of picture frames
- Testing spray patterns before turning the spray gun on a project.

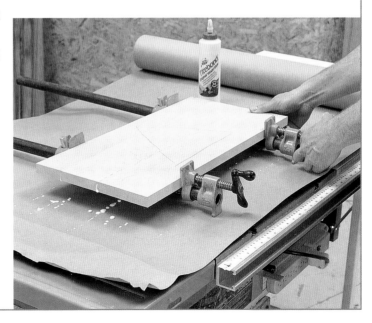

Eliminate Goggle Fogging

My goggles used to completely fog over in hot weather or whenever I wore a dust mask. Then a motorcyclist friend told me about a spray he uses on his face shield. Now, I simply treat my lenses with antifogging spray. Temperature and humidity determine how long each application works, so you'll have to experiment a little. The first time you use it, apply two coats. After that, spray on a fresh coat at the first sign of fog. A 2-oz. spray bottle contains about 150 applications.

Magnetic Pencil Holder

I used to have trouble hanging onto my pencil, but now it's always at arm's length. I simply place magnets on each side of my shirtsleeve and twist a nut onto my pencil (if the nut's too large, I wrap tape around the pencil shaft).

My shirtsleeve magnets are also great for keeping a couple of nails or screws handy during assembly or for work around the house. I admit it looks kind of goofy, but at least nobody can accuse me of having a screw loose!

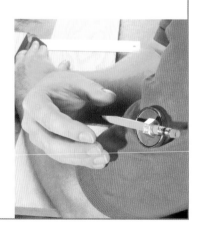

Never A Dull Pencil

Precise marks are one key to accurate cuts. Rather than mounting pencil sharpeners all around the shop, I just stick 120-grit PSA-backed sandpaper wherever I need a sharp pencil; at both ends of my workbench, right next to my miter saw, on top of my tablesaw's rip fence, etc.

Plug Your Wrenches

I know I should unplug my tools before changing blades and bits, but sometimes I forget. So far I've been lucky, but I'd rather be safe, so I came up with a simple solution. Using a hook-and-loop strap, I secured my tool wrenches to the end of the power cords. Now there's absolutely no way I can change a blade or bit without first unplugging the tool. And as an added bonus, I can't misplace the wrenches.

Pick-Up Stick

I like to work in my driveway when the weather is nice. To avoid flat tires, I built a magnetic tool to pick up wayward screws and nails. It captures and releases these hazards quite easily.

The pick-up stick is very simple. It's composed of a ¾" x 3' dowel, a plywood ring with a few rare-earth magnets epoxied to it, and a large plastic lid fastened to the end of the dowel. Drill a hole in the ring large enough to allow it to freely slide on the dowel.

To capture screws and nails, slide the ring down on top of the lid. To release them, slide the ring up the dowel.

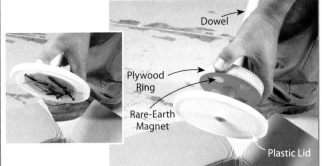

Dowel

Plywood Ring

Rare-Earth Magnet

Plastic Lid

Frankenstein's Pencil

I like to use carpenter's pencils until they're worn down to stubs. Stubs aren't very handy, though—they're hard to dig out of a pocket. To solve this problem, I gathered up all the stubs lying around the shop and cut scarf joints on them with a handsaw. I trued up the joints with a disc sander and glued the pieces together, making one new, longer pencil. I also duct-taped a paper clip to my new pencil, and glued on an old drafting eraser, for a little icing on the cake.

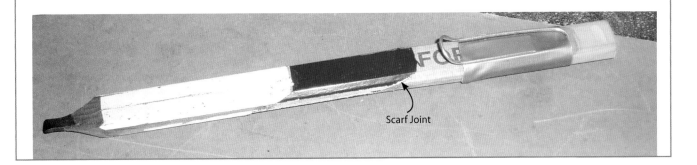

Scarf Joint

Sawdust Catcher

After years of sweeping under my contractor's saw, I finally devised a way to directly collect most of the sawdust in a large plastic trash bag. The bag is held by a ½" MDF frame. I drilled holes in the frame for machine bolts, and corresponding holes in my saw's base, then epoxied the bolts in the base's holes. The bag wraps around the frame, which is attached to the base with wing nuts.

Save the Straw!

A can of lubricant is very useful around the shop, and so is the little red straw...if you can find it after the first use! I figured out that the straw fits in the groove in the top of the can, and you can still put the lid on. No more lost straws!

Snow Shovel Dust Pan

I've tried out a lot of different kinds and sizes of dustpans but I like this child's snow shovel the best. The long handle means I don't have to bend over very far and it's a lot lighter than a full-sized shovel. I bought it for only two bucks at my local hardware store.

Practical Paraffin

Ordinary paraffin canning wax has dozens of uses in my shop. It's cheap at $2 a pound, available at any grocery store and easy to cut into small chunks. Unlike candle wax, which often contains beeswax, or some spray lubricants, which may have silicone in them, paraffin won't contaminate oil and varnish finishes because it's a completely petroleum-based product. Most wax residue gets sanded off anyway.

I often lubricate my jointer and planer beds with a paraffin wax squiggle. Wood is much easier to push down a waxed bed.

Glue doesn't adhere to paraffin. I rub wax on clamping blocks to keep them from sticking.

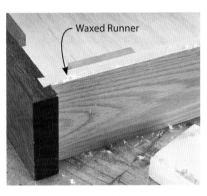

Waxed Runner

I always wax new and old drawers to make them run smoothly.

My plane is much easier to push when it's waxed, too. I rub paraffin on its sole every 10 strokes or so.

No More Bruises

My shop is so small that I often bump into my tools while navigating between them. Recently, I got a nasty scrape and bruise on my thigh from the end of the fence rail on my tablesaw. To prevent further injury, I plugged the end of the rail with a rounded-over block of wood. I still bump into it occasionally, but at least now it doesn't leave a scratch.

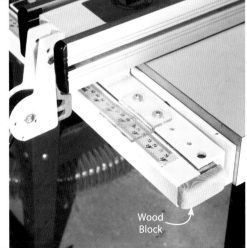

Wood Block

Vise

Benchtop Board Clamp

My father showed me this "bird's mouth" jig almost 60 years ago. It securely clamps ¼- to 3-in.-thick boards on edge. It's so useful that I've never bothered to add a vise to my workbench. I've been tempted to mount the jig permanently, but I prefer an uncluttered work surface. Besides, this jig is easy to install and remove.

To hold a board for planing or edge banding, simply engage one end on the sliding wedge (see photo at right). Slide the board and wedge forward until they lock between the fixed wedge and the fence (see photo inset). Support the back end of the board with a block the same thickness as the base.

I cut both wedges from a single board on the tablesaw, using a tapering jig and the blade tilted 45 degrees. I mounted the fence on the base and glued a stop on the sliding wedge. I positioned the two wedges by using a ¾-in.-thick spacer between the sliding wedge and the fence. Then I fastened the fixed wedge to the base.

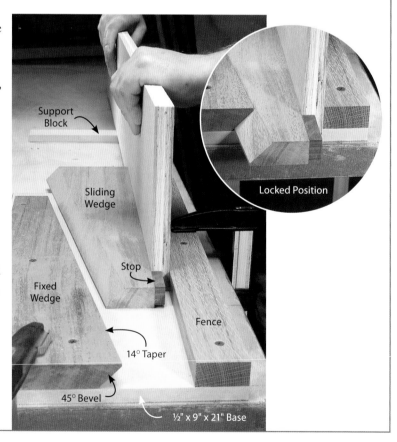

Support Block

Sliding Wedge

Fixed Wedge

Stop

Fence

14° Taper

45° Bevel

½" x 9" x 21" Base

Locked Position

Adjustable Board Support

In the good old days, when a woodworker wanted to plane a board's edge, he'd clamp one end in the bench's face vise and support the cantilevered end with a free-standing device called a "deadman". My modernized version mounts in the tail vise. After drilling holes in a 2-in.-thick post, I glued and screwed on a ¾-in.-thick top. By simply moving the dowel, I can support virtually any board or panel at a comfortable work height. And instead of taking up valuable floor space, my deadman stores compactly until the next use.

Tail Vise

¾" x 2" x 6" Top

1" Dia. Holes Spaced 2"

2" x 2" x 17" Post

Best Way to Mount a Face Vise

The back jaw of my face vise sticks out an inch from the edge of my workbench. I've noticed traditional benches have the back jaw set flush with the edge of the bench. Is there any advantage to this?

This vise question comes up all the time. The reason the back jaw was set flush on traditional benches is that it provides better support for a long board clamped on edge. Boards were held in this position so the edge could be jointed with a hand plane. The flush vise jaw allows the opposite end of the board to be clamped to the bench. The board is then continuously supported against the edge of the workbench. This allows you to work on the edge without wobble. Few of us still joint boards by hand anymore, but there are times when we modern woodworkers need to tightly clamp a long board to the bench.

Face Vise

Cam-Action Bench Dog

I made a clamping device for my bench that can quickly snug up a board just by swinging a lever. The lever has a cam that pushes a sliding stop tight against the board.

I made all the parts from ¼" thick stock. The total thickness of the device is ½", so I can use it for planing or sanding any piece that's more than ½" thick.

The base for the stop is 6" wide and 20" long. The guide rails are 6" long. The inner edges of the rails and the outer edges of the sliding stop are beveled at 10°. The bevels on the rails point up, while the bevels on the stop point down. This dovetailed arrangement keeps the stop from lifting up when it's tightened. The rails are glued to the base.

The cam lever is 2" wide and 6" long; its rounded end is a circle with a 1" radius. The lever rotates on an 8-32 FH machine screw, ¾" long. The hole for the screw is offset: It's located ⅝" in from the left side of the lever and 1" down from the lever's end. Drill this hole first, using a ⅛" bit, then align the lever with the sliding stop and continue the hole through the base. Countersink the bottom of the hole, insert the screw and fasten it with a wing nut.

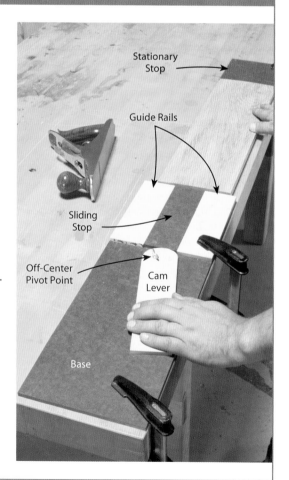

Stationary Stop

Guide Rails

Sliding Stop

Off-Center Pivot Point

Cam Lever

Base

Clamp Doubles as Tail Vise

After years of wishing my old workbench had a tail vise, I realized I could make one of my new Jorgensen Cabinet Master bar clamps do the job. All I had to do was reverse the sliding lower jaw (it's removable) and mount the bar and fixed jaw under the benchtop.

I drilled and chiseled out an elongated hole in the leg so the sliding jaw would extend only ⅝-in. above the benchtop. Then I lag-screwed a notched block and cap at the opposite end to act as a bearing surface for the fixed jaw. To finish my tail vise, I drilled a row of 1⅛-in.-dia. holes in line with the sliding jaw and fashioned a bench dog to fit.

When I need to use the clamp elsewhere, I just remove the sliding jaw and pull the fixed jaw and bar out from the other end.

Corner Molding Vise Pads

I've found that sections of 1" corner molding are ideal for padding the jaws of a machinist's vise. You can buy adhesive-backed magnetic strips at a craft supply store to hold the pads in place. Alternatively, you can just cut up refrigerator magnets and glue them onto the molding. When the pads get chewed up, it takes only a minute and a few cents to replace them.

No-Rack Vise

A workpiece always slips when placed vertically in my vise, because the vise racks. To solve the problem, I made a vise spacer from a 1"x 2"x 6" hardwood block, a ¼" T-nut, a ¼" x 4" bolt, and a couple pieces of ¾" dia. dowel. I drilled a 4" hole in one end of the hardwood block and inserted the T-nut to accept the bolt. Next I drilled two ¾" holes in the bottom of the block to line up with the bench's dog holes, and glued and screwed two ¾" dowels into them.

To prevent racking, I clamp the workpiece in the vise, then insert the spacer into two dog holes on the benchtop, on the opposite side of the vise from the workpiece. Next, I insert a bench dog into a hole in the vise. As I tighten the vise, I adjust the bolt in or out to keep the vise's front jaw parallel to the bench. This enables the vise to apply even pressure across the full width of the workpiece.

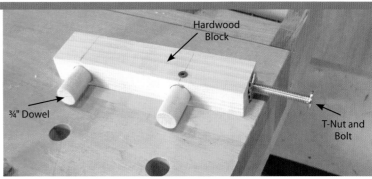

Hardwood Block

¾" Dowel

T-Nut and Bolt

Mobile Machinist's Vise

A little metalworking finds its way into my woodshop from time to time. When cutting metal, it's best to use a machinist's vise to get a better grip. Because it sticks up and is in the way, I can't permanently attach it to my woodworking bench. Instead, I built a simple platform from doubled-up ¾-in. plywood with a 2x2 cleat screwed to the bottom. The platform allows me to temporarily mount my vise to my bench when needed. It spends the rest of the time on the shelf below the bench.

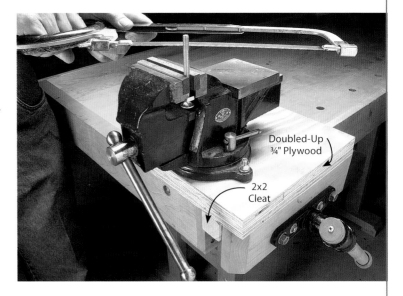

Doubled-Up ¾" Plywood

2x2 Cleat

Vise Crank Handle

I'm getting up in years but I still love woodworking. My hands aren't as limber as they used to be, so it was uncomfortable to twist my vise handle. I remembered the crank on my father's Model T, so I made one just like it for my vise. I drilled a hole slightly bigger than the diameter of the vise's rod in one end of a 1-in.-diameter turned wooden handle. I removed the endcaps from the rod and slid on my new handle. As a bonus, the handle swings out of the way so I won't bang my leg into it.

If your endcaps don't come off, you could split your new handle with a chisel, place it around the vise handle and glue the halves back together.

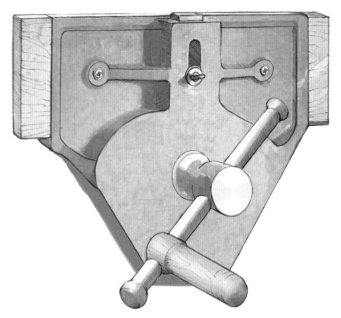

Snap-On Soft Jaws

I've been using an old metal-working vise in my shop for years. Occasionally I really do need a metal-working vise, but most often I use it to hold drawer sides up high when cutting dovetails. Unfortunately the metal jaws can be a hazard to edge tools and they can mar the surface of the wood. I solved these problems by adding a pair of soft jaws to the vise. The jaws are just two pieces of pine with a couple holes for recessed rare earth magnets. The soft jaws literally snap in place to provide a non-marring clamp surface for my stock plus a non-threatening surface for my edge tools.

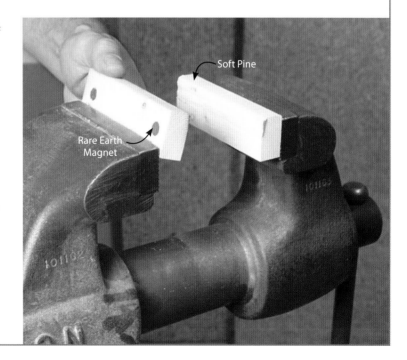

Soft Pine

Rare Earth Magnet

Rock-Solid Bench Support

The face vise on my workbench didn't hold long boards rigidly enough until I added this adjustable "bench slave." And it only cost about $30.

First I milled a board to attach to the leg, making sure it was thick enough to fit flush with the front edge of the benchtop. Then I cut a dado right down the middle of the board, to house a piece of T-track (slotted aluminum track that accepts T-bolts). When I installed the T-track, I left a gap at the top for installing and removing the support block.

Next I drilled two centered holes in the support block, one large enough for the T-bolt to slide through freely, the other small enough for the T-bolt to thread into. I attached a T-style knob to the free-sliding bolt and fastened a toggle clamp over the threaded-in T-bolt.

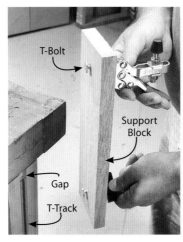

Installing and removing the support block is easy, thanks to a small gap for the T-bolts at the top of the T-track.

Quick-Change Vises

I use two vises mounted to separate boards when I drill pen blanks. I frequently switch the vises, but clamping and re-clamping the vise boards to the drill press table was a pain. Now I use Mag-Jigs, powerful magnets that can be switched on or off with the twist of a knob. I mounted two Mag-Jigs on each board.

If you use a standard cast-iron drill press table, you're all set. The Mag-Jigs will stick directly to it. My drill press setup is a bit fancier, though, as I've installed a large melamine table equipped with a fence. So, I mounted a steel plate on a third board. I clamp that board to the table and place the vise board on top of the steel plate.

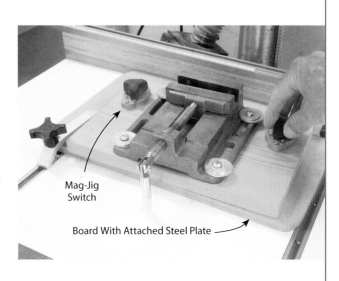

Mag-Jig Switch

Board With Attached Steel Plate

What's a Tail Vise?

I am really puzzled as to how the tail vise actually works as I have only used a front vise.

A tail vise's main purpose is to hold a board flat on the bench for planing, routing, sanding and so on. The tail vise pushes a board tightly against a bench dog so the board can't swivel or move. The bench dog fits in a series of holes cut in the top to accommodate different sizes of boards. Think of your bench as a big clamp: The bench dog is the fixed end or head of the clamp, and the dog in the tail vise is the clamp's adjustable end. Both the bench dog and the vise dog are adjustable in height so they won't stick above the board and get in your way.

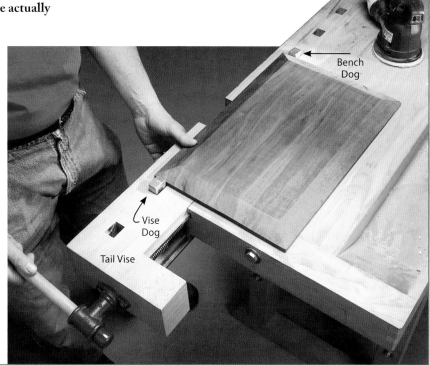

Bench Dog

Vise Dog

Tail Vise

What's Wrong With My Vise?

The jaws of my new vise aren't parallel, top to bottom. Is this OK?

Your vise is just fine. This design ensures that a board doesn't wiggle when you tighten the vise.

The lean in your vise's outer jaw is called toe-in. Toe-in corrects for up-and-down play in the guide bars. As you tighten a vise, the guide bars tend to angle down, so they're lower in front than in back. This makes the outer jaw lean away from the inner jaw.

Toe-in compensates for that lean. When you tighten a vise with toe-in, the outer jaw becomes parallel to the inner jaw. It puts even pressure along the entire surface of your workpiece, which is exactly what you want. If your vise doesn't have toe-in, or the toe-in is inadequate, plane the outer jaw's wooden face so it's thicker at the top than at the bottom. That creates the lean you'll need to hold work more securely.

Guide Bar

Outer Jaw

Wood

Attack of the Powder Post Beetle

I just noticed that my stack of air-dried oak is peppered with tiny holes. I also noticed little piles of fine dust on and around the stack. What can I do to save my wood?

You're probably looking at a powder post beetle infestation. These pests particularly love the sapwood in hardwoods like red oak and ash. The problem usually manifests itself when the beetles begin to exit the lumber in the springtime. They push the dust (called frass) that is packed into the holes out ahead of themselves.

You can help prevent future infestations by maintaining a tidy area around wood that's air drying outdoors. Remove scraps, sawdust, vegetation, etc.

Once an infestation is discovered you have two choices. You can take the wood to a kiln to finish the drying process. Kilns will heat the wood to 140 degrees F or more and that will kill the beetles. Your other recourse is to have the pile fumigated by a pest control company. You may have to call around to find a company familiar with the problem.

Beetle Hole

Frass

Inexpensive Blade for Suspect Lumber

I'm always on the lookout for orphaned boards. I've reclaimed lots of useful material from old pallets, downed trees, remodeling job sites and salvage yards; I've even rescued weathered siding from old barns. I try to remove all the nails, dirt and grit before sawing my salvaged treasures. But to make sure I don't damage one of my expensive blades, I cut these boards with an inexpensive 7¼-in. circular saw blade purchased at a home center. These blades can cut boards as thick as 1½ in. and they're designed for tough use, with teeth made from a softer but less brittle grade of carbide.

Is Blue-Stained Pine OK?

I have some pine that was given to me. The price was right but the wood is full of blue stain. Is it safe to use this wood for painted projects or as a secondary wood?

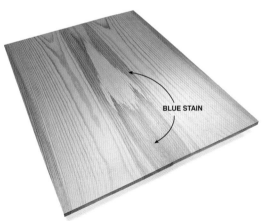

Blue stain is a common fungus that infects the sapwood of freshly sawn boards causing a blue discoloration in pine. The infestation most often occurs during the summer months when freshly sawn boards are exposed to the open air before kiln drying. The color can range from a striking blue to a dull gray or black. We asked Harlan Petersen at the University of Minnesota Department of Wood and Paper Science about blue stain.

Mr. Petersen told us that blue stain is a non-destructive fungus that has little or no effect on the structural integrity of the wood, so it is safe to use in terms of strength. However, because more destructive organisms thrive under the same conditions that lead to blue stain, it is advisable to inspect your boards for weakened wood fibers or punkiness.

The Western Wood Products Association encourages woodworkers not to think of blue stained pine as junk wood. Often your blue stained boards can be used like a spalted or figured wood to create dramatic effects (see photo).

Plain-Sliced Plywood

I'm building a project out of red oak plywood and I'd like to use the best plywood I can find. Is plain-sliced the best grade? It certainly costs more!

Plain-sliced plywood isn't "better" in any objective sense, but the face veneer (the oak, in your case) is more expensive and requires more work in the manufacturing process, so the plywood costs more. In simple terms, rotary-sliced veneer, the kind you find on standard home-center plywood, is peeled off the log like paper towels off a roll. Plain-sliced veneer is sliced off the log like miniature boards. The difference is in appearance: Rotary-sliced veneer has a grain pattern that is often very open, with the porous growth lines very far apart. Plain-sliced veneer duplicates the appearance of solid-wood boards, with arches. The multiple arches on a piece of plain-sliced plywood result from individual pieces of edge-glued veneer.

Most people find the look of plain-sliced to be more natural and appealing, though as you've noticed, you pay about 50 percent more for it in oak. However, sometimes rotary-cut plywood can look very much like plain-sliced, so it's worth looking at it first to see how wild and open the grain really is. And for some projects, like the Hoosier Cabinet we featured in AW #77 (December 1999), rotary-cut plywood is a more authentic choice. It looks great because we chose the sheets carefully.

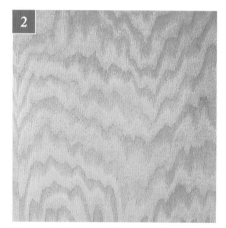

Plain-sliced veneer plywood

Rotary-sliced veneer plywood

Metal Detector for Recycled Lumber

When you use recycled lumber from old buildings, it's essential to find any embedded metal before you hit it with your bandsaw, or worse, the thickness planer. I use a hand-held, battery operated metal detector that's reliable to a depth of 6 to 8 in. I figure it has already paid for itself several times over.

Steamed vs. Unsteamed Walnut

Is it true that air-dried walnut looks a lot better than kiln-dried?

Kiln drying actually has little effect on walnut's color, but steaming does. Steaming blends the natural colors and distributes them evenly throughout the wood fibers. The result is a rather drab, grayish-brown board. Kiln-dried walnut is usually steamed because furniture manufacturers like the uniformity it gives to their furniture. That's why many people have been led to believe it's the kiln that kills walnut's natural beauty. Unsteamed walnut, whether it's dried by kiln or air, preserves the purples, reds, greens and browns that naturally occur in walnut.

As an individual craftsperson, you may sometimes want to avoid sifting through boards for good color matches. That's the time to pick steamed walnut. For special projects in which you really want the rich, true colors of walnut displayed, go for unsteamed.

Unsteamed Walnut

Steamed Walnut

Using Air-Dried Wood

Some of the glue joints failed on a project I built last winter from air-dried wood. Where did I go wrong?

You may have been hit with a double whammy: wood that wasn't ready for building and joints that weren't clamped long enough.

Wood that's been dried outdoors usually has 8 percent to 12 percent moisture content (MC). When you bring this lumber indoors in winter, its MC will drop further, ideally down to 6 percent to 8 percent. As wood dries, it can warp or twist. A large, rapid decrease in humidity and MC is particularly stressful. Your wood was probably drying and moving when you built with it, and this could have forced the joints apart later on. It's best to bring air-dried wood into your shop for a few weeks before milling in order to reduce its MC and stabilize it.

Clamping time for yellow and white glues should be extended if you're using wood with 8 percent and higher MC, for an outdoor project or to go in a relatively humid environment, for example. White and yellow glues dry and build strength as they lose water; the higher the wood's MC, the longer this process takes. A few hours of clamp time may be needed, with full strength developing after two to three days.

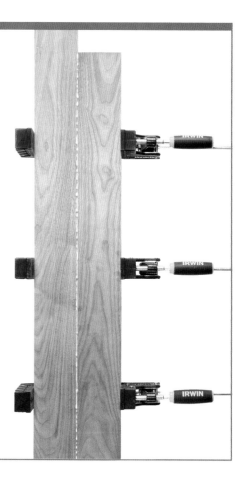

Warped Wood Woes

I ordered a milled piece of ebony through the mail last winter. It looked great upon arrival, but after a few days it was so warped and twisted that I couldn't use it. What gives?

Watching your prized ebony turn into a potato chip must've hurt! Chances are this board had a fairly high moisture content (10 to 12 percent) when it was shipped. It arrived in a dry winter environment, where wood can have a moisture content as low as 5 or 6 percent. Your board started to dry out as soon as

you unwrapped it. Attempting to keep a board from changing shape while drying is a bit like trying to stop a glacier, but here are some things to try next time:

Buy rough lumber. You'll need a jointer and planer to mill it, but if you start out with thicker wood you'll have more leeway if it warps.

Use a moisture meter. Compare the moisture content of your new wood with old wood stored in your shop. Don't mill your new wood until it's about the same moisture content as the old stuff.

Paint the ends. Wood dries out faster through its ends and can crack if it dries too fast. Paint slows down the rate at which end grain loses moisture.

Stack your wood off the floor. Concrete floors can be very damp.

Place stickers between the boards. All sides of your wood should be equally exposed to air so they dry at equal rates.

Weight your boards. This helps keep them flat and straight, but it's no guarantee. You've done about all you can do.

Sticker

Painted Ends

Raise Lumber Above Floor

Stack and sticker mail-order wood as soon as it arrives.

Where Can I Find Information on Different American Woods?

The best place to start is to assemble a set of sample pieces. Pictures in books are fine, but if you really want to get to know a wood, you've got to hold it in your hand to judge its color, texture, and hardness.

One of the most comprehensive sets available comes from the Wood Smart Co., which contains 46 domestic species. Here you'll find typical samples of just about every wood you'd want to consider for a woodworking project, from American elm to willow. Each piece is a generous ½-in. thick by 3-in. wide by 6-in. long, unfinished, and clearly labeled with the wood's common name, botanical name,

specific gravity, and figures to calculate how much a flatsawn or a quartersawn board will shrink or swell. The 46 pieces come packed in a tailor-made cardboard box. A complete list of species is available on the website below.

If you want to know more facts and figures about these woods, the best source (and a terrific value) is The Encyclopedia of Wood, written and updated many times by the Forest Products Laboratory, a unit of the U.S. Forest Service. It contains almost 500 pages of technical data on domestic and imported woods, ranging from hardness to bending strength to decay resistance, and lots more.

Wood for Humidors

Why is Spanish Cedar used to line humidors? Can other woods be substituted?

Aging of premium cigars, like the aging of fine wines, requires a controlled environment. Humidors are designed to keep cigars at 70 degrees F with a relative humidity of 70 percent—perfect for cigars, not so good for most woods. Actually a member of the mahogany family, Spanish cedar's name comes from its spicy, cedar-like odor. Surprisingly, this pungent scent does not impart any unpleasant taste to the cigars. Spanish cedar's ability to absorb and moderate moisture without excessive dimensional change makes it the wood of choice for lining humidors.

Honduran mahogany is an acceptable substitute for Spanish cedar with one notable exception: The tobacco beetle, which uses tobacco as a host for its larvae, can't stand Spanish cedar but doesn't mind Honduran mahogany. Sometimes there's more to tradition than just tradition.

Tip: If you use Spanish cedar, look for Cedrela mexicana which doesn't have the pitch problems of the less expensive Cedrela odorata.

Workbench

Collapsible Work Stands

In a small shop, the more things that can be folded up and moved out of the way, the better. These work stands are easy to build, easy to store and cheap. They're especially good for finishing and gluing up panels. One sheet of 5/8-in. AC plywood will yield six stands. If you make them the same height as your tablesaw they will double as infeed and outfeed supports.

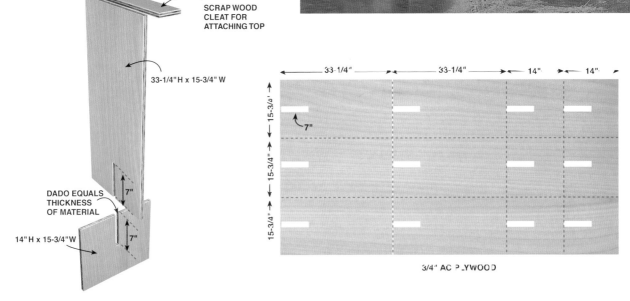

SCRAP WOOD CLEAT FOR ATTACHING TOP

33-1/4"H x 15-3/4" W

DADO EQUALS THICKNESS OF MATERIAL

7"

14" H x 15-3/4"W

7"

33-1/4"   33-1/4"   14"   14"

15-3/4"

7"

15-3/4"

15-3/4"

3/4" AC PLYWOOD

Bar Clamp Holdfast

A bar clamp makes an excellent bench holdfast. Just grind the end of the clamp so the sliding jaw can be slipped off the bar. Drill holes in the bench at convenient intervals, push the bar through one of the holes, and reinstall the sliding jaw. You can put the handle above or below the bench—whichever is more convenient.

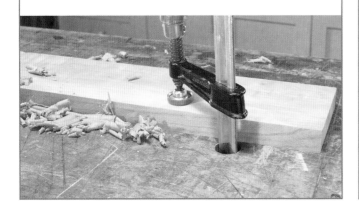

Deadbolt Bench Stop

For a quick and simple bench stop, I mounted a sliding bolt taken from an old door to the end of my workbench. In the locked position, the bolt stays put; in the unlocked position, it's completely out of the way.

Adjustable Support

I frequently need an outfeed table or work support for long pieces, so I built this T-shaped assembly to use in conjunction with my Black & Decker Workmate.

The table is just a horizontal board that's dadoed, glued and screwed to a vertical board. Not all my tools are the same height, though, so I devised an adjustment to the support that's quick and easy to use. Just drill different pairs of 1" holes for each tool in the vertical board. Set the height by inserting 1" dowels into the holes. Slide the table into the Workmate's jaws and clamp.

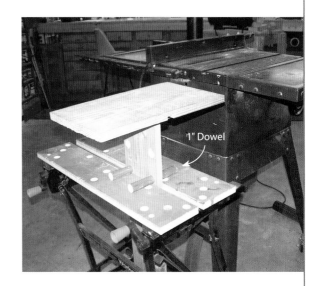

1" Dowel

Classic Sawhorse

I've found a sturdy sawhorse that's great even if you have limited space. When I'm done working with them I just stack them on top of each other and store them out of the way. Here's all it takes to build one horse:

- One 42-in.-long 2x6 for the top board
- Four 28-in.-long 1x8 boards for the legs
- Four 9⅞-in.-long 1x8 boards for the gussets
- Thirty-six 2-in. wood screws.

Notch the top board so the legs angle outward and toward the ends. Legs A and B are mirror images of each other and have compound 14-degree angle cuts at both ends. The four gussets are identical.

To assemble, predrill screw holes in the legs and gussets. Loosely screw the legs in the notches and screw and glue the gussets to the edges of the legs. Because the legs are not screwed tight, it's easy to line up the gussets. Tighten the screws that hold the legs to the top board and you're done.

14-DEGREE NOTCHES IN SIDES OF 2x6

4-1/2"

28"

LEG B

3/4"

6"

7-1/4"

9"

14-DEGREE BEVEL END CUTS

LEG A

2x6

GUSSET

14 DEGREES

1x8

LEG A

14 DEGREES

LEG B

14 DEGREES

7-1/4"

9-7/8"

Get Support on the Left Side

For crosscutting long pieces of plywood by yourself, rig up some kind of support on the left side of your saw. Sometimes a shop cart will do the trick, especially if your floor is smooth. However, a cart can get hung up, ruining your cut. A more sure-fire approach is a piece of plywood clamped to a sawhorse at just the right height. Make it long enough to support your work both before and after the cut.

Double-Duty Planer Stand

I love two-for-one deals. Even my shop is a twofer; it doubles as a garage (sometimes) when I'm not woodworking. My recent purchase of a benchtop planer inspired me to create another two-for-one deal. I built a mobile outfeed table for my tablesaw that doubles as a stand for my planer.

The cart is designed so the outfeed table on the planer equals the height of my tablesaw. This gives me a beautiful, long outfeed extension for the planer. Never one to leave well enough alone, I built up the sides so the top of a pair of 22-in. rollers equals the height of my saw. Now, my planer stand acts as an extension table for my saw and my tablesaw acts as an outfeed extension for my planer. There's lots of room under the cart to store the planer and the saw is perfect for stacking wood while planing.

2" Locking Caster

22" Roller

Convenient Benchtop Protection

My workbench is beautiful and I want to keep it that way, so I cover the top with builder's paper ($7 per 140-ft. roll at my local home center) whenever I'm gluing or staining. But the heavy roll was hard to handle and a nuisance to store until I devised this simple holder made from 4-in. PVC drain pipe (10-ft. length, $3).

The holder is no wider than the roll, so there aren't any protruding hangers or rods.Using my chop saw, I cut the PVC pipe and the roll of paper to the width of my workbench. Then, on my tablesaw, using the fence, and with the blade set just high enough to cut through the pipe, I carefully cut a lengthwise slot.

I screwed the pipe to the end of my bench, using the drain holes for access. Then I slid in the roll of paper. It was a tight fit at first, because the new roll was the same diameter as the pipe, but once I'd covered the bench a couple times, the paper pulled out easily.

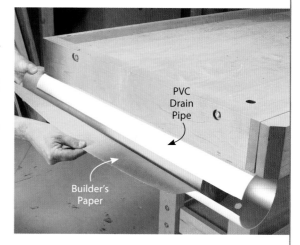

PVC Drain Pipe

Builder's Paper

Combo Cart

Hauling my benchtop planer or miter saw out every time I needed to use one or the other was hard on my back until I devised this mobile base. It makes both of them readily accessible and stores neatly in the corner when I don't need it.

I positioned the tools so the planer provides outboard support for the saw. I made sure the planer blades and dust hood were accessible, and I extended the planer's outfeed capacity. I store a bunch of my portable power tools in the cabinet below.

The cabinet costs about $100 to build. It takes about 1½ sheets of ¾-in. plywood and four double-locking swivel casters. You'll have to adjust the dimensions of your cabinet to suit your work habits and tools.

I built my cabinet so the bed of the miter saw sits 42 in. from the floor, a comfortable working height for me. To locate the planer shelf, I subtracted the planer's height from the height

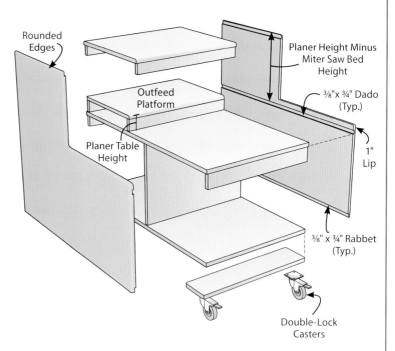

Rounded Edges

Planer Height Minus Miter Saw Bed Height

Outfeed Platform

⅜"x ¾" Dado (Typ.)

Planer Table Height

1" Lip

⅜" x ¾" Rabbet (Typ.)

Double-Lock Casters

of the miter saw's bed. To make the outfeed extension, I measured the height of the planer's outfeed table and built a platform to match. I slid it into the cabinet and screwed it in place.

Fold-Away Outfeed Table

Like many of you, I don't have room in my shop for a
large outfeed table, although sometimes I need one. Using
heavy duty folding brackets purchased from Rockler (12"-
$22, 16" - $30), I made an outfeed table for my saw that's
available when I need it and stowed out of the way when
I don't. I made the top out of ¾" x 36" x 36" MDF. The
top is the same width as the saw's table; it's as long as it
can be without hitting the floor when folded down. Rout
grooves in the top that line up with your saw's miter slots.
I notched one corner of the top so, when folded, the table
clears my in-floor dust collector pipe. I screwed 2 x 4's to
the underside to attach the brackets and to add strength
and stability to the top. (This design won't work on a
contractor saw, because its motor is in the way.)

Drawbridge Outfeed Roller

In my small shop, most of my tools are on mobile bases. The problem I ran
into was my outfeed roller required readjusting every time I brought out my
tablesaw. I solved this irritation by rigging an outfeed roller directly to my saw
with chain and screw hooks. Because it adjusts in and out and telescopes up
and down, the roller support can accommodate almost any length
material, and it folds up for easy storage. Best of all, the
roller stays true with the saw even on my rough
floor. Because my saw is so light, I screwed its
legs to my homemade mobile base and added a concrete
block to keep it from tipping forward. I put feet on the front side
of the base to keep the base from rolling during use.

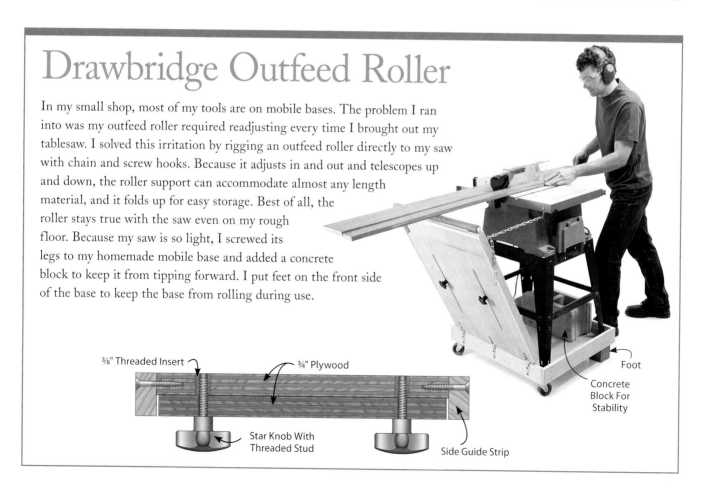

Drawer-Slide Outfeed Table

In my garage shop, large tools have to be mobile and storable, so I attached this collapsing outfeed support to my saw. It slides on 100-lb. full-extension drawer slides. Extended, the roller sits 36 in. behind the blade, so I can rip boards as long as 6 ft. I can clamp the arms in any position to support shorter boards. Closed, the roller rests 16 in. behind the blade, so it doesn't interfere with the blade guard assembly or with the miter gauge bar during crosscuts.

The support is built like an inside-out drawer. First I bolted support arms onto the saw's cabinet. I had to extend the left arm to allow tilting the motor. Then I installed the drawer slides and the extension arms. On my saw, 20-in. slides were the longest that would fit. I fastened the extension arms securely with a wide board to minimize racking. I mounted the roller on top, centered behind the blade. To position everything correctly during construction, I clamped the roller flush with the saw table.

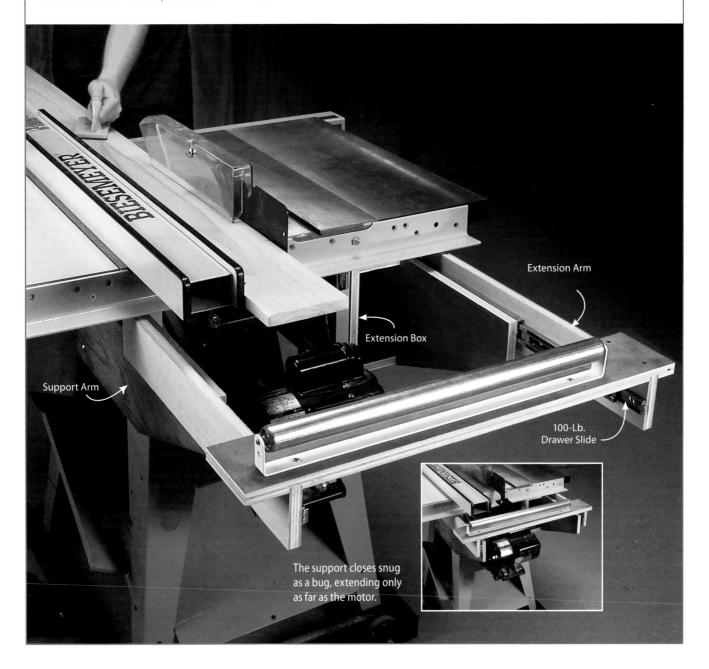

Extension Arm

Extension Box

Support Arm

100-Lb. Drawer Slide

The support closes snug as a bug, extending only as far as the motor.

Flip-Top Sawhorses

I got tired of rummaging around for a blanket or anything soft to lay my finished projects on, so I rigged up these simple carpet caps that fit on top of my sawhorses. They just flip out of the way when I'm back to rough work.

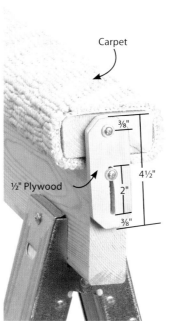

Carpet

1½" x ½" Dado

#8 x 1¾"
Round-
Washer-
Head Screw

½" Plywood

⅜"

4½"

2"

⅜"

Heavy-Duty Plywood Sawing Support

While crosscutting a full sheet of plywood, I found that I had no way to support the left side as it hung off the side of the tablesaw. I tried a regular roller stand but it just tipped over. As I looked around my shop for a solution, I noticed that the fence on my jointer was almost the same height as my tablesaw. I wheeled the jointer into position and clamped a board to its fence to support the sheet of plywood. It makes a perfect side support that won't tip over.

Jointer
Fence

Support
Board

Clamp

Jointer

Heavy-Duty Workbench on Wheels

My shop is so small that even my workbench is on wheels! I used Delta's mobile base kit and it worked great. The directions call for 1½ in. by 1½-in. wood connecting rails up to 30-in. long. If these wood rails are made longer, they tend to bow. For my 62-in.-long workbench I used square metal tubing instead. It cost me about $20 from a metal distributor. This tubing is even strong enough to support a lower shelf. This doubles my tool storage area and it's all mobile!

If you're not up to sawing and drilling your own metal tubing, here's another option: Grizzly makes 36-in. metal connecting tubes that can be added to their mobile base. This extends the Grizzly base to a 44-in.-long capacity.

Plywood Shelf

Square Metal Pipes

Mobile Base Kit

Kicker Chock Block

I love the convenience of mobile bases, but I hate it when they wobble on the floor even when they're locked down. I got my chock block idea at the airport where the ground crews use something similar for parked aircraft. My chock block locks the fixed casters on my mobile bases so they don't budge. It's a great improvement.

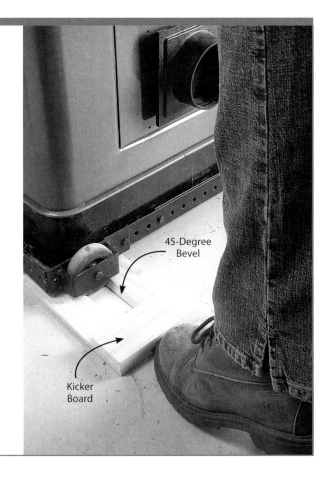

45-Degree Bevel

Kicker Board

Hinged Frames Give Broad-Based Support

Whether I need support for cutting plywood or bases for an assembly table, I reach for my hinged frames instead of sawhorses. The hinged frames open into stable, double-armed platforms that can be used individually or together.

Each assembly consists of two identical frames and two identical gates made from ¾-in. fir plywood using half-lap joinery. Four continuous hinges hold the parts together and facilitate opening and closing. Hook-and-eye screw latches lock the assembly in the open position.

Hinged frames fold flat for storage.

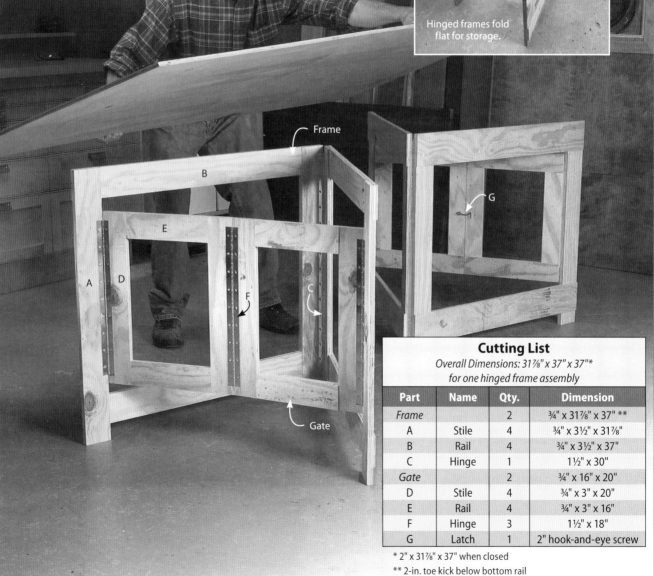

Cutting List

Overall Dimensions: 31⅞" x 37" x 37"*
for one hinged frame assembly

Part	Name	Qty.	Dimension
Frame		2	¾" x 31⅞" x 37" **
A	Stile	4	¾" x 3½" x 31⅞"
B	Rail	4	¾" x 3½" x 37"
C	Hinge	1	1½" x 30"
Gate		2	¾" x 16" x 20"
D	Stile	4	¾" x 3" x 20"
E	Rail	4	¾" x 3" x 16"
F	Hinge	3	1½" x 18"
G	Latch	1	2" hook-and-eye screw

* 2" x 31⅞" x 37" when closed

** 2-in. toe kick below bottom rail

Knock-Apart Utility Table

I couldn't do without this knock-down stand for my benchtop tools and accessories. It's made from ¾-in. plywood (two 36-in. high x 48-in.-wide base boards and a 48-in. x 48-in. tabletop). Cut ¾-in.-wide slots halfway into each base piece using a bandsaw or saber saw. Slide the parts together and check that the bottom sits level on the floor. Add leveling feet, if necessary. Add blocks of wood to the top corners of each base piece. Secure the top with screws run through pocket holes in each block.

You can design a table to suit your needs; just be sure the base is wide enough to be stable.

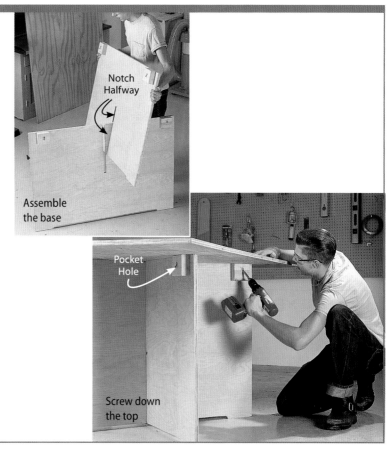

Notch Halfway

Assemble the base

Pocket Hole

Screw down the top

Lightweight Extension Wings

Extension wings on the miter saw make cutting long stock a breeze. My shop-made wings install and knock down in seconds and they're as light as feathers. My secret? The wings are made from a hollow-core door. After ripping the door to width, I pushed the internal honeycomb pieces back and glued new pine side rails between the faces. Then I installed swing-down legs for stability. Steel bed-rail fasteners hold the wings level with the saw table. After engaging the fastener, I drop a nail behind the hook to lock the wing in place.

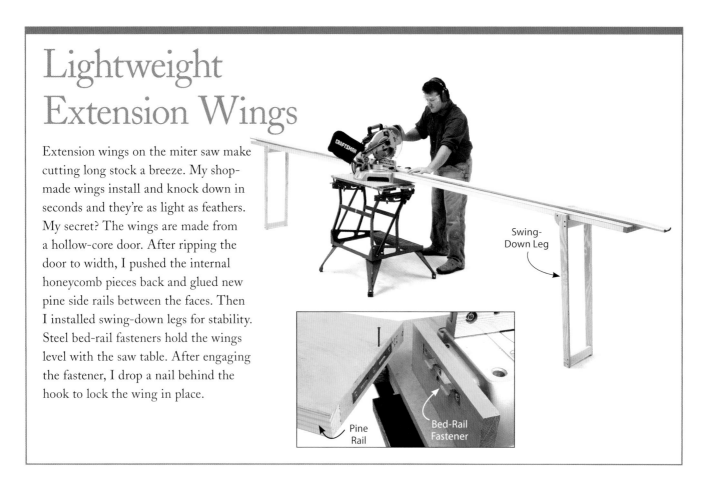

Swing-Down Leg

Pine Rail

Bed-Rail Fastener

Mobile Bandsaw

Horsing my bandsaw out of the way was a real pain until I installed a pair of large casters (see Source, below). Now my saw has a built-in two-wheel cart. During use, the saw sits firmly on the floor, because the wheels don't touch the ground. They're also out of the way.

Tipping the saw and balancing it while moving is tricky until you get the hang of it, because the saw is top-heavy and awkward to hold. Although casters make this cumbersome piece of machinery much easier to move, you should only install them if you're comfortable handling heavy loads.

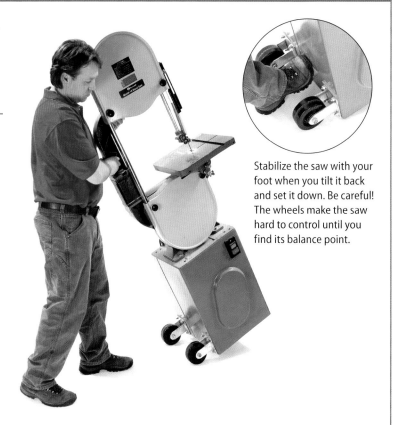

Stabilize the saw with your foot when you tilt it back and set it down. Be careful! The wheels make the saw hard to control until you find its balance point.

Mobile Machine Caddy

My shop space is so limited—only 12 feet square—that I designed this system to house four machines: belt-disc sander, miter saw station, drill press and planer. Each machine has an accessory storage tray below. With all the machines down I have a clear working surface above. Each machine is wired to a central outlet so it's always ready for use.

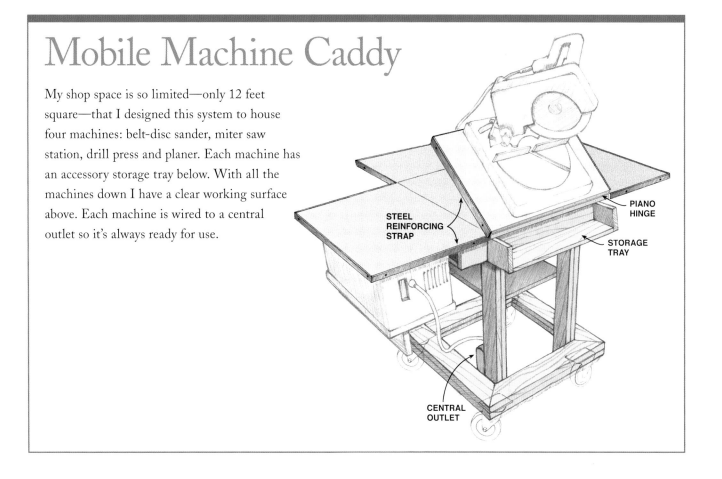

STEEL REINFORCING STRAP

PIANO HINGE

STORAGE TRAY

CENTRAL OUTLET

Nesting Sawhorses

Here's a real lifesaver in a small shop. These horses are lightweight, strong and designed to nest tightly together for easy storage. They can be built from 2x4s and put together with biscuits for less than $10 a pair. (Mill the 2x4s to 1¼ in. by 3-in. so they're flat and square.) I've been using a pair of horses like these for years and they continue to serve without complaint. Size your horses however you like, keeping the angle of the legs at 98 degrees for stability. Cut the notches that join the foot to the leg on your bandsaw. Attach the foot with glue and a screw run up through the bottom.

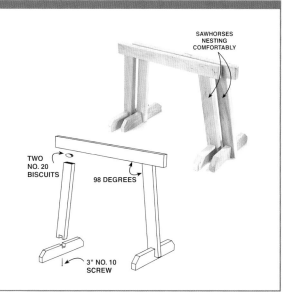

SAWHORSES NESTING COMFORTABLY

TWO NO. 20 BISCUITS

98 DEGREES

3" NO. 10 SCREW

Old Door Workbench

I thought I didn't have enough room for a second work surface, until I made this one from a salvaged pre-hung door. Look for a flush, solid-core door with the jamb (door frame) attached. A solid-core door is sturdy, provides strong attachment for the bench legs and is heavy enough to take a pounding. I reinforced the jamb with screws and added stock where the threshold used to be. Then I screwed a 1 in. x 4-in. flange onto the back edges of the jamb with #8 x 2-in. screws. The jamb is hung on the wall at a comfortable working height with #10 x 3-in. screws. For convenient tool and accessory storage, screw perf-board to the flange that's inside the door opening. Make two legs from ¾-in.-threaded pipe and screw them into two ¾-in. pipe flanges to support the workbench when it's down. Support the bottom jamb with angle brackets and add a hasp to hold the door shut.

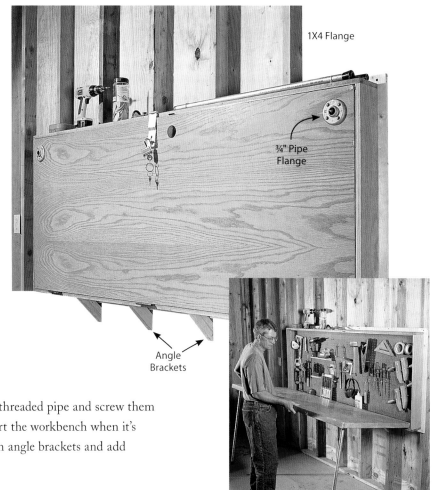

1X4 Flange

¾" Pipe Flange

Angle Brackets

Sawing Rack

My shop is simply too small to cut full-size sheets of plywood on the tablesaw. After many a bitter battle using a circular saw to cut floppy sheet stock perched on sawhorses, I developed this handy rack for cutting those full-size sheets down to size. One side is designed for crosscutting while the other is used for ripping. The rack makes a sturdy platform for supporting the plywood while rough cutting with a circular saw.

To build the rack: Rip scrap ¾-in. plywood to 3-in. Cut 1-in.-deep dadoes every 12-in. or so to create the half-lap joints. Assemble with glue so there are no metal fasteners to ruin a misguided blade. Topped with a sheet of plywood, the rack can also serve as an assembly table.

CROSS-CUT SIDE

RIP SIDE

Pivoting Outfeed Support

I recently saw an outfeed stand that had a pivoting top. The pivoting action prevents a workpiece from catching the front edge of the outfeed top. Instead, the top just pivots up level as the workpiece passes over it. I figured I could make something similar that would work just as well.

For the base I used a sawhorse with a concrete block for extra stability. I screwed a couple of stop blocks to the top of the horse to keep the outfeed top from pivoting too far forward or backward. The top is a ¾-in.-thick by 12-in.-wide by 36-in.-long melamine shelf that I bought at a home center for $6. The 1x4 end brackets are set toward the back of the braces by 1 in. to make the outfeed top tip toward the tablesaw. The brackets are attached to the horse with a screw at each end. When the outfeed top is level, there is a ¾-in. gap between it and the stop blocks. I trimmed the horse's legs so the outfeed top is level with my tablesaw.

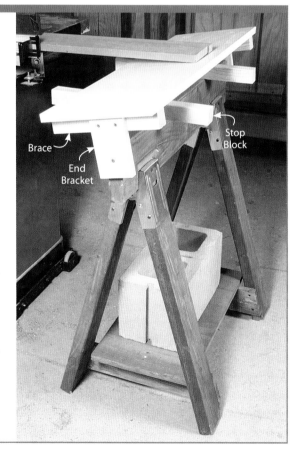

Brace

End Bracket

Stop Block

Stackable Sawhorses

I built these lightweight, stackable sawhorses from ¾-in.-thick lumber, a handful of screws and several squirts of glue. The glue and screws make the horses very strong. A hardwood block for the base of the triangle ensures joint strength, but to make them even stronger, you could also nail triangular pieces of plywood over the ends. The legs are 28½ in. long by 3-in. wide with a 20-degree miter cut at the top. The horizontal board is 26 in. by 4 in. The pair of horses cost me about $20 to build.

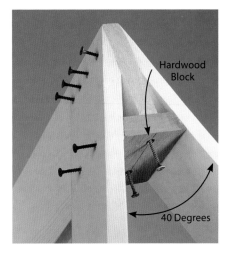

Hardwood Block

40 Degrees

Support Arm for Crosscut Sled

I got tired of trying to keep my crosscut sled flat on the table when I cut wide panels. At the beginning of each cut, I had to support the sled's back end to keep the front end from lifting—sometimes the runners would lift right out of the top's grooves.

My solution was to fasten this hinged support arm to my saw's cabinet. It also stores my rip fence and other accessories. To use the support, I simply unfold the arm and flip up the hinged block. The block has a strip of ultra-high-molecular-weight plastic (UHMW) fastened on top, so the sled slides smoothly.

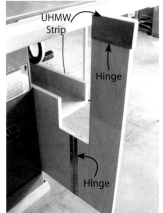

UHMW Strip

Hinge

Hinge

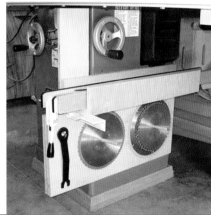

Stowable Outfeed Table

I share my shop with my car, so everything has to be portable. My outfeed table installs in a minute and folds up flat for storage. It bolts onto the back of my saw and has adjustable feet, so it sits flat anywhere on my uneven garage floor.

The table is ¾-in. melamine with hardwood edging. It measures 3 ft. wide by 4 ft deep, so it's big enough to support full sheets of plywood or 8-ft. boards, yet small enough for one person to maneuver. I built it in less than a day for less than $50.

I routed dadoes for the miter gauge bar in the top and cut a slot for the blade-guard assembly. Then I attached the legs (see photo, below left). To mount the outfeed table flush with my saw table, I milled spacer blocks to the correct thickness and fastened them on each side of the blade-guard slot (see photo, below right). Then I drilled holes for the ¼-in. carriage bolts that connect the table to the saw. First I drilled stopped holes in the top to recess the bolt heads. Then I clamped the table in position behind the saw and drilled the shank holes through the spacer blocks and the L-bracket. Washers and wing nuts lock the table in place.

Folding leg brackets fasten the legs. A spring-loaded lever locks the legs open and closed.

Carriage bolts connect the table to the saw's L-bracket.

Sliding Mobile Bases

My mobile bases slide on low-friction, ultrahigh molecular weight (UHMW) polyethylene pads. Fastened to these sliding bases, my tools glide easily over the concrete floors in my shop, yet there's enough resistance to keep them stationary during use. The bases are compact, so I don't whack my toes on them, and I don't have to worry about forgetting to lock or unlock casters.

Each sliding base costs about $20 to make, much less than a caster-equipped mobile base. The pads (see photo, right) cost only about $2 apiece, because they're cut from a sheet of UHMW polyethylene.

I've found that a push-pull method keeps top-heavy tools, like my drill press, stable. I push lightly with my top hand to keep the tool from tipping forward and pull with my bottom hand to slide it.

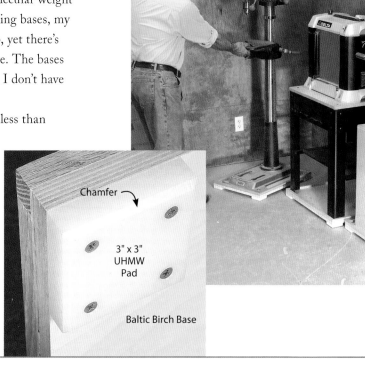

Chamfer

3" x 3"
UHMW
Pad

Baltic Birch Base

Space-Saving Cutting and Finishing Bench

In order to save space and make plywood cutting easier, I made this hinged bench. Laying out and cutting the interlocking joints required some careful work, but slipping them together during assembly was a cinch. The perimeter boards are attached with screws. Keep the screws at least ¼-in. from the top edge. The legs pivot up for storage and the bench is held to the wall with a wooden turnbuckle. Be sure the turnbuckle is solidly attached to the wall so the table doesn't flip down and bean someone!

The gridwork provides solid, even support for sawing. I set my circular saw to cut only ⅛-in. into the table. That way I don't hit any of the assembly screws or weaken the table. This bench is also ideal for finishing.

Turnbuckle

Hinge

Leg
Pivots
Up

Tool Trolley with Brakes

Mobile tool bases are a must in my small shop. Here's how I built one for my drill press:

I screwed together a shallow box (¾-in. plywood bottom and 2x2 sides), added heavy-duty casters ($3 each at a hardware store or home center) and two adjustable vertical-style toggle clamps ($17 each from Woodcraft Supply, 800-225-1153). For easy steering, use swiveling casters on one end and rigid casters on the other.

Now I roll my drill press into position and push down the clamp levers to lock it in place.

Toggle
Clamp

Swivel
Caster

¾"
Plywood

Rigid Caster

Trash Can Outfeed

To save space, my trash can doubles as a work support. I made a dolly with locking casters to fit the can's bottom, so I can roll the unit to wherever it's needed.

The work support is adjustable in height. It's just a round-nosed board with two ¼" x 6" slots, held in place with ¼" bolts and jig knobs. I routed curved grooves in the support's feet to match the trash can's rim, so the support doesn't slide off the can. When I want to empty the trash, I just lift off the support. I've made reference marks on the support for the correct height of each tool.

Radiused
Groove

Stowing Table

Now and then I need extra bench space for assembly or finishing. My garage shop is cramped so I made this easy-to-stow bench add-on. The tabletop is built of ½-in. plywood and 1x4 aprons. The legs are hinged and connected to the tabletop with a collapsing brace to prevent the legs from being accidentally kicked in. The add-on table connects to my workbench with a beveled cleat—a 2x4 cut at 45 degrees. Storage is a snap—it slides against the wall behind my bench.

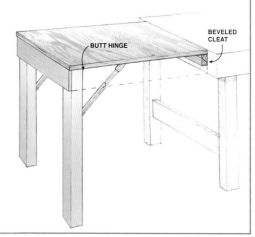

BUTT HINGE

BEVELED
CLEAT

Workbench Joint

Plans for my knock-down workbench called for the 2x4 stretchers to be fastened with bolts and hex nuts. I'd have to rout huge pockets, weakening the stretcher, in order to get a wrench on the nuts. Yuck! I rummaged through my jelly jars of spare hardware and came up with this nifty solution.

First I counterbored a hole, large enough to fit my socket wrench, in the leg. Then I drilled a hole for a ⅜-in. bolt through the leg and into the stretcher. Finally, I drilled a ¾-in. hole through the side of the stretcher. This hole is just big enough to slide in a ⅜-in. wing nut. When the bolt engages the wing nut, the wing nut jams against the sides of the hole. No more need for a wrench!

⅜" Wing Nut

⅜" Bolt

What's the Ideal Workbench Height?

Is there a standard or recommended height for a workbench?

For most people, a height that allows you to lay the palm of your hand on the benchtop with a slightly bent elbow works best. If you have back problems, you may want to raise that height to your belt line.

The ideal workbench height is really the one that works best for you. It's a function of what kind of woodworking you do and how tall you are. Traditional workbenches were built low to get the user's full body weight and muscle power behind their tools. It's effective for pushing a hand plane but uncomfortable for almost all other work. With handheld power tools, a higher bench height is more desirable and less of a strain on the ol' back.

If possible, try mocking up a bench with plywood and sawhorses. Start with our ballpark height and see what you think. Adjust the height accordingly until you find the height that's best for you and what you do.

Prescription Safety Glasses

I hate fumbling with goggles over my prescription glasses, so I've given up. Don't regular glasses protect my eyes well enough in the workshop?

No. Normal prescription glasses, even if they have plastic lenses, are no substitute for safety glasses. Bite the bullet and buy a pair of prescription safety glasses with polycarbonate lenses and permanent side shields. They're available wherever you buy your regular glasses. They can be made in any prescription and cost no more than a regular pair of glasses.

Safety glasses are different from regular glasses in three important ways.

First, the lenses are thicker and have much greater impact resistance. Polycarbonate lenses are by far the strongest.

Second, the frames are built differently. They won't allow a lens to pop out toward your face.

Third, safety glasses have side shields that wrap around your face like goggles. Side shields not only protect your eyes, they help prevent other accidents, too. They keep distracting dust out of your eyes far better than standard glasses, so you can concentrate on what you're doing. (Safety glasses are available without side shields, but we don't recommend them. There's no reason to go around half-protected.)

You can get safety glasses with side shields that are detachable, so one pair of glasses could serve you both in the shop and on the street. The problem is, detachable side shields are easy to lose or misplace.

Side Shield

Unhinge Hollow-Core Doors

Economical and light in weight, hollow-core doors make great temporary work surfaces, because they're so easy to maneuver. Used with sawhorses and a couple 2x4s for support, they can handle a surprising amount of weight. Workshop doors don't have to be good-looking, so bargain-shop at salvage yards or scratch-and-dent bins.

Hollow-Core Door

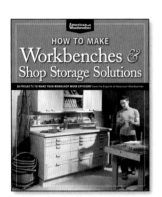
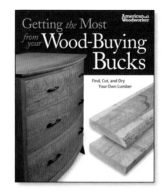
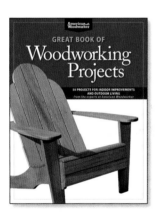
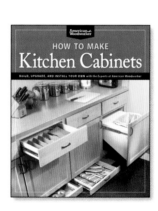